*Women's Movements in
Twentieth-Century Taiwan*

Women's Movements in Twentieth-Century Taiwan

DORIS T. CHANG

University of Illinois Press

URBANA AND CHICAGO

Library of Congress Cataloging-in-Publication Data
Chang, Doris T., 1969–
Women's movements in twentieth-century Taiwan / Doris T. Chang.
p.   cm.
Includes bibliographical references and index.
ISBN 978-0-252-03395-7 (cloth : alk. paper)
1. Women—Taiwan—History—20th century.
2. Women—Taiwan—Social conditions—20th century.
3. Women's rights—Taiwan.
4. Feminism—Taiwan.
5. Feminist theory—Taiwan.
I. Title.
HQ1777.C43   2009
305.42095124'9—dc22   2008035914

Contents

Acknowledgments

I wish to thank the Chiang Ching-kuo Foundation for International Scholarly Exchange for the Visiting Fellowship to Taiwan in the summer of 2006. I also wish to express my sincere gratitude to Chung Shu-min and Hsu Hsueh-chih of the Institute of Taiwan History for inviting me to conduct research at Academia Sinica. I am really grateful to Yu Chien-ming of Academia Sinica and Lin Wei-hung of National Taiwan University for providing me with copies of their work. I also would like to acknowledge Lee Yuan chen, Yu Mei-nü, Huang Chang-ling, Tseng Chao-nuan, Sun Ruei-suei, and Fan Yun of the Awakening Foundation for updating me with important information about the autonomous women's movement in post–martial law Taiwan.

Special thanks to James Bartholomew and Christopher A. Reed of The Ohio State University, Leila Rupp of the University of California at Santa Barbara, and both reviewers of this manuscript for providing me with valuable suggestions for its improvement. I would like to acknowledge the editors of the University of Illinois Press, Laurie Matheson, Rebecca Crist, Angela Burton, and Phyllis Brashler, for supporting this research project and working with me toward its completion. I also wish to thank Kristie Bixby for copyediting my manuscript and my colleagues at the Center for Women's Studies and Religion for offering me guidance and support since I joined the faculty of Wichita State University in 2003. I am especially indebted to James Ho of Wichita State University and Grace Lin of National Taiwan University for introducing me to scholars and feminist leaders in Taiwan. In addition, I would like to acknowledge Denny Roy. My chronology of Taiwan's history is based on a modification of the "Chronology of Major Events" in his book *Taiwan: A Political History.*

Lastly, I dedicate this book to my parents, Philip and Susan Chang, my sister, Amelia Chang Wright, and my best friend, Karen DaSilva, who has been my kindred spirit since our days in high school. Without the unconditional love and strong support of my parents over the years, the completion of this manuscript would not have been possible.

Chronology of Taiwan's History

1544	Portuguese sailors named Taiwan Ilha Formosa (Beautiful Island). Before the arrival of European explorers and Chinese immigrants, Taiwan's original inhabitants were Malayo-Polynesian indigenes.
1624	Dutch colonization of southern Taiwan; migrant workers and merchants from coastal Southeastern China are encouraged to settle in Taiwan in large numbers.
1662	Koxinga (Zheng Chenggong) of Ming China captures Taiwan from the Dutch and sets up an exile government on Taiwan after fleeing the Manchu (Qing) conquest of China.
1683	Qing forces from China seize Taiwan.
1885	Taiwan becomes a province of Qing China.
1895	Japan defeats Qing China in the first Sino-Japanese War. China cedes Taiwan to Japan pursuant to the Treaty of Shimonoseki.
1921–34	Taiwanese elites establish the Taiwan Cultural Association in 1921 and participate in the petition movement for the establishment of a Taiwan parliament within the legal framework of imperial Japan's Meiji constitution. Feminist discourses and autonomous women's movements emerge (1920–31).
1927	Advocates for a Taiwan parliament establish the Taiwan Populist Party.
1928	Hsieh Hsueh-hung and others establish the Taiwan Communist Party.
1937–45	The second Sino-Japanese War; Taiwanese are recruited into Japanese armed forces during the imperialization movement.
1945	After Japan's surrender, Taiwan is brought under the control of the Chinese Nationalist (Kuomintang) government of the Republic of China (ROC) headed by Chiang Kai-shek.

1947   Mass protest during the February 28th Incident leads to the Kuomin-
        tang government's massacre of 20,000 Taiwanese civilians and politi-
        cal activists.

1949   Chinese Communist troops defeat the Kuomintang in the Chinese
        civil war. The Kuomintang transfers its government and troops from
        mainland China to Taiwan and imposes martial law on the island.
        Chairman Mao Zedong of the Chinese Communist Party declares the
        creation of the People's Republic of China (PRC) on the mainland.

1949–53 The Kuomintang government on Taiwan implements a land reform
        program to transfer land ownership to tenant farmers.

1954   The United States and Taiwan establish a Mutual Defense Treaty.

1960   Democracy activist Lei Chen is incarcerated.

1964   P'eng Ming-min, professor of political science at National Taiwan Uni-
        versity, is arrested for advocating Taiwan independence and challeng-
        ing the Kuomintang's reunification policy with mainland China.

1971   The United Nations expels the ROC diplomats from Taiwan and re-
        places them with representatives from the PRC on mainland China.

1972   Hsiu-lien Annette Lu launches the autonomous women's movement
        in postwar Taiwan.

1975   ROC President Chiang Kai-shek dies.

1978   Chiang Kai-shek's eldest son, Chiang Ching-kuo, becomes the ROC
        president on Taiwan.

1979   The United States switches its diplomatic recognition from the ROC
        government on Taiwan to the PRC government on mainland China.
        In order to safeguard Taiwan's security vis-à-vis the PRC, the U.S.
        Congress passes the Taiwan Relations Act.

        Democracy activists stage a mass rally in the city of Kaohsiung against
        the Kuomintang's authoritarian rule and Taiwan's diplomatic isolation.

1980   Eight dissident leaders of the Kaohsiung incident, including Hsiu-lien
        Annette Lu, are court-martialed and sentenced to long prison terms.

1982   Feminist activists in Taiwan launch the magazine *Awakening*.

1986   Political activists of the Democratic Opposition establish the Demo-
        cratic Progressive Party (DPP).

1987   The Kuomintang regime lifts martial law and ushers in Taiwan's de-
        mocratization in the post–martial law era.

1988   Chiang Ching-kuo dies. Lee Teng-hui becomes the ROC president on
        Taiwan.

1991   Lee Teng-hui ceases the state of war with communist China on the
        mainland.

1991–92 Senior members of the National Assembly and Legislative Yuan re-
        sign. They are replaced by a new generation of elected representatives
        in Taiwan.

1996   The PRC launches test missiles toward the coast of Taiwan as Lee Teng-hui wins Taiwan's first direct presidential election through universal suffrage.

1999   Lee Teng-hui characterizes the relationship between the ROC on Taiwan and the PRC on the mainland as "a special state-to-state relationship." Consequently, the PRC suspends its semiofficial cross-strait talks with the Taiwan government.

2000   DPP candidates Chen Shui-bian and Hsiu-lien Annette Lu are elected the ROC president and vice president. The Kuomintang transfers power to an opposition party for the first time in more than fifty years.

2008   The Kuomintang candidate, Ma Ying-jeou, is elected the ROC president on Taiwan.

Note on Transcription

In accordance with Taiwan's customary practice, I use the Wade-Giles system of Chinese romanization to transliterate names of persons, places, and universities in Taiwan. For all other Mandarin Chinese terms, the pinyin system of romanization is used, in keeping with the current practice in Chinese scholarship.

*Women's Movements in
Twentieth-Century Taiwan*

Introduction

Since the 1970s, several books in the English language have discussed women's movements in mainland China during the twentieth century. The Chinese origin of most Taiwanese notwithstanding, no comparable study in the West has examined the political factors that contributed to the emergence of a Taiwanese women's movement in the 1920s, its collapse in the early 1930s, and its reemergence and continuance in the early 1970s and thereafter within the context of Taiwan's contested national identities in the twentieth century. This is the first book in English to fill this gap. As a case study of a non-Western society's selective appropriation of Western feminist ideas to meet the needs of women in a Confucian culture, this book contributes to cross-cultural feminist scholarship, integrating Taiwanese feminist discourse into the mainstream of historical narratives on international women's movements.

In 1895, China ceded the island of Taiwan[1] to Japan after the former was defeated in the first Sino-Japanese War. Fifty years later, following its defeat in World War II, Japan returned Taiwan to the Chinese Nationalist government (Kuomintang). In 1949, the Kuomintang fled to Taiwan and imposed martial law on the island's population after it lost the civil war to the Chinese Communists. From 1949 through 1987, the Kuomintang's policy of no contact and no negotiation with China ensured that Chinese communism exerted virtually no influence on postwar Taiwan's autonomous women's movement. Martial law in Taiwan was lifted in 1987. Throughout the 1990s, continuing tension between the two governments across the Taiwan Strait also limited the scope and depth of dialogue between feminists in mainland China and in Taiwan.[2]

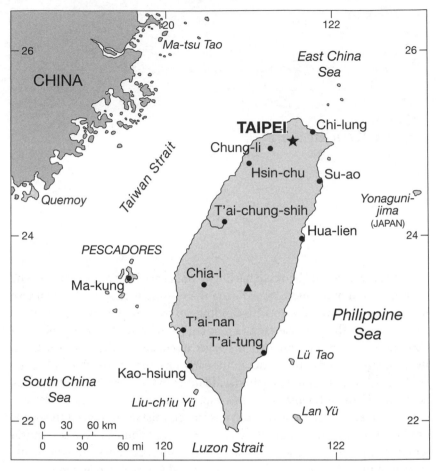

Map of Taiwan

Since 1949, the Kuomintang-led Republic of China (ROC) on Taiwan
and the Chinese Communist–led People's Republic of China (PRC) on the
mainland have vied for international recognition as the sole legitimate government of China. To maintain the international legitimacy of the Kuomintang government on Taiwan, state-sponsored historiography emphasized
the continuity of the ROC from its founding in 1911 on mainland China to
the transfer of its government to Taiwan in 1949 and thereafter. Domestically,
the Kuomintang launched a re-sinicization program to eradicate traces of
Japanese culture from postwar Taiwan. With the Kuomintang-sponsored
Chinese historiography as the hegemonic discourse in the research and
teaching of history in postwar Taiwan, research on the Japanese colonial

era (1895–1945) was severely circumscribed until the lifting of martial law in the post–1987 period.[3] Under martial law, virtually all historical narratives of Chinese feminist discourses and women's movements were written within the conceptual framework of pre-1949 women's movements in mainland China and post–1949 women's movements in Taiwan.

In 1993, in the post–martial law period, Yang Ts'ui wrote a book titled *The Taiwanese Women's Liberation Movement under Japanese Colonial Rule,*[4] which deals with feminist discourses in autonomous women's movements during the 1920s. The same year, Academia Sinica, the premier research institute in Taiwan, launched a journal, *Research on Women in Modern Chinese History,* which included articles about women's experiences in colonial Taiwan. In 2004, Yu Chien-ming published a book chapter on women's movements in the Taiwan area. A collection of essays by multiple authors, *Women in the New Taiwan* (2004), was the first project in Western scholarship to discuss gender issues from a Taiwanese historical perspective.

As a historical study, this work approaches Taiwanese women's movements from the perspective of twentieth-century Taiwan, describing the ebb and flow of Taiwanese feminist discourses and women's movements from the Japanese colonial era to the postwar Chinese Nationalist period. To reflect the larger trend in the field of Taiwanese history in recent years, this book spans the 1945 divide to include the autonomous women's movements during the 1920s and the post-1972 period. To a large extent, the emergence, collapse, and reemergence of autonomous women's movements in twentieth-century Taiwan can be attributed to the changing political dynamics on the island. During periods of soft authoritarianism, autonomous women's movements emerged and operated within the political parameters set by the authoritarian regimes.[5] In contrast, during periods of hard authoritarianism,[6] the autonomous women's movement collapsed and was not given the political space to reemerge.[7] Thus, the purpose of this study is to situate the Taiwanese advocacy of women's rights within the broader context of Taiwan's authoritarian political culture over the century. This book also discusses ways in which Taiwan's democratization in the post–martial law era (1987 and thereafter) facilitated the diversification of feminist discourses.

Under Japanese colonial rule, feminist discourse emerged within the context of the colonial government's greater tolerance of political dissent during the early 1920s. In 1919, a civilian governor-general replaced his Japanese military counterpart and granted Taiwanese a certain degree of freedom and cultural autonomy within the Japanese Empire.[8] From the 1920s to the early 1930s, the autonomous women's movement was an integral part of Taiwan's social and political movements.[9] Yu Chien-ming distinguishes autonomous women's movements from their government-affiliated counterparts in Taiwanese society. Whereas government-affiliated women's organizations played the passive role of mobilizing women to carry out the government's policies, the autonomous women's movement emerged from Taiwan's civil society in the 1920s with its own objectives of promoting women's rights and status. It was thus independent of the colonial government's direct control and patronage.[10]

With the Japanese invasion of Manchuria and the rise of Japanese militarism in 1931, the intensified repression of the colonial government toward Taiwan's sociopolitical movements in general and independent women's organizations in particular led to the decline and collapse of the women's movement.[11] From the early 1930s to Japan's defeat in World War II, the highly repressive political climate under the hard authoritarian rule of the colonial government during wartime mobilization was not conducive to political dissent or the reemergence of an autonomous women's movement. In this period, the government-affiliated women's organizations that promoted the war effort and the assimilation of Taiwanese women into Japanese culture were the only organizations that flourished.[12]

With the defeat of Japan in 1945, Taiwan was restored to the Kuomintang government of the Republic of China. In 1946, Taiwanese women leaders affiliated with the Kuomintang established the Taiwan Provincial Women's Association. Henceforth most intellectuals engaged in discussions of women's rights and status were Kuomintang-affiliated Taiwanese women or officials and social commentators from mainland China between 1945 and 1949.[13] As a consequence of the Kuomintang's suppression of political dissent in Taiwan during the February 28th incident of 1947, most Taiwanese intellectuals refrained from criticizing the regime or the society for fear of being persecuted.

After the regime fled to Taiwan in 1949, several more government-affiliated women's organizations were established to mobilize women for its military campaigns to recover mainland China from Communist occupation.[14] Conversely, the postwar autonomous women's movement emerged after a change in the Kuomintang's leadership from the hard authoritarianism of Chiang Kai-shek to the soft authoritarianism of his eldest son, Chiang Ching-kuo. In response to demands for political reforms voiced by an emerging Taiwanese middle class, Chiang Ching-kuo softened his father's authoritarianism in 1972 and thereafter. Even with one-party rule, the younger Chiang's greater tolerance for social and political dissent in Taiwan created some limited space, beginning in 1972,[15] for the emergence of an autonomous women's movement. Since the autonomous movements in the 1920s and the post–1972 period advocated women's self-determination, this study places greater emphasis on the analysis of feminist discourses within the autonomous women's movements rather than on the policies of government-affiliated women's organizations.

Changes in Women's Status in Chinese History

In the twentieth century, feminists in Taiwan attributed the gender inequality found in Taiwanese society to the Neo-Confucianism first articulated in the Song dynasty (960–1279).[16] Previously, from the collapse of the Han dynasty in 220 C.E. to the end of the Tang dynasty in 907 C.E., Chinese women had enjoyed relatively high social status. During this period, central Asian nomadic influences from the steppe elevated Chinese women's status with regard to divorce, remarriage, and activities in the public domain.[17]

After the end of the Han dynasty (206 B.C.E.–220 C.E.), China entered a period of political disunity known as the Six Dynasties (220–589). The conquest of China's northern plains by nomadic peoples from the steppe, known to the Chinese as "barbarians," forced many Chinese to flee to the region south of the Yangzi River. For those who remained in northern China, elite political families from Chinese and nomadic backgrounds intermarried and appropriated each other's cultures. In contrast to the Confucian ideal of gender segregation, many women in elite families of northern China were active in social and political arenas. Confucian scholars and imperial historians in subsequent Chinese dynasties portrayed elite "barbarian" women in the north during the Six Dynasties as shrewd and jealous in their political meddling. Conversely, elite Chinese women in the south were depicted as genteel ladies who transmitted Confucian values and literary traditions to their children.[18]

With reunification of China during the Sui and Tang dynasties (589–906), elite women retained their privilege and right to a Confucian education in classical Chinese poetry and prose. If there were no male offspring in the family, daughters, both single and married, could inherit their father's property. During this period, widows also had the choice to remarry. The women of Sui and Tang also inherited the practice of horseback riding from northern women in the Six Dynasties. In contrast to the Confucian ideal of female seclusion in the domestic realm, this practice allowed some women freedom of mobility outside the home.[19]

Since Confucianism conceptualized women as managers of household expenditures and educators of children in the home, elite women of the Song dynasty (960–1279) were known for their roles as maternal tutors and managers of household budgets and family estates. As in other dynasties in China's imperial past, palace women played influential roles as courtesans, concubines, regents, and consorts to the emperor. Economically, the Song dynasty witnessed imperial China's incipient commercial revolution in maritime trade, economic growth, and urbanization. In market towns and cities, women from non-elite backgrounds defied the Confucian restrictions on women's participation outside the home. They obtained gainful employment as prostitutes, entertainers, cooks, maids, tailors, waitresses, and restaurant managers. Because married women and widows retained control over their own dowries, some widows were able to negotiate a remarriage for their future. The tension between Confucian ideals and the reality of women's opportunities in the job and marriage markets could be a reason that motivated Neo-Confucian philosophers in the Song period to emphasize women's seclusion in the domestic realm and the importance of widow chastity.[20]

Based on their reinterpretation of Chinese cosmology in *The Book of Changes* (*I Jing; I Ching*), Song Neo-Confucianism rigidified the masculine yang in the public domain versus the feminine yin in the domestic realm. Thus, women were confined in the domestic realm as managers of households and nurturers of children. In contrast to classical Confucianism's cosmological conception of yin and yang as two reciprocal and complementary parts that made up a rounded whole,[21] Neo-Confucians emphasized the moral inferiority of the feminine yin to the masculine yang. The Song Neo-Confucians used this metaphysical reinterpretation to justify a woman's obedience to her father before marriage and deference to her husband and his parents after marriage. Also, they envisioned the cloistering of women in the domestic realm as a safeguard to female chastity.[22]

Based on the Song Neo-Confucians' interpretation of widow chastity, the cult of widowhood became a common practice during the Mongol Yuan dynasty (1279–1368) and thereafter. After the Mongols invaded China from the northern steppe region, they brought with them the practice of the levirate. As an institution of marriage, the levirate could take several forms. Since the Mongol elite practiced polygamy, the practice could involve a son's marriage to his stepmother after his father's death or a widow's marriage to her deceased husband's nephew or brother. Since most Chinese found this "barbarian" practice to be both alien and objectionable, the insistence on widow chastity became a Chinese strategy for deterring the Chinese population from practicing the levirate. To preserve Chinese women's chastity from sexual assault by Mongol invaders, the Song Neo-Confucian ideal of cloistering women in the home became widely practiced among the Chinese population during Yuan times. Chinese women would bind their daughters' feet during early childhood to mark their distinctiveness from the unbound feet of Mongol women and girls and to accentuate the cultural difference of Chinese women from their "barbarian" counterparts. Thus, the Yuan period was the watershed that marked the decline in women's participation in the public domain, their freedom of physical mobility, and their choice to remarry.[23]

In the Ming and Qing dynasties (1368–1911), also known as late imperial China, the rise of an urban print culture facilitated the spread of female literacy among the non-elite classes. For young males, passing the civil service examination as a career path to achieve gentry-scholar status (and thereby obtaining the academic credential for serving in the imperial bureaucracy) motivated many parents to transmit knowledge necessary for passing the examination to their sons. Whereas sons would be sent to private academies to receive the appropriate education for passing the examination, women and girls were barred from taking the test. They were often homeschooled and trained in Confucian precepts on the ways to be good mothers and faithful wives and daughters-in-law. They were also taught classical Chinese poetry and prose, calligraphy, painting, music, embroidery, and practical skills of household management. It was hoped that education would make them more valuable and competitive in the marriage market and also prepare them to be educators of their own children in the future.[24]

In late imperial China, the practices of footbinding and cloistering women in the domestic realm continued unabated. It was not until the nineteenth century that modern Chinese reformers among the Confucian scholarly elite began to critique these practices as hindering China's capability to resist Western domination. Some reformers vowed not to bind their daughters' feet in order to set a good example for others in their community. By the early twentieth century, the practice was virtually eliminated in urban China. With the collapse of the Qing dynasty in 1911 and thereafter, young women without their feet bound participated in gainful employment outside the home and contributed to the economic modernization of the new Chinese republic.[25]

While mainland China was transformed into a nascent republic, Taiwan became Japan's first modern colony. In the early twentieth century, Taiwanese physicians collaborated with the Japanese colonial government to launch public health education campaigns for the abolition of footbinding. The colonial government encouraged Taiwanese parents to unbind their daughters' feet and send them to public schools to obtain functional literacy as a preparation for them to become wise mothers and productive wage laborers in the plantations and light industries of the Japanese Empire. Because higher education was inaccessible for most Taiwanese in colonial Taiwan during the 1920s, an elite minority of students managed to further their studies in major cities of Japan proper and mainland China. It was in these cosmopolitan centers of learning that Taiwanese students came to familiarize themselves with liberal feminism and transmitted the idea to the Taiwanese public.[26]

Definitions of Feminism

In the 1920s and post–World War II Taiwan, the liberal individualist strand of feminism from the West made a significant impact on Taiwanese feminists' formulation of their critique of Confucian society's gender inequities. As a middle-class reformist ethos, liberal feminism (*ziyoupai nüxing zhuyi*)[27] envisioned gender equality in every respect—socially, politically, and economically. In both Taiwan and the West, liberal feminists sought to humanize the capitalist market economy rather than to overthrow it. By and large, they operated within the boundaries set by the state's legal and political systems.

To improve women's status in the family and society and to protect women from gender discrimination, liberal feminists advocated the replacement of gender-biased civil codes with gender-egalitarian legislation. They also advocated the passage of legislation ensuring men's and women's equal employment opportunities, and safeguarding equal pay for equal work. In the 1920s and the post–1972 era, liberal feminists in Taiwan advocated women's freedom to realize their potential in the male-dominated public domain.

In the West, liberal feminism idealized personal independence, women's rights, and individual freedom to pursue paid work in the public domain. Due to the strength of Confucian family-centered ideology in Taiwanese society,[28] most liberal feminists attempted to strike a balance between their advocacy of women's self-realization in the public arena and women's fulfillment of obligations within the familial context of interpersonal relationships.[29] Comparatively, this emphasis on familial relationships and fulfillment of gender-specific obligations as mothers and wives resembled relational feminism in the West.

According to Karen Offen, relational feminism and liberal individual feminism historically have been two distinct strands of thought in Western feminist discourses.[30] Based on Shu-ju Ada Cheng's application of Offen's definitions of relational and liberal feminism to her analysis of Taiwanese feminism, the same two strands may be identified in post–1972 Taiwan.[31] I contend that both strands of feminism were also evident in Taiwanese feminist discourse of the 1920s. Thus, this study demonstrates that relational feminism coexisted alongside liberal individualist feminism in Taiwanese feminist discourses of the 1920s and the post–1972 era.

In contrast to liberal feminism's idealization of women's freedom from familial constraints,[32] relational feminism's pro-family ideology advocated gender equity between husband and wife without eliminating their distinct gender roles in the familial context. In a similar vein to relational feminism in the West, the concept of yin and yang in traditional Chinese cosmology validated the two genders' interdependent and complementary relationships, reciprocal obligations in the family, and women's mothering roles.[33] For three thousand years, Chinese philosophers in both the Taoist and Confucian traditions have conceptualized yin and yang as two complementary and indispensable parts that constitute a rounded totality. Despite the influence of yin and yang in Taiwanese relational feminists' vision of gender relationships, feminists objected to Confucianism's ascription of superiority to the masculine yang and the ascription of inferiority to the feminine yin. Thus, relational feminists in Taiwan envisioned the transformation of gender hierarchy into a new gender-egalitarian ethos where wives, mothers, and working women could all enjoy equity with men without forsaking their gender-specific qualities, such as feminine gentleness and capacities for compassion and nurturing.[34]

In the final analysis, the coexistence of gender difference and gender equity in relational feminism differed from liberal feminism's belief in women's assimilation into the male-dominated culture.[35] Although there was no evidence to suggest that the post–1972 feminists in Taiwan derived their feminist discourses from their predecessors in the 1920s, the postwar feminists' borrowing of Western-inspired liberal feminism turned out to be remarkably similar to their counterparts in the 1920s. Meanwhile, Confucian society's emphasis on behaving in accordance with one's familial roles and fulfilling one's social obligations[36] provided the cultural context for Taiwanese feminists in the 1920s, 1970s, and thereafter to formulate their indigenous strand of relational feminism independent of Western influence.

According to Offen's conceptualization of relational feminism in nuclear families of Western societies, a married woman's primary obligations were associated with her gender roles as the mother of her children and the wife of her husband. As urban dwellers in a newly industrialized society since the 1980s, many young couples in Taiwan have decided to move away from their parents and establish their own nuclear families. Nonetheless, a married woman's gender roles in a complex weave of relationships in her extended family remain an important feature of many women's lives in contemporary Taiwan.[37]

As more married women in Taiwan have become gainfully employed and have contributed to family finances, they also have gained more power in their relationships with their husbands and their parents-in-law. In recent decades, specific powers and obligations have been attributed to women's roles as wife, mother, daughter, and daughter-in-law. Although the Chinese culture in Taiwan has traditionally been patrilocal, some divorced women in recent years are returning to their natal families, soliciting financial help and moral support from their siblings and parents. In this context, these divorced women resourcefully tapped into their relationships as daughters and sisters of their biological families as a strategy for survival during times of personal hardship. Since Taiwanese women play diverse gender roles in their extended families, relational feminism in Taiwan encompasses the empowerment of women as wives and mothers in their nuclear family, as daughters-in-law in their husband's family, and as sisters and daughters in their natal family.[38] In accordance with the Confucian vision of social harmony, most Taiwanese feminists in the 1920s, 1970s, and thereafter promoted equal and harmonious relationships between men and women in the family and society.

According to Lee Yuan-chen, a Taiwanese feminist leader beginning in the 1980s, the relative moderation of feminists' demands in Taiwan in comparison with the agendas of their feminist contemporaries in the United States could be attributed to Taiwan's authoritarian political culture in the 1970s and 1980s. In the bipolar context of the Cold War, the Kuomintang sided with the United States. Inspired by American feminist discourse in the 1960s and 1970s, feminist activists in Taiwan selectively appropriated Western concepts and synthesized them with Taiwan's indigenous cultural values and sociopolitical conditions.[39] In contrast to Taiwanese feminists' ideological concessions to the authoritarian regime under martial law, the same activists threw off self-censorship during the era of democratization in the post–martial law period. Since 1987, Taiwan has witnessed the emergence of diverse strands of feminist discourse previously suppressed within the authoritarian political milieu.

Among the major strands of Western feminist thought, socialist feminism (*shehui zhuyi pai nüxing zhuyi*) did not become an explicit category of analysis in Taiwanese feminist discourse until 1988. Because of the Kuomintang's unceasing efforts to weed out communist and leftist elements in Taiwanese society from the late 1940s onward, socialist influence on Taiwanese feminist thought prior to 1988 was only implicit and circumscribed. Beginning in 1988, however, several feminists explicitly applied Marxism in their analyses of the long-standing alliance between Confucian patriarchy and industrial capitalism in the exploitation of Taiwanese women workers.

Moreover, many radical concepts pertaining to women's sexuality previously suppressed under martial law were openly discussed during Taiwan's democratization in the 1990s. For the first time in Taiwanese history, the concept of *woman-identified woman* (*nüren rentong nüren*) in lesbian feminism and the ideology of sexual liberation (*xing jiefang*) emerged as strands of radical feminist discourse (*jijin pai nüxing zhuyi*). The ideas of American radical feminists—Audre Lorde, Adrienne Rich, and Gayle Rubin—were discussed in Taiwan's feminist circles.

As components of a newly industrialized society and a nascent democracy, Taiwanese feminist discussions in the post–1987 era are in many ways similar to feminist agendas of the industrialized nations in northeast Asia, Europe, and North America.[40] In these democratic societies and industrialized economies, feminist goals tend to include gender equality in employment opportunities, environmental protection, women's right to reproductive choice, the prevention of domestic violence and sexual assault, the civil rights of same-sex couples, and the advancement of women into leadership roles in the political arena. To achieve these goals, feminist activists in these countries have regularly battled in the court systems or lobbied for legislative reforms in parliamentary bodies.[41]

Definition of Autonomous Women's Movements

According to Shu-ju Ada Cheng and Yu Chien-ming, Taiwan's autonomous women's movements (*zifaxing de funü yundong*)[42] are social movements that maintained a high degree of ideological and organizational independence from the state and were therefore different from collective institutional mobilizations by women that were directly under the state's control and patronage.[43] Yu Chien-ming's narrative describes the pioneering contributions of girls' schools established by Christian missionaries to the advancement of women's rights in late nineteenth century Taiwan.[44] According to Yang Ts'ui, colonial Taiwan's autonomous women's movements emerged in the 1920s and disintegrated by the 1930s. A postwar autonomous women's movement did not reemerge until the 1970s.[45] In concert with Yang's periodization, this study argues that the first and second waves of the autonomous women's movement in the twentieth century emerged from Taiwanese society in 1920 and 1972, respectively. As such, they were indigenous social movements that consisted of collective actions and the formulation of feminist thought aimed at challenging the patriarchal status quo in order to improve women's status and eliminate gender inequities in family and society.[46]

In respect to periodization, this study divides twentieth-century Taiwan's autonomous women's movement into two phases. The first wave consisted of the autonomous women's movement in the Japanese colonial era. In the

1920s, the number of Taiwanese students studying in mainland China and Japan proper increased dramatically. The Taiwanese students in urban centers of learning in Japan and China were transmitters of feminist ideas (*nüxing zhuyi; nüquan zhuyi*) to Taiwan.[47] During this period of greater political freedom in imperial Japan, feminist discussions began to appear in colonial Taiwan's magazines and newspapers.[48]

Between the mid-1920s and early 1930s, several autonomous women's associations were established in colonial Taiwan. The autonomous social and political movements in the same period—the Taiwan Populist Party, the Taiwan Farmers' Union, and the Taiwan Communist Party—also had explicit policies aimed at advancing women's status. To a large extent, colonial Taiwan's autonomous women's movement relied on women activists in anti-colonial labor and farmers' movements to propagate the ideology of women's liberation among the masses. In the face of the Japanese government's campaigns to suppress leftist radicals in the aftermath of the Manchurian Incident in 1931, the autonomous women's movement in colonial Taiwan precipitously declined along with left-wing organizations.[49]

In contrast to the decline and collapse that overcame the first wave of the autonomous women's movement in the early 1930s, the second wave has survived the authoritarian political culture since its inception in 1972 and has flourished during the era of Taiwan's democratization in the post–1987 era.[50] Ku Yen-lin, a feminist scholar and associate of both Lu Hsiu-lien and Lee Yuan-chen, subdivides the second wave of the autonomous women's movement into three stages. Led by Lu Hsiu-lien (Hsiu-lien Annette Lu), the first woman vice president of the Republic of China on Taiwan (2000–8), the first or "pioneering" stage lasted from 1972 to 1977. With the initial publication of the feminist magazine, *Awakening,* in 1982, the second or "awakening" stage then lasted from 1982 through 1987. In 1987, the Kuomintang lifted martial law and ushered in Taiwan's democratization. Thus, the post–martial law or third stage extends from 1987 to the present.[51]

As the formative stage of Taiwan's autonomous women's movement in the postwar era, the pioneering stage laid the ideological foundation and provided feminist activists with the crucial experience necessary for the continuation of their struggle during the awakening and post–martial law stages. In the post–martial law era, Taiwan's pluralistic democracy enabled feminist activists to organize numerous nongovernmental women's organizations. Since most of the women's organizations were situated in Taipei, their proximity to the center of political power in Taiwan's capital facilitated feminist activists' access to legislative lobbying.[52]

As mentioned previously, autonomous women's movements in both the

1920s and the post–1972 era emerged within the context of authoritarian political cultures. Because of hostility from the Japanese colonial government and the Kuomintang toward the autonomous women's movements, no mass-based women's movements emerged in the 1920s, 1970s, or 1980s. Rather, their organizational character resembled the elite-sustained women's movement in the United States. During the Second Red Scare in the United States (1948–57), the women's movement survived in an environment where socially conservative public opinion and an anti-feminist political climate were not conducive to the mobilization of women for mass protests. Instead of organizing a broadly based movement with thousands of members, the women's movement relied on the commitment of a small number of feminist activists to ensure its survival.[53]

Similar to their counterparts in the United States, most Taiwanese feminists of the Japanese colonial era and the post–1972 period were from upper- or middle-class backgrounds. Most feminist activists in the 1920s came from colonial Taiwan's literate minority.[54] In postwar Taiwan most feminists were either college educated or had obtained graduate degrees in Taiwan or the West.[55] Because of their educational and class backgrounds, most activists in the autonomous women's movements of the 1920s, 1970s, and thereafter can be regarded as the elite minority with a pro-woman agenda. Whereas the American Women's Liberation movement was transformed into a broadly based mass movement in the mid-1960s,[56] the Awakening Association, a leading feminist organization in post–martial law Taiwan, did not have its first mass membership drive until 1994.[57]

With the new opportunity presented by the political liberalization in the post–martial law era, college students established women's studies clubs, and in response to their interest and demand, many college courses in women's studies then came to be offered for the first time. Prior to the lifting of martial law in 1987, the autonomous women's movement relied on informal friendship networks to recruit activists. In the post–martial law period, many college students chose to participate in the autonomous women's movement after joining campus women's studies clubs or taking women's studies courses.[58]

Plan of the Book

Chapter 1 discusses the feminist discourses and autonomous women's movements within colonial Taiwan's social and political movements of the 1920s and early 1930s. In addition, I distinguish the autonomous women's movements from their government-sponsored counterparts. According to Hsin-yi Lu, the concepts of *good wife, wise mother* and *new woman* coexisted in colonial Taiwan's intellectual discourses of the 1920s. Inspired by the Western concept of the *new woman* in the liberal democratic culture of Taisho Japan, feminists in colonial Taiwan visualized a new woman as one who would assert her financial autonomy, support universal suffrage, and practice free-choice marriage.[59]

Based on my analysis of colonial Taiwan's feminist discourse in the 1920s, the concept of the New Woman was derived from liberal individualist feminism. Conversely, Taiwanese intellectuals discussed *good wife, wise mother* in terms of women's gendered obligations as primary educators of children within the context of familial relationships, thus representing the relational strand of Taiwanese feminism. I assert that relational feminism, liberal feminism, and a Marxist-Leninist perspective on the woman question were the main strands of feminist thought in colonial Taiwan's autonomous women's movement. In contrast, government-sponsored women's organizations functioned as an institutional means for the colonial government to assimilate Taiwanese women into Japanese culture.[60] I contend that the Japanese colonial government's wartime policy served to exacerbate women's double burden in the public domain and the domestic realm.

Chapter 2 provides a historical overview to illustrate the continuities of the Chinese Nationalist or Kuomintang's policies toward women and its government-affiliated women's movements from the 1920s in mainland China to its rule in postwar Taiwan (1945–2000). Specifically, the chapter discusses the programs of the Kuomintang-affiliated women's organizations in postwar Taiwan under the leadership of Madame Chiang Kai-shek, the First Lady of the Republic of China on Taiwan (1949–75).

After the Chinese Communists defeated the Kuomintang in 1949, the latter transferred its anti-communist campaign from mainland China to the island. In order to support the Kuomintang regime's prospective military re-conquest of mainland China from Communist occupation, Madame Chiang mobilized members of government-affiliated women's organizations in postwar Taiwan to provide social services to the Kuomintang troops, make military uniforms in factories, and raise funds for building government-subsidized housing for soldiers.[61] Among the government-affiliated women's organizations, some Taiwanese members created rural childcare facilities.[62] Whereas most beneficiaries of rural daycare facilities were Taiwanese women and girls, most beneficiaries of the state-subsidized housing were male military personnel and their dependents.[63] I contend that the former's chronic shortage of funds in comparison to the latter attested to gender inequality in an authoritarian state.

In chapter 3, I present a narrative of Hsiu-lien Annette Lu's early life experiences that culminated in her decision to pioneer the autonomous women's movement in postwar Taiwan. Then I describe Lu's leadership role in the pioneering stage (1972–77) of the autonomous women's movement. The impact of the Kuomintang's authoritarianism in shaping the elite-sustained character of the autonomous women's movement is also discussed. For the purposes of cross-cultural and historical analysis, I compare and contrast postwar Taiwan's elite-sustained autonomous women's movement with its counterpart in the United States.

Chapter 3 also discusses the content of Lu's *New Feminism* (*Xinnüxing zhuyi*). Similar to the impact of Betty Friedan's *Feminine Mystique* on the Women's Liberation movement in postwar America, it was Lu's *New Feminism* that laid the theoretical foundation for Taiwan's feminist discourse in the 1970s. I conduct a textual analysis of Lu's *New Feminism* to look at her selective incorporation of various strands of Western feminism with Confucianism to formulate an original, multifaceted feminist discourse. To understand the influence of the Kuomintang's authoritarian political culture on the formation of Taiwanese feminism in the 1970s, I analyze the arguments that Lu devised to negotiate and compromise with the authoritarian government in the 1970s. Here, I examine her selective adoption of those aspects of Western feminism that she deemed acceptable to the regime.[64] As an original research approach, I analyze the nature and extent of Lu's selective appropriations of Western feminist ideas from the Anglo-American liberal tradition, such as those expressed by Mary Wollstonecraft, Margaret Mead, and Betty Friedan. The socialist ideas of American feminist Charlotte Perkins Gilman and French Marxist existentialist Simone de Beauvoir also exerted considerable influence on Lu's conceptualization of socialized childcare and housework.

In 1982, Lu's feminist associate, Lee Yuan-chen, and other feminist activists founded *Awakening* (*Funü xinzhi*), a monthly magazine for feminist intellectuals and activists to contribute to the feminist discourse in Taiwan. In this study, the group of committed feminists who regularly contributed essays and financial resources to *Awakening* were designated as the Awakening feminists. For more than a decade, the magazine was the single most important feminist monthly dominating Taiwan's feminist discourse.[65]

Chapter 4 examines the Awakening feminists' strategies in general and Lee Yuan-chen's feminist ideas in particular. To this end, I analyze Lee's feminist theoretical work entitled *Women's Forward March* (*Funü kaibuzou*) and numerous essays in *Awakening* from the year of the monthly's initial publication in 1982 through 1989, the year that Lee stepped down from her position as chairperson of *Awakening*'s board of trustees. In regard to cross-cultural influences, Lee stated that Simone de Beauvoir, Margaret Mead, and American feminist Jean Baker Miller's women-centered perspective all exerted considerable influence on her formulation of feminist thought in the 1980s.[66] I examine Lee's selective borrowing from these three theorists' ideas and the influence of Lu Hsiu-lien's *New Feminism* on Lee's writings in the 1980s. This chapter also evaluates the changes and continuities in the autonomous women's movement's strategies and discourses from the pioneering stage in the 1970s to the awakening stage in the 1980s.

Chapter 5 discusses the various ways in which Taiwan's democratization in the post–martial law era facilitated the diversification of feminist discourses and the creation of non-governmental women's organizations in 1987 and thereafter. I compare them with the earlier feminist discourses and organizational strategies in the authoritarian political milieu of the martial law period.

According to Hwei-syin Lu, Taiwanese feminists in the post–martial law era were not as radically individualistic and oppositional to men as their counterparts in the West. This is because Taiwanese women by and large strive to achieve self-empowerment within the context of familial relationships.[67] While Lu's assessment is applicable to the relational strand of Taiwanese feminism, her analysis did not take into account the critiques of Confucian family-centered ideology by radical feminism and Marxist feminism.

As occurred during the 1920s, Marxism once again became an explicit category of feminist analysis in the post–martial law era. In 1989, Ts'ao Ai-lan published *The Perspectives of a New Generation of Taiwanese Women* (*Xinshidai Taiwan funü guandian*). I analyze the text to see the ways in which Ts'ao applied the theory of Marxist feminism to explain the mutually reinforcing relationship between industrial capitalism and patriarchy's exploitation of women's unpaid labor in the domestic realm and low-wage labor outside the home.

In 1994, the publication of Ch'un-jui Josephine Ho's *The Gallant Woman* (*Haoshuang nüren*) propelled her sexual liberation ideology onto the center stage of radical feminist discourse in Taiwan.[68] I evaluate Ho's writings to show the ways in which she used the metaphor of a buffet (help yourself meal; *zizhucan*) to illustrate a woman's right and freedom to determine her own sexual behavior. During the same decade, lesbian feminism critiqued the mutually reinforcing relationship between Confucian patriarchy and heterosexism and the imposition of compulsory heterosexuality on the Taiwanese society. The concluding chapter restates the influences of Taiwan's political cultures and different strands of Western feminism on feminist discourses in the autonomous women's movements of the twentieth century.

1. Feminist Discourses and Women's Movements under Japanese Colonial Rule, 1895–1945

In the early 1920s, Taiwanese feminist discourse emerged in the context of the Japanese colonial government's limited tolerance of political dissent. Beginning in the 1920s, the Taiwanese students who studied in China and Japan served as transmitters of a liberal strand of feminism and women's rights ideology (J: *joken shugi*; C: *nüquan zhuyi*) from the cosmopolitan centers of Western learning in Tokyo, Shanghai, Guangzhou, and Beijing to colonial Taiwan. Just as Taisho Japan imported Western ideas to enrich the pluralistic discourse of its democratic experiment, the May Fourth movement (1915–23) in China also imported Western ideas to launch a radical critique of Confucian patriarchy.[1]

From the 1920s to 1931, enhancement of gender equality and women's status were important objectives of colonial Taiwan's social and political movements. As such, autonomous women's movements (*funü yundong*) had overlapping membership with other social and political movements.[2] This chapter distinguishes the autonomous women's movements and organizations from their government-sponsored counterparts. Whereas the government-sponsored women's organizations served the purpose of carrying out the Japanese government's policies, the autonomous women's movements emerged from Taiwan's nascent civil society. The latter were independent of the government's direct control and patronage.[3] Further, I analyze the ways in which gender, class, and ethnic inequalities in Taiwan were part of the discourses of the sociopolitical movements, and I discuss the impact of the government's policies on Taiwanese women's experiences.

Despite moderate toleration of political dissent in the 1920s, by the early 1930s the colonial government's intensified repression toward Taiwanese sociopolitical movements, led to the decline and collapse of the autonomous women's movements. From the early 1930s to Japan's defeat in World War II, a highly repressive political climate discouraged political dissent and the re-emergence of the independent women's movements. In this period, only government-sponsored women's organizations could flourish.[4]

In order to situate women's experiences in a broader context, it is essential to understand Taiwan's historical background. Taiwan was the place of origin of Malayo-Polynesian (Austronesian) languages. The indigenous inhabitants of Taiwan (*yuanzhumin*) [5] were islanders who shared a common linguistic and ethnic heritage with Malays and Polynesian islanders in different parts of the Pacific.[6] Taiwan (*Tayouan*) was the Malayo-Polynesian name of a bay area on the southwestern plain of the island where early immigrants from coastal southeastern China first settled. As the Chinese settlers expanded their land claim and commercial activities in different parts of the island, they began to refer to the entire island as Taiwan. In 1544, Portuguese sailors witnessed the lush vegetation on the island and named it *Ilha Formosa* (Beautiful Island). A century later, the Dutch colonized the island and built Fort Zeelandia on Tayouan to facilitate the Dutch East India Company's maritime commercial activities.[7] In 1623, the Chinese government of the Ming dynasty (1368–1644) recognized Dutch control over Taiwan. The Dutch colonial administration governed the island until 1662—the year that the Ming loyalist and pirate, Koxinga (Zheng Chenggong), drove the Dutch out of Taiwan and created his own exile government on the island.[8]

When the Dutch arrived in southern Taiwan in 1624, the Chinese immigrant community on the island was still relatively small. To neutralize the aboriginal population's fierce resistance against Chinese settlers and traders, the Dutch East India Company launched military campaigns to suppress its aboriginal neighbors. During its four decades of rule, the Dutch administration encouraged large-scale immigration of Chinese farmers, laborers, traders, and artisans to provide the necessary labor force for developing the island's fishing industry, commercial deer hunting, irrigation projects, and sugarcane and rice plantations. The result was a Sino-Dutch hybrid colony where the Chinese offered the necessary labor force and tax and trade revenues for the Dutch East India Company. Reciprocally, the Dutch provided Chinese colonists with military protection and administrative governance.[9]

Due to the large influx of Chinese bachelors who settled in Taiwan and the practice of intermarrying with indigenous women to acquire the land and property of their wives' families, many bicultural couples served as bilingual interpreters. Historically, aborigine women with Chinese husbands played critical roles in conducting diplomacy and mediating trade between Chinese and indigenous communities.[10]

Beginning in the seventeenth century, the majority of Chinese immigrants in Taiwan spoke the Hoklo (Minnan) dialect of coastal Fujian province in southeastern China, which lies across the Taiwan Strait from the island. In addition to the Fujianese community, a minority of Chinese were Hakka (Kejia) immigrants from the Guangdong (Canton) province. In 1683, the government of the Qing dynasty (1644–1911) incorporated Taiwan into the Chinese Empire. In the subsequent century, Chinese culture emerged as the dominant culture of the island. Because the Fujianese community comprised 70 percent of the island's population, the Fujianese majority regarded their dialect as "the Taiwanese language."[11]

After the mid-eighteenth century, the Qing government permitted Chinese men and women to emigrate to Taiwan as a family unit. Consequently, the number of Chinese women who permanently settled in Taiwan increased significantly. By virtue of residing on a maritime frontier of the Chinese Empire, women in Taiwan have historically enjoyed a higher status than their counterparts in mainland China. In the nineteenth century, Taiwan's customary law granted married women the right to own land. Due to the shortage of Chinese women in nineteenth-century Taiwan, it was also more common for Taiwanese widows to remarry.[12] Yet, as ethnic Han Chinese, most people in Taiwan and mainland China shared the Confucian heritage from China's traditional past. As a patriarchal ideology, Confucianism ascribed inferior status to women and superior status to men in both family and society. While there were private academies for boys in Taiwan, girls were mostly home-schooled.

The advocacy of modern education for girls did not begin in Taiwan until the 1880s, when Presbyterian missionaries from Canada and Britain created girls' schools in Tamsui (Tanshui) and Tainan. In the girls' boarding school in Tainan, the traditional Chinese practice of footbinding was prohibited. Pupils were taught gender-specific knowledge and skills, such as home economics, methods of childcare, and family hygiene. In addition to preparing them to be future homemakers and mothers, the school was also committed to offering girls a well-rounded curriculum. In some respects, the curriculum of the Tainan girls' school was analogous to that of their male counterparts. Although boys and girls attended separate schools, students of both genders were taught reading, writing, arithmetic, and natural sciences. Because the missionaries devised a Romanization system to translate the Bible into the Minnan dialect (Hoklo Taiwanese), pupils of both genders were taught the

Romanization system to enable them to read the Bible in the Taiwanese vernacular. In addition, physical education and field trips were integrated into the extracurricular activities of the school. Despite the Christian missionaries' efforts in promoting education for girls, their influence remained limited within a small community of Christian converts.[13]

Girls' education in Taiwan did not become more widespread until the early twentieth century within the context of imperial Japan's modernization program. After China's defeat in the first Sino-Japanese War (1894–95), it ceded Taiwan to Japan under the terms of the Treaty of Shimonoseki in 1895. As a new Asian power striving to be accepted as an equal among the Western powers, Japan was mindful of its national prestige and was eager to convert Taiwan into an ideal colony through modernization.

Yet before the Japanese colonial government could launch its modernization program in Taiwan, it had to focus on the suppression of organized resistance against Japanese colonial rule. During the first two decades of the twentieth century, the Japanese government replaced traditional Taiwanese district heads with Japanese officials and Japanese-educated Taiwanese collaborators. In the economic realm, the colonial state conducted comprehensive island-wide land surveys and confiscated farms and forestlands in order to attract Japanese capital investments in camphor and sugarcane industries. Modern Japanese sugar factories gradually replaced traditional Taiwanese-owned sugar mills. Many Taiwanese sugarcane growers were reduced to tenant farmers who had no other choice but to sell their produce to Japanese-owned sugar companies at a fixed price. Deprived of their former status and livelihood, discontented Taiwanese elites and small farmers staged organized rebellions against the Japanese colonial state.[14] In order to ensure that the legislative, executive, and military powers were concentrated in the office of the governor-general, the Imperial Dict in Tokyo passed Law No. 63 in 1896 to grant the governor-general the power to enact executive orders to be enforced in Taiwan. In this way, the Japanese state imposed a military dictatorship to suppress dissent, control the native population, and maintain social order on Taiwan until 1919.[15]

Autonomous Women's Movements as Integral Parts of Colonial Taiwan's Social and Political Movements

In 1919, the Japanese government appointed a civilian governor-general and terminated military rule in Taiwan. In the era of Taisho democracy in Japan,[16] the new governor-general tolerated limited political dissent in Taiwanese society within the parameters of his authoritarian rule. According to Ts'ai P'ei-huo, a Taiwanese political leader in the 1920s, the spirit of liberal democracy under a constitutional monarchy (*minponshugi*) contributed to Taiwanese liberal reformers' quests for universal suffrage and political equality with their Japanese counterparts.[17] To achieve this end, liberal reformers stepped up their efforts to petition for the creation of a Taiwan Parliament within the legal framework of imperial Japan's Meiji Constitution. Between 1922 and 1934, Taiwanese activists gathered signatures on both Taiwan and Japan's home islands for the annual submission to the petition committee of the Imperial Diet in Tokyo. To legitimize their cause, the Taiwanese solicited the political support of liberal-minded Japanese intellectuals, politicians, and journalists.[18] Inspired by Woodrow Wilson's advocacy of national self-determination in 1918, the Taiwanese liberal reformers hoped that the creation of a Taiwan Parliament could enable Taiwanese home rule and preserve the island's cultural autonomy in the Japanese Empire.[19] Encouraged by the passage of the bill for universal suffrage of Japanese male citizens at the Imperial Diet in 1925, the number of people who signed the petition increased significantly after 1926.[20]

In Japan, the passage of Article 5 of the Revised Police Security Law in 1921 lifted the ban on women's participation in political gatherings. Consequently, Taiwanese women students in Japan were able to participate actively in the petition movement for a Taiwan Parliament. In the post–World War I era, Taiwanese students and intellectuals were keenly aware of the profound impact of the Great War on shaping the advancement of women's status in Europe and the United States. The passage of woman suffrage legislation in Britain (1918) and the United States (1920) became subjects of interest and discussion among the Taiwanese intelligentsia.[21] On April 28, 1928, the Woman Suffrage movement in Japan obtained the endorsement of more than eighty members of the House of Representatives in the Imperial Diet to introduce and promote the passage of the Woman Suffrage Bill.[22] Because Taiwanese men and women were denied the right to the franchise in the 1920s and early 1930s, liberal reformers envisaged the attainment of universal suffrage for Taiwanese of both genders as a means to legitimize self-rule on the basis of popular sovereignty.[23] Yet, most liberal reformers prioritized the cause for the creation of a Taiwan Parliament over women's movements and issues.[24]

Most writings on universal suffrage, improvement of Taiwanese women's status, and the creation of a local parliament were published in either *The Taiwan Youth* (*Tai Oan Chheng Lian*) or *Taiwan People's News* (*Taiwan min-bao*). *The Taiwan Youth* was a magazine published by a group of Taiwanese liberal reformers in Tokyo from 1920 to 1922. It was published in both the

Japanese and Chinese languages to inform the public about the necessity of a Taiwan Parliament and to preserve Taiwanese language and culture. In 1923, *Taiwan minbao* (*Taiwan minpo*) was published in Tokyo as a bimonthly periodical with Chinese and Japanese columns. It became a weekly in 1925. In 1927, the colonial government granted *Taiwan minbao* permission to be published in Taiwan. By 1929, *Taiwan minbao* was replaced by *Taiwan xin-minbao* (*Taiwan shinminpo*). During the 1920s and the 1930s, *Taiwan min-bao* and its replacement were the only indigenous newspapers of Taiwanese sociopolitical movements owned and managed by the Taiwanese.[25]

Throughout the 1920s, progressive Taiwanese intellectuals and students wrote numerous articles in *The Taiwan Youth* and *Taiwan minbao* to raise the awareness of women's issues. Most contributors to the magazines were members of the Taiwan Cultural Association (*Taiwan wenhua xiehui*). Established in Taihoku (Taipei) in 1921, the Taiwan Cultural Association was the home base of the Taiwan Petition movement for the creation of a local parliament. Its activists gathered signatures in Taiwan for the annual petitions to the Imperial Diet in Tokyo. To resist Japanese assimilation, its members often served as speakers in lecture tours throughout Taiwan seeking to promote Taiwan's culture and language.[26]

As an organization dominated by liberal reformers of the Petition movement in the early 1920s, the Taiwan Cultural Association's membership nevertheless included many left-wing radicals. In both the radical and reformist wings, numerous women leaders and speakers emerged. They traveled throughout urban and rural Taiwan giving lectures on women's rights and various issues pertaining to women and labor. In other words, the Cultural Association provided these women a platform for disseminating ideas about women's rights and promoting the solidarity of the Taiwanese peasantry against the exploitation of Japanese-owned industries.[27] Thus, the women's movements emerged within the sociopolitical context of the Taiwanese intelligentsia's protest against the second-class citizenship of the Taiwanese in the Japanese Empire. The goals of the women's movements were the emancipation of Taiwanese women from colonial domination, patriarchal oppression, and capitalist exploitation.[28]

As a result of growing industrialization in colonial Taiwan there were increasing incidents of strikes and confrontations between Japanese capitalists and Taiwanese laborers beginning in the mid-1920s. In response to this trend, radical youths in the Cultural Association sought to redirect the financial and human resources of the Petition movement to mobilize workers and the peasantry against Japanese business owners. However, many moderate members of the older generation in the Cultural Association were landlords, wealthy merchants, and veterans of the Petition movement for a Taiwan Parliament, and they objected to the youths' reallocation of resources. Despite this opposition, the youth outvoted their elders in 1927.[29]

After most moderate members of the Cultural Association either withdrew their membership or were expelled, they established the first political party in colonial Taiwan, the Taiwan Populist Party (*Taiwan minzhongdang*, 1927–1931).[30] Its moderate reformist strategies notwithstanding, the Taiwan Populist Party nonetheless adopted several policies regarding women from the left-wing political parties in Japan. Like its Japanese counterparts, the Taiwan Populist Party demanded home rule for colonies as well as freedom of speech, of the press, and of assembly. Its members opposed the trafficking of women and advocated gender equality and universal suffrage. Moreover, the party advocated the enactment of labor legislation to protect workers' and peasants' rights and enhance their standards of living.[31]

But unlike the left-wing political parties in Japan, the Taiwan Populist Party also formulated policies that reflected colonial Taiwan's unique conditions. It advocated a united front of the Taiwanese populace from all classes and backgrounds to resist colonial domination and establish a Taiwan Parliament. The party also called for the abolition of the traditional practice of offering cash gifts to the bride's family for betrothal. In the place of traditional arranged marriages, its members advocated monogamous free-choice marriages.[32]

Women's Independence in Marriage and the Family

In the 1920s, Taiwanese feminist discourses[33] were influenced by Japanese left-wing ideologies of socioeconomic egalitarianism, the Japanese concept of universal suffrage in *minponshugi,* and various strands of liberal and left-wing ideas espoused in the May Fourth movement (New Culture movement) in China (1915–23).[34] Even though Taiwanese intellectuals were not as radically anti-Confucian as the May Fourth intellectuals in China, they nevertheless emulated their Chinese counterparts' call for a new modern culture to replace the outdated Confucian rites of conduct (*li*). Inspired by the movement in China, Taiwanese intellectuals launched Taiwan's New Culture movement in the 1920s.[35]

As New Culture advocates, Taiwanese intellectuals critiqued the Confucian rites. In Confucianism, interpersonal interactions in society were based on five types of human relationships, including those between ruler and subject; father and son; husband and wife; older brother and younger brother; and between friends. In this male-centered social and familial hierarchy, each person had specific duties and status in his or her relationship with others.

Among these relationships, only those between friends were egalitarian. To ensure that every person in society fulfilled his or her roles and obligations in accordance with his or her station, every individual was expected to conform to the Confucian rites. These rites were a comprehensive set of socially prescribed behavioral codes for regulating behavior.[36]

To challenge the inferior status of women in the traditional Confucian framework, Taiwan's New Culture advocates stated in numerous newspaper articles that Heaven (*Tian*) endowed human rights, liberty, and equality to every man and woman. In Confucianism, *Tian* was the supreme and universal moral consciousness that presided over the hierarchical world order. By using the term to convey and legitimize men's and women's common humanity and gender equity, these intellectuals reinterpreted and modernized the concept of *Tian* along the lines of Western liberalism.[37]

Moreover, New Culture advocates called for women's independence in marriage and the family.[38] Rather than settling for a marriage arranged by the parents of the bride and the groom, a woman should have the freedom of choosing her own spouse. In instances where parents attempted to force their daughters into unwanted marriages, a female intellectual, Su Yi-chen, urged women to courageously resist coercion. She stated that traditional arranged marriages should be replaced by marriages based on love freely chosen, mutual respect, and equality between two individuals.[39] This perspective was a direct challenge to the Confucian rites of conduct still widely practiced in both China and Taiwan during the 1920s.

Traditionally, daughters and sons were obligated, through filial piety, to defer to the decisions made for them by their parents. Marriages were perceived as an agreement between two families, rather than an agreement between a young couple. As a result, daughters were often married into families capable of paying the highest prices for betrothal (*pinjin*). In general, a single woman would be evaluated based on her youth, physical appearance, capability in household management, education level, family background, and the locality in which her family lived. These factors would determine the amount of *pinjin* that the prospective bridegroom should pay to her family. Due to the nature of arranged marriages, most couples were strangers to each other on their wedding days. Consequently, it was not unusual for a couple to remain incompatible for the rest of their lives.[40]

Whereas a well-to-do man had the option of purchasing a concubine, a married woman had no choice but to tolerate the sharing of her husband with other women. As Mencius stated in the fourth century B.C.E., there were three instances in which a person was considered unfilial. Of these, failure to produce an heir was the greatest offense against one's ancestors.

Based on this Confucian tenet, a man would purchase a concubine on the grounds that his first wife was incapable of producing a male heir for his family. While society expected women to preserve their chastity at all costs, the same moral standard did not apply to men. During Taiwan's New Culture movement, this double standard became a target of intellectuals' cultural critique and discontent.[41] In a published essay in 1928, Ts'ai Tun-yao considered it odd that men were socially permitted to take concubines, while women were not allowed to have more than one husband.[42] To refute the Confucian rite's designation of a wife as socially inferior to her husband, the movement promoted the equality of husband and wife. To eliminate the notion of the bride as a commodity to be exchanged between two families, Taiwanese intellectuals advocated the abolition of the traditional practice of sending money for betrothal to the bride's family.[43]

The commodification of young girls for economic advantage by two families also contributed to the centuries-old practice of selling daughters to the families of their future husbands. These girls were traditionally known as *tongyangxi*.[44] When a poor family could ill afford to raise many children, selling or giving away a daughter to the family of her future husband could spare the parents the costs of raising the daughter. Upon her arrival to her future husband's family, she is expected to do housework. When both the *tongyangxi* and her betrothed came of age, a simple ceremony would be performed to formalize the marriage. Because the Chinese tradition expected a bridegroom's family to pay for both the betrothal and the wedding ceremony, purchasing a *tongyangxi* at a low cost could save the bridegroom's family a considerable sum of money.[45]

In some cases, the bridegroom's family would sell off the *tongyangxi* to another family or into prostitution. In 1918, the Japanese civil code outlawed the selling and purchase of persons in Taiwan. In order to evade the government's policy, poor families would put their daughter up for adoption as a legal means to transfer ownership of the child to her future husband's family. To curb the abuses and trafficking of adopted daughters, the Bureau of Social Education in the Japanese colonial government enacted policies to use police intervention as a strategy and also launched public educational campaigns to enlighten the public about the social evils of these practices.[46] This campaign, along with the government's efforts to eliminate footbinding and urge Taiwanese parents to send their daughters to school, demonstrated that the Japanese administrators in colonial Taiwan were in many ways more progressive than the Taiwanese populace. As early as 1914, the government issued and enforced an official order prohibiting footbinding. Japanese laws also granted Taiwanese women the right to divorce and remarry. To eliminate the traditional practices of purchasing or adopting *tongyangxi,* paying for betrothals, and purchasing concubines, Taiwan's New Culture intellectuals advocated legislation banning these practices.[47]

The influence of Western liberal feminism on Taiwanese intellectuals can be seen in their advocation of modern marriages based on love freely chosen (*ziyou lianai*), gender equality (*nannü pingdeng*), and free-choice marriage (*ziyou hunyin*).[48] As colonists, most of these intellectuals acquired knowledge about Western liberal feminism from their educational experiences in universities and colleges in urban Japan. In the 1920s, much of Taiwanese male intellectuals' discussion of women's status and roles was shaped by a larger discourse over the meaning of *modern.* Japan proper, the metropolis of the empire, signified modern civilization and enlightened culture where educated women resided. The modern way of life in urban Japan was the ideal culture that most Japanese-educated Taiwanese intellectuals aspired to emulate as a way to achieve upward mobility. As a symbol of Japan's modernity, women in urban Japan were often depicted in Taiwanese writing as school teachers who transmitted modern ideas or as objects of the Taiwanese male intellectuals' romantic interests. Symbolically, the modern Japanese woman represented the opposite of Taiwan's tradition-bound society, where parents still arranged marriages for their children.[49]

Underlying Taiwanese intellectuals' idealization of modern marriages based on free choice between two individuals was their belief in the sanctity of erotic love (*lianai*). A major proponent of erotic love in the West was the Swedish feminist, Ellen Key. In *Love and Marriage,* Key conceptualized love freely chosen as a synthesis of erotic and spiritual love. This interpretation received a positive reception in Japan's feminist circles. Between 1911 and 1916, excerpts of the Japanese translation of *Love and Marriage* appeared in a liberal feminist literary magazine in Japan, *Seito* (*Bluestockings*).[50] Upon completing their studies in Japan, several intellectuals promoted Key's concept of erotic love to challenge the practice of arranged marriages. They advocated the belief that carnal and spiritual union between two compatible individuals should be the foundation for a successful and happy marriage.

However, as a Japanese colony politically separated from China, colonial Taiwan's New Culture advocates were not as unanimous in their radical rejection of Confucianism as their iconoclastic counterparts in mainland China during the 1920s. In other words, different New Cultural advocates in Taiwan expressed varying degrees of disapproval of Confucianism in their essays in *Taiwan Youth* and *Taiwan minbao.* For example, in an essay in *Taiwan Youth,* Yang Wei-ming visualized an ideal marriage based on a young couple's mutual respect and understanding. In contrast to Ellen Key's emphasis on the primacy of an individual's decision to marry, Yang still urged young Taiwanese couples to seek parental consent after reaching the decision to marry. In cases where a son confronted his parents about their objection to his decision to marry the woman he loved, Yang chastised such an individual as a son who had forgotten where he came from. He suggested that the son should be attentive to his parents' feelings and the parents should be reasonable rather than authoritarian when presenting their point of view.[51] In an attempt to integrate the modern Western concept of free-choice marriage with the Confucian concept of filial piety, Yang did not offer a clear solution to a young person who could not persuade his or her parents to consent to the marriage. This article also illustrates Yang's reservations about the wholesale adoption of Western individualism.

In contrast to Yang's attempt to incorporate the modern Western concept of erotic love with the Confucian notion of filial piety, a radical Taiwanese woman intellectual, Yu Chuan, suggested that society should not pass value judgments on a young couple's decision to elope without parental consent and should not condemn men and women who had more than one lover. As long as all the parties involved are honest and respectful to each other, Chuan stated, she would support their lifestyle.[52] Similarly, at a time when arranged marriages were still the norm and divorces were almost unheard of in Taiwan, an iconoclastic Taiwanese intellectual, Ts'ai Hsiao-ch'uan, concurred with Ellen Key's assertion that a loveless marriage ought to be grounds for a "free divorce" (*ziyou lihun*)—that is, a divorce based on a person's free will.[53]

As Key provided Taiwanese intellectuals with the definition of erotic love, the character Nora in Henrik Ibsen's play, *A Doll's House*, became a symbol of female self-determination. Set against the backdrop of nineteenth-century Norwegian society, Nora made the courageous choice of leaving her unhappy married life behind to step into an unknown future. In the 1920s, Tsu Chuan, a Taiwanese student in the Chinese city of Nanjing, introduced the character to the Taiwanese public. In an article published in *Taiwan minbao* in 1929, she quoted several lines from the last act of the play. When Nora's husband confronted her about her sacred duties as a mother and a wife, Nora replied that her sacred duty was to herself. From Tsu Chuan's perspective, Ibsen's creation of this character was his way of critiquing the patriarchal social structure from a woman's perspective. After the translation of his play into several Asian and Western languages, Nora became a symbol that galvanized generations of women worldwide to choose their independence.[54]

In order to cultivate girls' independence and enable young people to befriend the opposite gender, another female scholar, Huang P'u-chun, advocated replacing the gender-segregated educational system with a coeducational system that would allow young men and women to interact freely in a gender-integrated egalitarian environment. She also argued that in the modern age, the Confucian precept dictating "males and females ought not to sit or eat together from the age of seven" should no longer be applicable.[55]

Women's Education

In addition to reforming the institution of marriage, the intellectuals also promoted women's education in colonial Taiwan. In the early 1920s, several women, including Ch'en Ying and Wu Suo-yun, emphasized women's traditional gender roles as managers of domestic affairs and educators of children at home. Similar to the argument for republican motherhood in the early years of the American republic, Ch'en and Wu argued that educated mothers could improve the quality of family education and thus elevate the quality of a nation's citizenry.[56]

While Wu saw mothers as transmitters of Confucian morality to the next generation, Ch'en, imbued with the Meiji notion of *good wife, wise mother* (*ryosai kenbo*), believed in mothers' crucial role in the intellectual preparation of children to compete for survival in a modern society. She believed that modern Taiwanese women should emulate the Confucian virtues of Mencius's mother. It was said that Mencius's mother admonished her son not to interrupt his study and was willing to relocate three times to new residential environments where he could improve his learning experiences. Hence, Ch'en attributed the excellence of Mencius's scholarship as a Confucian philosopher to his mother's educational commitment and persistent effort.

Although Ch'en endorsed women's gender-specific familial obligations in Confucianism, she nevertheless objected to the claim that "women who lacked talents were virtuous." She argued that it was illogical to expect women to be effective educators of children without availing them of the same educational opportunities as their male counterparts. Thus, whereas traditional Confucians expected women to follow and obey their husbands, Ch'en and Wu reinterpreted Confucianism to embrace the modern notion of gender equity without eliminating gender distinctions in familial relationships.

In contrast to Ch'en's and Wu's adherence to the duality of male and female gender roles, an avant-garde woman intellectual, Huang P'u-chun, asserted that men's and women's physiology and behavioral patterns were fundamentally alike at the beginning of human history. Influenced by the Marxist interpretation of historical evolution, Huang traced the genesis of men's control and domination of women and the usurpation of women's rights to the emergence of the patriarchal concept of private property. Huang contended that human rights in general and women's rights in particular were still not being acknowledged or respected in the East (*toyo*), unlike modern Western societies. She argued that Taiwanese adherence to gender roles and the presumption of women's dependence on men are by and large the consequences of the patriarchal educational system's ideological indoctrination.[57]

Contrary to Wu Suo-yun's belief in training women to be wise mothers, Huang believed that both genders should learn the same knowledge in a co-educational environment. Inspired by Western individualism's concept of self-realization, Huang asserted that it was only through a woman's acquisition of modern knowledge that she could strive for her independence.[58] Reflecting the Western concept of liberal individualism, the editorials in *Taiwan minbao* reminded women that a good education was the means of enhancing one's employment opportunities and breaking the cycle of financial dependence on one's husband and family. According to one editorial, the women who had leverage to resist unwanted arranged marriages and make free-choice marriages a reality were financially independent wage earners and professionals.[59] To empower women financially, another editorial urged women to pool their financial resources in order to establish a women's bookstore and a publishing house.[60]

Comparatively, the individualist strain of feminism evident in these editorials and in Huang P'u-chun's essay stand in direct contrast to Ch'en Ying and Wu Suo-yun's conceptualization of women's gender roles within the context of Confucian familial relationships. As it was in Taiwanese feminism, individualist feminism and relational feminism were the two main strands of feminist thought in the West. Whereas individualist feminism emphasized women's rights to self-realization outside the home, relational feminism emphasized gender equity and women's obligations in the context of interpersonal relationships within the family and society.[61]

Similar to the coexistence of Western individualism and Confucianism in colonial Korea during the 1920s, the influence of Western individualism in Taiwan's intellectual circles coexisted with Confucianism's emphasis on an individual's obligations to familial relationships and societal roles. In 1928, a Taiwanese intellectual, Chang Yueh-ch'eng, indicated that every individual, regardless of one's gender, should have the right to self-expression, individual freedom, economic independence, and political participation. On the other hand, he or she should manage the household and contribute to society.[62]

In addition to articulating the gender-egalitarian vision of Taiwanese men's and women's rights and obligations, Taiwanese intellectuals demanded that Taiwanese men and women enjoy equal access to all levels of educational institutions.[63] In 1926, while 98 percent of Japanese boys and girls were attending elementary schools in Taiwan, only 43 percent of Taiwanese boys and 13 percent of Taiwanese girls were enrolled in the colonial school system. Despite the fact that the vast majority of taxpayers in colonial Taiwan were Taiwanese, the elementary schools with predominantly Japanese children had double the financial resources of their Taiwanese counterparts.[64] To rectify this disparity, activists demanded that Taiwanese children be accorded the same rights and opportunities to universal compulsory education as Japanese children.[65] Furthermore, Taiwanese reformers demanded that the colonial government enforce the promises made in the governor-general's Integration Rescript of 1922. The rescript stated that Taiwanese and Japanese children should attend the same middle and high schools. It also stated that ethnicity should no longer be a factor in school admissions.[66]

In reality, only a small number of Taiwanese pupils were admitted to middle schools in comparison with a large number of Japanese nationals in Taiwan. The girls' high school also privileged Japanese applicants over their Taiwanese counterparts. In 1929, 60 percent of Japanese applicants were admitted to girls' high school. In contrast, only 44 percent of Taiwanese applicants were admitted.[67] By the early 1940s, most Taiwanese students still attended schools with a predominantly Taiwanese student body. Conversely, Japanese nationals in Taiwan still attended schools with a predominantly Japanese student body.[68]

The liberal reformers of the Petition movement used the failure of the Japanese government to fulfill the promise of ethnic equality to strengthen their case for the creation of a Taiwan Parliament.[69] Based on their rationale, a Taiwan Parliament's legislative power could counter-balance a governor-general's executive power. Not only could the Taiwan Parliament abolish the colonial laws that relegated the Taiwanese to second-class citizenship, it could also verify the colonial government's enforcement of the Integration Rescript to fulfill the promise of ethnic equality. Lastly, the reformers argued that legislators of the Taiwan Parliament ought to be elected via universal suffrage of all adult residents of Taiwan.[70]

Despite the colonial government's tacit acceptance of de facto discrimination and ethnic segregation, it was successful in promoting Taiwanese schoolgirls' functional literacy. In 1922, only 12 percent of Taiwanese school-age girls were enrolled in common schools (ko gakko). By 1944, Taiwanese girls' enrollment rose to 61 percent. Under the system of Japanese colonial education, the graduates of common schools received the equivalence of elementary education.[71]

The goal of colonial education was to provide Taiwanese girls with basic skills and knowledge to be competent workers in labor-intensive industries and to socialize them to be good wives and wise mothers capable of educating the young. Colonial schools also served to instill Confucian ethical values, socialize children to be loyal subjects of the Japanese Empire, assimilate them into the Japanese culture, and improve their proficiency in the Japanese language.[72]

Since Japanese was the common language spoken in colonial schools, it became the lingua franca of both Chinese and Malayo-Polynesian indigenous populations from diverse linguistic backgrounds in colonial Taiwan. Young Taiwanese of both genders used the Japanese language to articulate their shared grievances as colonial subjects. The development of Taiwanese nationalistic consciousness became an unintended consequence of Japanese colonial education.[73]

In the colonial educational system, Taiwanese girls had the option of applying for admission to a girls' high school after graduation from the common schools. The high school curriculum included Japanese,[74] Confucian ethics, natural sciences, music, physical education, sewing, and handicrafts. As a school created for the purpose of training Taiwanese women teachers for common schools, it required three years less schooling than their male counterparts. Consequently, they were paid less than Taiwanese male teachers.[75]

Although the colonial government educated Taiwanese schoolgirls in basic skills and functional literacy, it nevertheless attempted to discourage women from obtaining higher education. In 1918, a conference of Japan's Ministry of Education concluded that Japanese women with higher education tended to harbor dangerous thoughts. Moreover, they contended that women with more education generally bore fewer children and were less dutiful wives and daughters-in-law than less educated women.[76] In 1928, a Taiwanese student, Han Shih-lin, criticized the emphasis in Japanese colonial education on the socialization of females to be good mothers, wives, and daughters. According to Han, both male and female students should be socialized to become good citizens as well as complete human beings who could realize their individual potential.[77]

Confronting the dual obstacles of ethnic chauvinism and sexism, Taiwanese women were denied the educational opportunities as available to Japanese and Taiwanese men. The only institution of higher learning in colonial Taiwan, Taihoku Imperial University, strongly favored Japanese applicants for admission. Consequently, the majority of Taiwanese who aspired to obtain a higher education had to gather enough financial resources for their studies on Japan's home islands.[78] Under these adverse circumstances, it was no small feat for some Taiwanese women to succeed in passing the highly competitive entrance examinations for admission to women's colleges on Japan's home islands. From the late 1910s to 1945, women studied medicine, nursing, dentistry, education, commerce, home economics, performing and fine arts, and social and natural sciences at Japanese institutions of higher learning. Upon their graduation, some entered professions such as civil service, teaching, journalism, nursing, midwifery, medicine, and bookkeeping.[79]

Women's Economic Independence and the Rights of Women among the Working Class and the Peasantry

The experience of Ts'ai A-hsin offers a notable example of the crucial role of women's higher education in fostering women's economic independence and contribution to society. Born in 1896, the marriage of Ts'ai's mother to her wealthy stepfather enabled her to obtain the best education in Japan. In 1915, she was admitted to the Tokyo Women's Medical College. Upon her graduation in 1921, Ts'ai returned to Taiwan and completed her residency at the Taihoku Hospital and became colonial Taiwan's first female physician. In 1925, Ts'ai established her own hospital at her residence in Taichu (*Taichung*). Based on Ts'ai's observation, many Taiwanese women were imbued with the traditional concepts of gender segregation and female propriety. They were thus resistant to the idea of visiting male physicians. Because of the underdeveloped facilities and shortage of well-trained personnel in obstetrics, women too often died in childbirth. To improve their health and prenatal care, Ts'ai created a seminar for the purpose of training midwives in obstetrics. To ensure the trainees' mastery of all relevant skills, the seminar was integrated into her hospital. From 1928 to 1938, it was estimated that five hundred students graduated from Ts'ai's training program.[80]

With the Japanese invasion of northern China in 1937, the colonial police periodically came to Ts'ai's seminar and randomly selected young women to serve as nurses on the front line. These occurrences caused much fear and anxiety among Ts'ai's students. Consequently, many withdrew from her seminar. Faced with this situation, Ts'ai had no other alternative but to terminate the training program in 1938. Despite the occasional setbacks, Ts'ai successfully attracted many female patients from the rural peasantry to her hospital. Inasmuch as Ts'ai offered the best medical care to impoverished peasant women without demanding payment, many peasants who could ill afford to pay a doctor would send their home-grown vegetables, fruits, and poultry to her residence. Apparently, her altruistic spirit and medical ethic had won her the trust and affection of Taichu's peasantry.[81]

At the turn of the twentieth century, Taiwanese physicians cooperated with the Japanese colonial government to abolish the traditional Chinese custom of footbinding in Taiwan. The government saw the liberation of Taiwanese women from this physical constraint as a way for the female population to contribute to the economy.[82] Beginning in the 1930s, urban women of both Japanese and Taiwanese backgrounds were employed in a variety of female-oriented service jobs as well as several male-dominated occupations—they were construction workers, bus conductors, drivers, radio broadcasters, telephone operators, waitresses in teahouses and restaurants, bar girls, entertainers, musicians, licensed prostitutes, massage workers, barbers, dressmakers, washerwomen, domestic maids, babysitters, office workers, store clerks, and factory workers.[83]

Meanwhile, Japanese capitalists took advantage of Taiwanese women's cheap labor in the light industries and farming sector. In colonial Taiwan, the vast majority of workers who engaged in the cottage industry's labor-intensive piecework were women. Among the factory mill hands, women and girls comprised a quarter of the industrial labor force in the early 1920s. Female workers in industries producing garments, textiles, sugar, tea, and other processed foods were required to work between ten and twelve hours a day. According to Yamakawa Hitoshi's study of several Japanese-owned industries in Taiwan during the 1920s, Taiwanese male workers generally received half the pay of their Japanese male counterparts for performing the same tasks. Among the Taiwanese, female workers tended to receive half of male workers' pay for performing the same tasks.[84]

Due to the acceleration of urban industrialization in colonial Taiwan from the mid-1920s onward, there were increasing instances of labor disputes between Japanese capitalists and Taiwanese laborers. Most women strikers protested against adverse working conditions, increased work hours, wage reductions, and unreasonable terminations of employment.[85] For guidance in the strategies of staging strikes and collective bargaining, many women solicited help from left-wing intellectuals in the Taiwan Cultural Association. As police suppression of strikers increased, the Taiwanese Communists and other left-wing activists conceived of a united front of Taiwanese from all sectors and strata of society to overthrow Japanese capital and the colonial government. In 1928, this was seen as a militant strategy for achieving Taiwanese independence from the Japanese Empire.[86]

The leftists' revolutionary approach to self-determination was contrary to the moderate non-violent approach of the Taiwanese liberals in the Petition movement. The latter advocated Taiwan's home rule as a constituent part of the Japanese Empire.[87] Since the mid-1920s, many liberal reformers actively supported female strikers by offering legal assistance to them in colonial courts. Whereas many liberal reformers still adhered to the belief of reforming the colonial economy and the political system within the Japanese legal framework,[88] the leftist radicals envisioned a nationalistic and proletarian revolution for the liberation of Taiwanese workers and peasants from colonial domination and capitalist exploitation.

In the late 1920s, two of the most influential left-wing organizations for the promotion of women laborers' rights were the Taiwan Farmers' Union (*Taiwan nongmin zuhe*) and the Taiwan Communist Party.[89] With the Bolshevik women's movement as their model, the Taiwan Farmers' Union and the Taiwan Communist Party trained female students and intellectuals to organize women laborers for the struggle to improve their working conditions and fight for equal pay for equal work. Based on the agendas of the Soviet women's movement, the Taiwan Farmers' Union and the Taiwan Communist Party advocated an eight hour work day; women workers' full pay during maternity leaves; the creation of free childcare facilities for women laborers; and women's freedom and equality to participate in wage labor and politics.[90]

To disseminate these policies and implement them among the masses, both left-wing organizations established women's departments in 1928. Women activists from the Taiwan Farmers' Union regularly gave speeches throughout Taiwan to awaken women farm laborers' consciousness and inform them of the need to unite with male laborers against exploitation by Japanese capitalists. Yet, due to the government's nationwide campaigns to arrest suspected Communists in Japan, Korea, and Taiwan, many leaders of the Cultural Association, the Farmers' Union, and the Communist Party either served prison terms or went underground in 1929 and thereafter. Consequently, most of the aforementioned policies for women laborers' rights and welfare were not implemented among the masses.[91]

In the 1920s, both the radical left-wing and the liberal reformist wing of Taiwan's social and political movements incorporated into their discourses the demands for women's liberation to achieve full economic and political participation, equal educational opportunities, and freedom and independence in the institutions of marriage and the family. However, most women activists who rose to positions of leadership and prominence belonged to the radical left-wing organizations, such as the Taiwan Farmers' Union and the Taiwan Communist Party.[92]

The most notable example of female leadership in Taiwan's proletarian movement was Hsieh Hsueh-hung (1901–70), a leader of both the Taiwan Communist Party (1928–31) and the Taiwan Farmers' Union (1926–36). Orphaned at the age of twelve, Hsieh went to live with her relatives. A year later, she was sold to her first husband as a concubine. At the age of sixteen, she ran away from her husband's family to work as a mill hand in a sugar factory. Though she was not yet able to articulate her political beliefs, her firsthand experiences as a concubine and a factory worker nevertheless sowed the seed for her future resistance to patriarchal oppression and the exploitation of Taiwanese women workers.[93]

In 1917, Hsieh traveled to Kobe, Japan. For the next three years, she improved her proficiency in Japanese and learned Mandarin Chinese. When the Taiwan Cultural Association was established in 1921, she became one of the activists in the women's movement of the association. After being harassed by the colonial police in Taiwan, she fled to China in 1925. In Shanghai, she befriended several Chinese Communists and attended Shanghai University to study Marxist sociology. Shortly thereafter, she traveled to Moscow and attended the Communist University for the Toilers of the East for two years. There she enrolled in courses on Marxist-Leninist revolutionary strategies. It was in Moscow that Hsieh befriended several Japanese Communist leaders and paved the way for the creation of the Taiwan Communist Party under the guidance of the Japanese Communist Party.[94]

As a founder of the Taiwan Communist Party in 1928, Hsieh imagined a united front of progressive men and women from middle class, working class, and peasant backgrounds to wage a nationalistic struggle against Japanese capital and the colonial government. Inspired by the Soviet women's movement, Hsieh advocated the creation of women's departments in all the local branches of the Taiwan Farmers' Union and the Taiwan Communist Party. The tasks of the women's departments were recruitment, Marxist-Leninist ideological training, and the mobilization of Taiwanese women to participate in the revolution. In accordance with the cosmopolitan worldview of Marxism-Leninism, Hsieh further envisioned a united front of women in Japan, Taiwan, Korea, and China. Many women students from these four societies had befriended each other and developed their leftist political orientations while studying in Tokyo. East Asian women also had the common experience of subordination under Confucian patriarchy. In addition, Korean women activists' participation in Korea's nationalistic struggle against Japanese colonial rule in the March First movement of 1919 galvanized many Taiwanese women students to struggle for Taiwanese self-determination.[95]

In the 1920s, many left-wing Taiwanese activists of both genders adopted the simplistic Marxist-Leninist presumption that gender equality would more or less be achieved after the dual domination of Japanese colonialism and Japanese capital was eliminated in Taiwan. They considered women's liberation (J: *fujin kaiho*; C: *furen jiefang*) as subordinate to and dependent on the larger goals of proletarian and nationalist revolutions. Due to this oversimplification, Taiwan's left-wing discourses on women's oppression in the 1920s did not treat women's oppression as an independent topic that deserved as much in-depth and independent analysis as the issues pertaining to capitalist exploitation and anti-colonialism.[96]

As a leader of the Taiwan Communist Party and the Taiwan Farmers' Union, Hsieh opposed the ideological and institutional separation of women's movements from the anti-colonial and proletarian movements. To her, any independent women's movement not part of Taiwan's anti-colonial and proletarian movements would be incapable of liberating the entire female population.[97] Due to the upper- and middle-class backgrounds of most feminists (*funü yundong zhe*) in the autonomous women's associations, Hsieh contended that their feminist agendas tended to prioritize the improvement of economically privileged women's status over that of women in the working class and the peasantry. Consequently, the vast majority of women could not identify with the agendas of these women's associations.[98]

According to Hsieh, a woman should seek emancipation through political participation in proletarian and peasant movements. In the process of awakening the nationalistic, gender, and class consciousness of women, the activists also gained the opportunity to improve their own leadership abilities and organizational skills. By recruiting rural women into the Taiwan Farmers' Union, Hsieh contended that merging the peasant movement with the women's movement could strengthen Taiwanese resistance to Japanese capital's exploitation of sugarcane farmers and confiscation of Taiwanese farmers' land. Through their political participation in the peasant movement, Hsieh asserted that women could develop their political consciousness and achieve equality with their male counterparts.[99] Despite Hsieh's refusal to identify herself as an advocate of the women's rights movement (*nüquan yundong zhe*), she was nonetheless committed to the concept of gender equality. The difference between Hsieh's radical revolutionary approach and the reformist agendas of autonomous women's associations from the moderate liberal perspective illustrated the lack of solidarity among women activists in regards to the means to liberate women in colonial Taiwan.

Autonomous Women's Associations

In contrast to Hsieh's negative portrayal of middle-class feminists in the autonomous women's associations, many feminist activists were aware of capitalists' exploitation of women workers.[100] Inspired by the women's rights associations in Japan proper, women activists in colonial Taiwan created several autonomous women's associations between 1925 and 1931.[101] In a typical women's association, activists were primarily upper- and middle-class professional women and wives of Taiwanese professionals, merchants, or gentry-scholars. Hence, homemakers and professional women created a space where they had ample opportunities to interact among themselves.[102]

Compared with the radical revolutionary goals of the Taiwan Farmers' Union and the Taiwan Communist Party, the goals of several autonomous women's associations were relatively moderate and reformist. Among their objectives were the promotion of women workers' rights and women's movements in Taiwan, the exchange of knowledge and ideas, and the provision of mutual assistance and emotional support among members through friendship networks.[103] Among these associations, both the *Funü gonglihui* in Takao (*Kaohsiung*) and the women's department of the Taipei Youth Study Society focused on women's issues and gender inequalities. They advocated cooperation between progressive men and women to oppose patriarchal values in Taiwanese society.[104] With the influence of Confucianism on women activists' consciousness, the cultivation of moral character through self-introspection became one of the goals of *Zhuluo funü xiejinhui* (Woman's Association for Mutual Assistance, Collective Action, and Advancement). On the other hand, the same activists called for the destruction of certain aspects of Confucian rites of conduct that had oppressed women in the family and hampered women's economic independence.[105]

To promote women's rights in the family and society, a Taiwanese intellectual, P'an Tse-hsiang, urged women's associations to organize lecture tours throughout the island for the promotion of women's liberation (*funü jiefang*).[106] As associations of women intellectuals, one of their goals should be to raise women's awareness of their rights and obligations in society. This feminist strategy was a legacy of the cultural-intellectual approach from the Chinese traditional past. Historically, Chinese gentry-scholars considered the transformation of cultural values and belief systems to be a precondition for other changes in society. According to Lin Yu-sheng, the cultural-intellectual approach was based on this line of thinking.[107] Thus, the activists' conviction of the need to change the cultural values and belief systems of the Taiwanese public was indicative of the cultural-intellectual approach. From the mid-1920s to the early 1930s, at least ninety-one women from various women's associations and the women's departments of left-wing organizations had given talks on various women's issues to sizable audiences throughout Taiwan.

Based on the investigative reports of several journalists in *Taiwan minbao*, the number who attended each lecture numbered between several hundred and more than two thousand.[108]

Whereas the cultural-intellectual approach influenced the strategies of Taiwanese women's movements, the absence of a Taiwan Parliament eliminated legislative lobbying as an option for the feminists to address their grievances and demands. Due to the governor-general's persistent opposition to the creation of a Taiwan Parliament on the premise that it was a movement with a strong tinge of Taiwanese nationalism, the annual petitions from 1921 to 1934 were never openly debated on the floor of the Imperial Diet.[109] Thus, whereas legislative lobbying was an important strategy of Japanese feminists' struggle for woman suffrage and other pro-woman legislation,[110] it was not a salient program of action for colonial Taiwan's autonomous women's movements.

In comparison with their Japanese counterparts, autonomous women's organizations in colonial Taiwan were relatively short-lived. Many Taiwanese activists succumbed to a shortage of funds and parental opposition to their involvement in the women's movement.[111] Notwithstanding the moderate nature of most women's associations in Taiwan, the Japanese colonial police placed activists in these associations under surveillance. With Japan's invasion of Manchuria in 1931, Japanese militarists stepped up their suppression of political dissent in Japan, Korea, and Taiwan. By the early 1930s, the colonial government suppressed the left-wing women's movements and the social and political movements that sponsored them, such as the Taiwan Cultural Association and the Taiwan Communist Party. Even though the Taiwan Farmers' Union was not completely dissolved until 1936, the imprisonment of its leadership greatly reduced the capability of its women's department to mobilize the masses of rural women.[112]

Government-Affiliated Women's Organizations

Whereas the autonomous women's movements in Taiwan were suppressed in the early 1930s, the government-affiliated women's organizations in Japan and its colonies flourished during Japan's military expansion. As early as 1887, the Nurses' Association of the Japanese Red Cross was established under the patronage of women in the Japanese imperial family. The purpose of the Nurses' Association was to promote the training of nurses and the visibility of the nursing profession. In 1889, the Japanese Red Cross established the curriculum, pedagogy, and guidelines for the training of nurses. On Japan's home islands, nursing students were required to undergo three and a half years of schooling and internship. During the duration of their study, they were taught human anatomy, dissection, disinfecting methods, and para-medic skills for emergency rescue. Beginning in 1899, local chapters of the Nurses' Association of the Japanese Red Cross were established in several cities in colonial Taiwan to train and recruit women into the profession. The memberships of each local chapter consisted of nurses, notable women in the Taiwanese community, and wives of Japanese government officials and civil servants. In 1904, the duration of study for nursing students was changed to three years.[113]

After Japan invaded northern China in 1937, the Japanese Red Cross sent both Japanese and Taiwanese nurses to the frontlines to provide emergency medical care to wounded soldiers. In order to reinforce the Taiwanese pop-ulace's identification with Japan's imperialistic project, the mass media in Taiwan emphasized the valor of Taiwanese nurses and soldiers who volun-teered to go to the frontlines in the service of the Japanese Empire. As Japan invaded Southeast Asia and confronted the Anglo-American Alliance during the Pacific War (1941–45), some nurses in Japan proper and colonial Taiwan received their training within two years instead of three. Meanwhile, the Japanese Red Cross also trained thousands of instant nurses within several months to meet the shortage of caregivers on the battlefields. On the home front, nurses in each locality organized rescue teams to treat wounded sol-diers who returned from the war zones.[114]

The government-affiliated women's association in charge of consoling wounded military personnel was the Patriotic Women's Association (*Aikoku fujinkai*). As early as 1901, the Patriotic Women's Association was created with the support of the Army Ministry, the president of the Upper House in the Imperial Diet, and the Home Ministry of the Japanese government.[115] With the outbreak of the Russo-Japanese War (1904–5), the Taiwan chapters of the Patriotic Women's Association were established under the guidance and support of the colonial government to mobilize women's auxiliary support for Japanese troops.[116]

After Japan's victory in the Russo-Japanese War, members of the Patriotic Women's Association focused their attention on consoling injured military personnel and visiting families of deceased soldiers who had participated in military campaigns to suppress the aborigines' armed resistance in colonial Taiwan. Since the mountainous regions where the indigenous population resided were wooded areas with the greatest source of camphor, the colonial authority waged a series of military campaigns to take control of this lucrative commodity in international trade. Camphor, "a white crystalline substance distilled from a species of laurel tree,"[117] was sold and used as an aromatic and a plasticizer for manufacturing photographic film. To control and limit the production output of camphor in the world market and thereby keep prices artificially high, the Japanese colonial authority deemed the production of camphor without a government-issued license illegal. Since most licenses were issued to Japanese camphor capitalists rather than to indigenous camphor producers, the indigenous communities that were the most economically devastated by this new policy organized armed resistance to assert their customary rights to the forests and the freedom to produce camphor without governmental restrictions.[118] Despite the Japanese armed forces' superior weaponry, the troops generally had to face fierce combat and suffer severe casualties. As members of a government-affiliated women's organization, the Taiwan chapters of the Patriotic Women's Association offered their financial and moral support to the troops and their families.[119]

In colonial Taiwan, the first three chapters of the Patriotic Women's Association were established in Tainan in the south, Taichung in the central region of the island, and Taipei in the north. Many more chapters were later established in different localities throughout the island. Typically, the wife of the chief administrative official in each locality would lead each chapter. Whereas most of the officers in leadership positions were Japanese, the vast majority of the Association's rank-and-file members were Taiwanese women and wives of civil servants and local elite who had developed strong ties with the colonial government.[120] In this sense, their educational and class backgrounds were similar to activists in the autonomous women's movements. Yet, contrary to the activists' promotion of Taiwanese culture in the autonomous women's associations, members of the Patriotic Women's Association functioned as an institutional instrument for the colonial government to reinforce Taiwanese women's identification with the Japanese nation.[121]

After the early 1920s, the colonial government enacted a policy of gradual assimilation of the Taiwanese into Japanese culture. From Japan's invasion of northern China in 1937 to its defeat in World War II, the government intensified its campaign to assimilate the Taiwanese through the imperialization movement (*kominka undo*). The Japanese term *kominka* may be translated literally as "to transform [the colonial peoples] into imperial subjects."[122] According to proponents of the movement, the Taiwanese people's total identification with Japanese culture and unequivocal loyalty to the Japanese nation could optimize the government's mobilization of Taiwan's human resources for waging a total war. In order to win the hearts and minds of the Taiwanese people, the colonial government expanded its programs for the building of power plants to promote rural electrification and transportation infrastructures to support the island's industrialization. During World War II, Japanese economic and industrial planners developed heavy industries in

Taiwan to use the island as a naval base for Japan's expansion into European and American colonies in Southeast Asia and the South Pacific. Factories were also equipped with machinery to process raw materials extracted from Southeast Asia.[123]

From 1936 to 1945, military rule was reinstated in Taiwan. To prepare the Taiwanese for a total war, phrases such as *imperial nation's spirit (kokoku seishin)* and *military nation's spirit (gunkoku seishin)* permeated every sector of public life, the educational system, and the mass media. In order to eliminate Taiwan's cultural autonomy from Japan, the Taiwanese were encouraged to change their family names from Chinese to Japanese surnames. Since most Taoist (Daoist) deities worshipped in Taiwan were originally from China, Taoist temples were either destroyed or replaced by government-sponsored Shinto shrines to promote the state religion of imperial Japan. The colonial state's attempt to replace Taiwan's folk beliefs with Shintoism notwithstanding, Taoist beliefs remained deeply entrenched in the island's local culture. Among the Taoists in Taiwan, the most venerated deity was Matsu, goddess of the sea and the patron saint of fishermen and seafarers.[124] During a series of air raids over Taiwan by U.S. forces in the Pacific War, a fabulous legend circulated throughout the island that "the Goddess Matsu appeared in the sky during an attack by American aircraft and caught the falling bombs in her uplifted skirt."[125]

After Japan invaded northern China in 1937, the colonial government sought to eradicate Taiwan's cultural affinity with China. It eliminated classical Chinese from the curriculum of the colonial school system and banned Chinese language publications.[126] Consonant with this colonial policy, the Patriotic Women's Association organized literacy courses to improve Taiwanese women's proficiency in the Japanese language. They regarded fluency in the national language (Japanese) as a means of fostering Taiwanese women's identification with the Japanese nation.[127] At home, Taiwanese mothers were urged to speak Japanese with their children.

To mobilize women for the industrialization of Taiwan's war economy in the 1930s, members of the Patriotic Women's Association encouraged women in all sectors of Taiwanese society to fulfill their patriotic duties by contributing their labor in cottage industries, factories, and agricultural sectors. The association established vocational schools for female family members of police officers and soldiers who were severely injured or who had died in the line of duty. In order to enhance the economic self-sufficiency of these families, women who enrolled were taught gender-specific skills and practical knowledge for making a living—raising silkworms for the silk industry, manufacturing handicrafts, tailoring, home economics, nursing, typing, and commerce. To encourage mothers' enrollment in these schools, the Patriotic Women's Association provided childcare facilities to alleviate their parental responsibilities while attending classes, and members volunteered their time to raise funds for childcare and vocational education.[128]

In 1904, the colonial government launched the Taiwan Women's Philanthropic Association (*Taiwan fujin jizenkai*) to raise funds for social welfare. Unlike the other government-affiliated women's associations that originated in Japan, the Taiwan Women's Philanthropic Association was the brainchild of Goto Shimpei, the head of civil administration in the colonial government. With Goto Kazuko, wife of Goto Shimpei, as its founding president, members of the Philanthropic Association were wives of colonial Taiwan's government officials, managers of government-owned enterprises, military officers, and the Taiwanese elite in Taihoku. Some of these women also had overlapping memberships in the Patriotic Women's Association.[129]

To solicit donations, the Philanthropic Association held numerous charity concerts featuring prominent Japanese singers, school children, and government officials and their wives singing Japanese and Western songs. The proceeds from these concerts were used to purchase hospital beds for the Japanese Red Cross and for disaster relief in colonial Taiwan. Some members raised funds to purchase bathtubs for the public baths at hot springs for therapeutic use by patients with skin ailments. In order to deter the growth of slums in the southern seaport of Takao (Kaohsiung), the Philanthropic Association contributed financial resources to demolish old buildings and build new apartments for slum dwellers. It also raised funds for the medical treatment of victims of contagious diseases and injured soldiers during the Japanese military campaigns to suppress the indigenous population's resistance in mountainous regions of Taiwan.[130]

In response to the Japanese army's invasion of Manchuria in 1931, housewives in Japan proper were urged to join the Greater Japan National Defense Women's Association (*Dai Nihon kokubo fujinkai*). The following year, the Army Ministry in Tokyo assumed control of the Association. Similar to the members of the Patriotic Women's Association, activists in the National Defense Women's Association saw themselves as mothers of the Japanese nation. As they extended their nurturing roles from the domestic realm to the public domain, they visited and consoled wounded military personnel and bereaved families of deceased soldiers.[131] In the aftermath of Japan's invasion of northern China in 1937, chapters of the National Defense Women's Association were created in several Taiwanese cities to mobilize women for their auxiliary support of the Japanese army's war effort. The chapters' missions were as follows: raising children to be mentally and physically strong for the future of the nation, mobilizing women in each community to send off soldiers to the battlefields, and filling in the jobs that men left behind when they were sent to war.[132]

In 1942, the Greater Japan Women's Association (*Dai Nihon fujinkai*) was established under the sponsorship of the Japanese government to promote the total mobilization of women on the home front for Japan's war effort. In the same year, the headquarters of the Greater Japan Women's Association in Taiwan was created in Taihoku with the support of the colonial government. Soon thereafter it established branches in every city and town in Taiwan. As on Japan's home islands, the purpose of establishing the Greater Japan Women's Association in Taiwan was to eliminate redundant functions of various government-affiliated women's organizations as well as to consolidate and streamline these women's organizations' human and financial resources. To this end, all the above-mentioned government-affiliated women's organizations were ordered to dissolve and merge their memberships and financial resources into the newly created Greater Japan Women's Association.[133]

During the Pacific War, activists in the association urged women to save money, conserve energy, and recycle used materials and scrap metals. In each community, women activists coordinated the basic training for evacuation of each neighborhood to bomb shelters during air raids. They also coordinated basic training in emergency rescue. As young men in Taiwan were sent to the battlefields, the association mobilized women on the home front to increase agricultural production and to work in war-related industries.[134] In response to labor shortages, women were recruited to work in plants that produced hydroelectric power, metals, fertilizers, coal, cement, alcohol, cigarettes, salt, canned foods, matches, paper, and medicine. By the early 1940s, more than 40 percent of all factory workers in colonial Taiwan were women.[135]

On the other hand, the militarists in the Japanese government praised married women's primary roles as good wives and wise mothers. In line with this ideology, the Greater Japan Women's Association in Taiwan rewarded exemplary matchmakers who had successfully introduced young couples to each other. Through these matchmakers, young couples tied the knot and produced potential soldiers for Japan's expanding empire.[136] In retrospect, the dual roles of motherhood and labor in the service of the empire contributed to the double burden of women in Japan proper and colonial Taiwan.

As adult women of Taiwan were mobilized to join the Greater Japan Women's Association, Taiwanese girls of high-school age were encouraged to join the Girls' Youth Corps (*Joshi seinendan*). Members of the Girls' Youth Corps attended seminars to acquire knowledge about tailoring, children's healthcare, home management (to minimize household expenditures), using first aid kits, participating in air raid drills, rescuing and treating the injured after an air raid, and physical training for firefighting during wartime mobilization. To meet the shortage of nurses at Lotung in northern Taiwan, local members of the Girls' Youth Corps volunteered to be nurses and received basic training to assist physicians during an outbreak of meningitis.[137] During the Pacific War, some nursing volunteers for the frontline came from the Girls' Youth Corps. Due to the combined effects of official praise for female volunteers, wartime ideological indoctrination, and peer pressure, it was quite common for Taiwanese girls to volunteer as nurses on the frontline during the early 1940s. For many Taiwanese, their exemplary service to the empire was a way for them to demonstrate their capability as equals of their Japanese counterparts.[138]

During World War II, Girls' Youth Corps in colonial Taiwan were organized into agricultural teams to work in rice fields for their extra-curricular activities. In preparation for a protracted war, the island was given the task of producing surplus rice for storage in granaries. Since some of the male farmhands were sent to the war zones, participation of adolescent girls and women in agricultural production became a key strategy for the government to respond to the shortage of farm labor. Members of the Girls' Youth Corps attended rice production seminars to receive instructions on the agricultural techniques for increasing the quality and quantity of rice production. Whereas some members of the Girls' Youth Corps joined agricultural teams, other high school girls with more technical aptitude and skills either volunteered or were selected to work in war-related industries. To prepare them for war work, these girls were taught the methods of camouflaging warplanes and military warehouses with large nets. They also acquired technical knowledge about how to fix electrical insulation materials and weld broken wings of warplanes. To meet the labor shortage in the mining industry during the Pacific War, young women were also employed as miners.[139]

Conclusion

In retrospect, the period of Japan's wartime mobilization provides a stark contrast to the era of the Taisho democracy. In the 1920s, the liberal democratic experience in Taisho Japan, the cultural critique of Confucian patriarchy in the New Culture movement in China, and Marxism-Leninism from Soviet Russia all exerted significant influence on social activists' visions of Taiwanese women's liberation. Although colonial Taiwan's intellectuals critiqued gender-biased aspects of Confucianism, many of them were still imbued with Confucianism's emphasis on a woman's gender-specific obligations to her familial relationships. Whereas relational feminism in Taiwan emphasized women's rights and obligations within the context of interpersonal relationships in the family and society, the Western-inspired liberal individualist strand of feminism emphasized women's rights to self-realization outside the home.[140] In the 1920s, the advocacy of autonomous women's movements for women's economic independence was derived from the dual influence of Western liberal feminism and Marxism-Leninism's emphasis on women's financial self-reliance as the main determinant of their emancipation.[141]

In the 1920s and early 1930s, the autonomous social and political movements' promotion of Taiwan's cultural autonomy mitigated the effects of the colonial government's assimilation policy. With the collapse of the autonomous social and political movements, the balance tilted in favor of the Japanization program. Ultimately, the policy of intensified cultural assimilation did not result in the complete Japanization of the Taiwanese population.[142] After the defeat of Japan in 1945, the Allies transferred control of Taiwan to the Chinese Nationalist government.

2. The Kuomintang Policies on Women and Government-Affiliated Women's Organizations

In 1949, four years after Taiwan was reintegrated into the Chinese polity, Chinese Communist troops defeated the Chinese Nationalists (Kuomintang) and the Kuomintang transferred the government to Taiwan. Prior to its arrival on the island, the Kuomintang promulgated civil codes and policies on mainland China dealing with women's issues. These codes and policies were transferred to Taiwan and implemented during the postwar era.

This chapter provides a historical overview of the continuities of the Chinese Nationalist ideology and the Kuomintang's policies toward women from the First United Front (1923–27) in mainland China to its rule in postwar Taiwan (1945–2000). Moreover, I will discuss the programs of the Kuomintang-affiliated women's organizations in postwar Taiwan and the similarities and changes between the government-affiliated women's organizations before and after the war. The Kuomintang-affiliated women's organizations that had the greatest impact were the Taiwan Provincial Women's Association, the Chinese Women's Anti-Aggression League, and the Kuomintang Women's Working Committee.

To examine the programs of the women's organizations, the Chinese Nationalist ideology, and the policies toward women, I analyze Madame Chiang's Confucian-oriented ideology toward women and her programs for the mobilization of women in postwar Taiwan. This chapter shows that the Kuomintang civil codes enacted in the early 1930s were an ideological compromise between traditional Confucian patriarchy and the May Fourth intellectuals' belief in the Western liberal concepts of individual rights and freedom.

The May Fourth (New Culture) Movement, 1915–23

During World War I (1914–18), the United States persuaded China to fight on the side of Allied Powers. In 1919, upon hearing the news that the Western Powers had transferred the German concession in Shandong Province to Japan based on the terms of the Treaty of Versailles, Chinese intellectuals and students launched the May Fourth demonstration in all major Chinese cities. They protested the Western Powers' failure to return the German Concession to China and the Chinese government's inability to stand up against the unequal treaty. The radical intellectuals saw the adoption of Western ideas and institutions as a way to strengthen and modernize China and thereby resist Western and Japanese imperialism. In the May Fourth movement (also known as the New Culture movement), radical intellectuals called for the total eradication of Confucian patriarchy and a wholesale adoption of Western values and institutions.[1]

Inspired by Western liberal individualism, feminist discourse in the New Culture movement in urban China was in many ways similar to its counterpart in colonial Taiwan during the 1920s. On both sides of the Taiwan Strait, women's rights advocates called for free-choice marriage, gender integration in social interaction and coeducation, women's economic independence in family and society, and gender equality in employment opportunities and political participation.[2] Given the fact that many women's rights advocates in colonial Taiwan studied in China during the New Culture movement and subsequently transmitted their ideas to the Taiwanese populace, the similarities are not surprising. On the other hand, in the 1920s Taiwan was a Japanese colony. Thus, its feminist discourse focused on inequalities between Taiwanese men and women as well as between the Taiwanese and Japanese in political rights and educational and employment opportunities.[3] Because Japan did not invade China until the 1930s, disparity between the Japanese and Chinese was not an integral part of feminist discourse in China during the 1920s.

In China, the radical intellectual circles and study groups of the May Fourth movement discussed women's issues in gender-integrated settings. Back in the 1910s, the vast majority of secondary schools, colleges, and universities were either single-sex or gender segregated. In 1919, a female elementary school teacher named Deng Chunlan petitioned the president of Beijing University to admit women based on the principle of gender equality. The following year, the elite university began to admit women students. Subsequently, many universities and colleges throughout urban China also lifted the ban on admitting women students. From 1919 through 1920, several female students went to study in France on a work-study program with the intention of bringing an understanding of European culture back to China. A couple of women students, Xiang Jingyu and Cai Chang, learned about Marxism in France and later played leadership roles in the early history of the Chinese Communist Party.[4]

In contrast to the personal freedom of women activists in the Chinese Communist movement, the majority of Chinese women in the early twentieth century were still expected to settle for marriages arranged by their parents. During the New Culture movement, some radical students, in their attempts to resist arranged marriages, chose to run away from home, elope with their lovers, or even commit suicide. In the journals of the May Fourth movement, radical youths advocated a woman's freedom to choose her husband without parental interference as well as her right to divorce and remarry. They also challenged traditional ideals of female chastity and gender segregation in Confucian rites.[5]

The First United Front, 1923–27

In the Chinese intellectual discourse of the May Fourth movement, Western liberalism and Marxism-Leninism were the two main strands of thought. In 1923, Soviet Russia was the only world power willing to offer its assistance to the Kuomintang government's military campaign to eliminate regional warlords for the reunification of China. In exchange for Soviet assistance, the Kuomintang agreed to forge a United Front with the Chinese Communist Party (CCP) in 1923. Under Soviet guidance, Chinese Communists were given permission to join the Kuomintang on an individual basis during the First United Front. Since the Kuomintang lacked organizational discipline and ideological cohesion, the party sought to draw from the Communists' organizational talents. With the assistance of the Soviet adviser, Mikhail Borodin, the Chinese Nationalist Party remodeled itself after the organizational structure of the Russian Communist Party. To tighten the Kuomintang's ideological discipline, the lectures of the founding father of the Republic of China, Dr. Sun Yat-sen, were declared the ideological orthodoxy of party members and the Kuomintang army.[6] In these lectures, he outlined the Three Principles of the People: nationalism, democracy, and people's livelihood. Some women activists from the CCP joined the Kuomintang's military campaign and worked alongside their Chinese Nationalist colleagues in the Kuomintang Women's Department.[7]

The Kuomintang created its women's department under the Party's Central

Committee in 1924, and modeled it after the organizational structure of the Women's Department in the Russian Communist Party (1919–30).[8] Many women activists of the May Fourth movement served as leaders of this department. Like its Soviet counterpart, the Kuomintang Women's Department trained women activists to be propagandists among the masses. It established girls' schools in Guangzhou to train young women in the necessary organizational and leadership skills needed for mass mobilization. The newly trained activists of the Women's Department were given the responsibility of galvanizing women's participation in the Kuomintang's military campaign to unify China. They were also responsible for organizing local women's unions nationwide to raise women's consciousness for the improvement of their status and working conditions.[9]

Under Chiang Kai-shek's leadership, the Kuomintang's Northern Expeditionary Force waged its military campaigns to unify China. Propagandists from the Women's Department followed the troops and effectively mobilized women for their active support of the Kuomintang's cause. The Women's Department also raised women's consciousness for their emancipation in the areas that were newly liberated by the Expeditionary Force. Women's unions offered temporary shelters and legal assistance to enslaved girls, prostitutes, and battered wives and daughters-in-law to secure their freedom from abuse. The women's unions also advocated shorter working hours, equal pay for equal work, and an end to corporal punishment in the workplace for women workers.[10]

In the cities and towns where Kuomintang troops had eliminated local warlords, labor and women's unions were established. In some cities and towns, the women's union became a department within a general labor union. With this structural integration, factory women participated in strikes alongside men to demand higher wages. In 1927, 15 percent of the members in Shanghai's labor unions were women factory employees.[11] At the height of the mass movements' expansion under Nationalist rule, it was estimated that 1.5 million women in over ten provinces were members of various Kuomintang-affiliated organizations.

As Thornton notes, local strongmen and elites in rural China who opposed the Northern Expeditionary Forces had their militia disbanded and their weapons confiscated. With the support of Communist activists, peasants' self-defense forces were created to replace the local militia.[12] The scope and impact made by the peasant, labor, and women's movements alarmed the Kuomintang's right wing, who valued sociopolitical stability and were wary of the mass movements' radical challenge to the status quo. The right wing of the Kuomintang was able to obtain large financial contributions from bankers and industrialists in urban centers of coastal China to wage an offensive against Communist elements in general, and labor and peasant unions in particular. The Kuomintang right-wingers and their allies accused the women's unions of attacking family values and inciting civil unrest in Chinese society.[13]

Because Chiang relied on the political and financial support of industrialists, bankers, and absentee landlords, their objection to the expansion of radical mass movements was a major factor that led to the rightists' purge of the leftists and the Communists within the Kuomintang. Beginning in 1927, the right wing of the Kuomintang allied with anti-communist militia in rural communities to suppress the self-defense forces of the peasant masses and reinstated the former status and properties of local landed elites. By co-opting local anti-communist militia into the Kuomintang's campaign for its anti-leftist purge, the regime's accommodation of autonomous local militia inadvertently sowed the seeds for local strongmen to undercut the political authority of Kuomintang-appointed officials in their localities.[14]

From 1927 through 1930, thousands of Kuomintang leftists, CCP members, peasant-union organizers, labor activists, and propagandists of the women's unions were executed. Based on eyewitness accounts and survivor testimonies, thousands of women propagandists were raped, mutilated, and executed in public.[15] In 1927, the Kuomintang expelled the Soviet advisors from Nationalist China, and the Soviet-inspired Women's Department in the Kuomintang was abolished.[16] After the collapse of the First United Front in 1927, the Kuomintang and the CCP's policies toward women took different paths. To escape persecution in urban China, the surviving women activists of the CCP fled to Mao Zedong's rural soviet. In the CCP-controlled areas of rural China, Communist activists mobilized women peasants for their political and socioeconomic participation in the public domain.[17]

The Nanjing Decade, 1927–37

Chiang's Kuomintang government established its capital at the city of Nanjing. In contrast to the CCP, which established programs for women in rural soviets, the Kuomintang endeavored to neutralize the left-wing agendas of the peasant, labor, and women's movements in the First United Front.[18] In 1928, there were still some remaining left-wing radicals in the Kuomintang who, based on the Leninist model of party dictatorship, advocated for a reassertion of the party's disciplinary authority to rein in the corrupt and ineffectual Kuomintang army and state bureaucracy. They criticized Chiang's policy of prioritizing the Kuomintang army's resources and power over the authority of the party and the national government. To generate popular support for the party-state, the radicals also urged the party to carry out rural land reform based on Sun Yat-sen's principle of reducing tenant farmers' rents and eventually redistributing large landlords' holdings to the tenants. Lastly, the radicals contended that the Kuomintang should encourage and nurture the development of autonomous organizations of workers, peasants, students, and women to create a solid base of support for the Nanjing government. Since Chiang perceived these left-wing radicals as a threat to his authority, he rejected their proposals and proceeded to purge the remaining left-wing radicals from the party.[19] Since all officials critical of Chiang's policies and leadership could be targeted for the purge, a culture of passivity and lack of policy initiative became the norm in the party and the state bureaucracy. [20]

To raise revenue for administrative and personnel costs it was not uncommon for state-appointed county magistrates to demand unreasonable land taxes from the local peasants. It was a common practice for county officials and local elites to embezzle tax revenues for personal gain, and as a result, self-serving county officials and local elites contributed to widespread popular discontent and sociopolitical instability in the vast countryside of Nationalist China.[21]

Meanwhile, in Chiang's attempt to unify China and consolidate his power, he invited the remaining regional warlords and their governments' officials to join the Kuomintang in an effort to co-opt them into his regime without inflicting further bloodshed. Consequently, most regional warlords and officials who opted to join the Kuomintang did so out of political expediency. The prevailing attitude of most officials was that they were getting promoted to a high rank and acquiring great wealth (*Shengguan facai*). Rampant corruption and nepotism became a severe problem at all levels of the government. Using a system of secret police to suppress political dissent, the Kuomintang regime became a self-serving institution without having to be accountable to the needs and demands of the general public.[22] Without a popular base of support in rural China, the Kuomintang relied mainly on its army to control its territories and population.[23]

Between 1929 and 1931, the Kuomintang promulgated the Factory Law and civil codes of the Republic of China (ROC). The Factory Law stipulated that men and women should receive equal pay for equal work. It also introduced the concepts of a minimum wage for a reasonable standard of living and outlawed night work for women. Lastly, it stipulated paid maternity leave for working women before and after childbirth.[24] The main reason behind the promulgation of these laws was to convince the Western Powers to revoke unequal treaties and their extraterritorial privileges in China.[25] In other words, the restoration of China's national dignity was the Kuomintang government's primary concern. Protecting the rights of Chinese citizens and workers was seen as secondary.

Just as the Factory Law protected working women's rights, the promulgation of civil codes in 1931 marked a step toward fulfilling some of the May Fourth intellectuals' demands for gender equality. The civil codes granted daughters and wives the same rights to property inheritance in the family as their male counterparts. The code also granted women the right to choose their husbands without parental interference. The traditional practice of selling a child bride (*tongyangxi*) to the family of a future husband was banned.[26] Moreover, the new codes eliminated the gender double standard of traditional jurisprudence by stipulating that both husband and wife had the mutual obligation to be faithful and chaste in marriage. If a husband were to commit adultery or bigamy, the new civil code granted his wife the right to file for a divorce without the traditional approval from the elders of the husband's family.[27]

Notwithstanding the legal gains that Chinese women had achieved, the new civil codes' stipulations on divorce, child custody, matrimonial property, and place of residence remained male-centered in the section that pertained to the relationships between family members (*minfa qinshupian*). Based on the stipulation of *minfa qinshupian,* a husband had the right to manage or collect earnings and interest from his wife's property and income.[28] A wife would need her husband's written endorsement to apply for a bank loan. Essentially, a woman lost financial independence upon marriage.[29]

If a married couple were living separately in different localities, the wife could only file for a divorce in the court of her husband's place of residence. Due to Chinese culture's emphasis on family unity over individual freedom, it was not unusual for a judge to order a battered wife to reconcile with her abusive husband. If the court were to grant a divorce, the civil code stipulated that the husband should have custody of the children, unless an alternative living arrangement for the children was agreed upon. Because divorce law did not include detailed provisions for visitation rights, many ex-husbands would deny their former wives the right to visit their children. With the prospect of losing children, most women trapped in unhappy marriages did not file for a divorce.[30]

Evidently, the civil codes were the product of the Kuomintang legislators' attempt to strike a compromise between Confucian patriarchy and the Western concepts of individual rights and gender equality espoused in the May Fourth movement. Since Confucian patriarchy and gender equality were mutually incompatible ideologies, the patriarchal aspects of the family laws contradicted the inclusion of gender equality.[31]

Because the Western concepts of individual rights and equality were alien concepts in rural areas of China, the vast majority of the Chinese remained unaware of women's new legal rights during the Nanjing decade. Moreover, rural women's illiteracy presented an obstacle to the dissemination of civil codes among the masses of women.[32] Because the Kuomintang government did not attempt to implement these new laws in all strata of Chinese society, most beneficiaries of the civil codes were upper- and middle-class women in urban China.[33]

Whereas the civil codes of Nationalist China were based on a compromise between Western liberalism and Confucianism, beginning in the late 1920s fascism also emerged as a dominant strand of thought. In 1932, Chiang Kai-shek organized the "Blue Shirt" secret society (*Lanyishe*) to eliminate political opponents and corrupt officials and to tighten ideological discipline in Chinese society. Most members of the Blue Shirt Society were military officers and alumni of the Huangpu (Whampoa) Military Academy, where the young Chiang served as the commandant. All members of the Blue Shirts swore unconditional loyalty and obedience to Chiang Kai-shek. As admirers of European fascism, Chiang and the Blue Shirts believed that Chinese fascism should consist of fervent nationalism, restoration of Confucianism and traditional culture, one-party dictatorship, absolute loyalty and obedience to the supreme leader, military discipline of a nation's citizenry, subordination of individual will to the collective will and spiritual unity of the nation-state, and glorification of state-sponsored terror and violence to weed out elements of decadent material culture and political dissent. To stamp out political opponents, many individuals were arbitrarily branded as Reds without due legal process. Meanwhile, a branch of the Blue Shirts, the Kuomintang secret police, carried out numerous political assassinations of Chiang's political opponents, suspected communists, editors of major newspapers, and civil rights leaders.[34]

According to Lloyd Eastman, Blue Shirts in the Kuomintang dominated the leadership of the nation's political indoctrination and cultural programs in the public schools, government agencies, and the military in an effort to create a stronger and healthier nation along fascist lines. These programs emphasized personal hygiene, public sanitation, physical training, military discipline, and sacrifice for the nation.[35] In contrast to Eastman's interpretation, Robert Culp observed a dialectical interaction between the Kuomintang policymakers and student activists. According to Culp, patriotic students in

urban China demanded that the Kuomintang leadership offer military training in secondary schools in the wake of Japan's increasing military intervention in northern China in 1928, and the Kuomintang leadership assented.
By the mid-1930s, the military training program had become a nationwide
phenomenon in secondary schools throughout urban China. However, the
Kuomintang-sponsored program followed the gender division of labor along
European fascist lines. That is, only male students were given military training
and conducted military drills for combat. Female students were given nursing
training and knowledge of first aid for war zones and the home front.[36]

In 1934, Chiang launched the New Life movement (*Xin shenghuo yundong*)
to enhance the nation's wealth and power and to wage effective military campaigns against the Chinese Communists. The movement attempted to reduce
corruption and increase productivity and efficiency in the Kuomintang, the
military establishment, and the Chinese population.[37] According to Robert
Culp, European fascism, Western liberalism, and Confucianism all coexisted
in the eclectic ideologies of the movement. Culp attributed this ideological
diversity to different philosophical perspectives among different individuals
and factions within the Kuomintang. As a consequence, the proponents of
fascism in the regime were never able to exert complete control over the entire
government and thereby eliminate rival factions and ideologies. Comparatively speaking, Chinese fascism during the Nanjing decade never achieved
the same level of totalitarian control over the government and society as its
counterparts in Europe.[38]

One of the New Life movement's principles was drawn from the Confucian
emphasis on moral cultivation (*xiuyang*), mastery of self-control, reciprocal
obligations in interpersonal relationships, and responsibilities for mutual
assistance. According to New Life advocates, the four cardinal virtues of
Confucianism were *li* (propriety in rites of conduct), *yi* (righteousness, justice, and duty), *lian* (integrity and honesty), and *chi* (conscience and sense of
self-respect). In the secondary schools of central China's lower Yangzi region,
Kuomintang policymakers drew on the late imperial Chinese model of the
teacher-student mentoring relationship to cultivate in students a sense of
reciprocal obligations in a hierarchical relationship and the habit of moral
reflection.[39] Whereas moral self-cultivation was generally considered a pre-
rogative of the male gentry-elite in imperial China, advocates of the New
Life movement desired the moral reformation and cultural elevation of the
entire Chinese people, regardless of gender, age, or class.[40]

Due to the influence of the Western liberal concept of gender equality in
the New Life movement, aspects of Confucianism that prohibited women
from participation outside the home were de-emphasized. In an effort to

promote women's contribution to national development, the Kuomintang encouraged women's attainment of vocational training or professional education. Consequently, women's enrollment in all levels of education and participation in the workforce increased significantly in the 1930s.[41] By 1949, there were between 300 and 400 thousand career women in urban China. The majority of them were civil servants, teachers, nurses, clerks, and secretaries. But there were also some women doctors, dentists, lawyers, journalists, self-employed businesswomen, and managers of business and industrial enterprises.[42]

Even though the Kuomintang valued women's contribution to the national economy, the New Life advocates tended to overlook the working women's dilemma and the double burden they bore in paid work and the family. A case in point was the New Life advocates' adoption of the emphasis in Western liberal feminism on women's role in the public domain and the emphasis in Confucianism on women's role in the domestic realm. According to Madame Chiang, women should be active participants in the socioeconomic development of the nation as well as good mothers and wives in the domestic realm. At home, women were expected to be the primary transmitters of Confucian moral values to the young.[43]

The coexistence of the two mutually incompatible ideologies, Confucianism and liberal feminism, inadvertently contributed to tensions and pressures in working women's lives.[44] The career of Madame Chiang Kai-shek offers a notable example. Born to a Christian family in Shanghai in 1897, Madame Chiang's parents sent her to study in the United States during her childhood. In 1917, she graduated with distinction from Wellesley College with a major in English literature and a minor in philosophy. As a bicultural woman who spent all her adolescent years in the United States, she was also well versed in modern and classical Chinese.[45] In 1927, she settled for a political marriage to Chiang Kai-shek when he achieved renown as the pacifier of warlords and the unifier of China.

As the first lady of Nationalist China, Madame Chiang exhibited the social voluntarism and philanthropy she learned from her Christian upbringing and her experience of the American Progressive Era (1890–1920). During the New Life movement, she was instrumental in introducing Christian missionaries from the West into the movement. With their Christian and liberal democratic values, these missionaries de-emphasized military discipline and instigated tension with the Blue Shirts.[46] Despite these contradictions, Madame Chiang effectively galvanized many upper- and middle-class women in urban China to raise funds for charities, orphanages, and hospitals. She also organized seminars for the purpose of training middle-class women in the methods of educating rural women about personal hygiene, environmental sanitation, domestic sciences, reading, and writing.[47]

Madame Chiang expected female activists to participate in fields that had been traditionally designated as women's work, such as women's vocational training, nursing, social services, and the resolution of domestic problems.[48] In 1928, just as the Nanjing government proposed the abolition of coeducation in secondary and higher education, Madame Chiang envisioned the socialization of male and female students in their gender-specific roles. She conceived of home economics as a course specifically designed for female students, whereas males would acquire basic knowledge in agriculture.[49] In her remarks about schools for the children of Chinese revolutionary martyrs, Madame Chiang stated that students in the girls' school should be properly trained in handicraft-manufacturing, weaving, and sewing skills in order to provide clothing for themselves and students in the boys' school. In contrast, the boys should be taught carpentry and methods of planting fruits and vegetables in order to provide for themselves and the pupils in girls' school.[50]

Despite Madame Chiang's advocacy of traditional female gender roles, some of Chiang Kai-shek's advisors criticized her for failing to live in accordance with what she preached. In 1943, at the height of World War II, Madame Chiang toured the United States and addressed a joint session of Congress to galvanize American support for China's war effort against Japanese aggression. As an adviser, English interpreter, secretary, and propagandist for her husband's government, her outspokenness and political influence in both national and international politics offended conservatives in the Kuomintang.[51] These underlying tensions in the government between Madame Chiang's high-profile presence and the traditional ideal of women's behavior would persist for years to come.

Central in the New Life movement's revival of Confucianism was the Kuomintang's prioritization of married women's roles as virtuous wives and good mothers (xianqi liangmu) over their participation in paid work outside the home.[52] As a reaction against the rejection of Confucian family values in the May Fourth movement and the First United Front, the New Life movement reemphasized the importance of women's traditional roles.[53] As was the case in Nazi Germany, the New Life advocates' glorification of motherhood was repeatedly emphasized in the Kuomintang educational system and the mass media.[54] The New Life advocates feared that working mothers' absence from family life could undermine the discipline and moral upbringing of children. This in turn would jeopardize social stability.[55]

As upper- and middle-class New Life advocates urged married women to prioritize their roles as xianqi liangmu over their paid jobs in the public domain, they failed to realize that working-class women's paid work was an absolute necessity for maintaining their family's lifestyle. In 1930, the average monthly living expenses and incomes of working-class families in Shanghai were 32.5 yuan and 32.6 yuan, respectively. Since female members of each working-class household contributed up to 34.7 percent of a family's total monthly income, many working-class wives had to work 12 hours a day just to maintain a subsistence lifestyle for themselves and their families.[56] This example illustrates that the New Life advocates in the Kuomintang elite were by and large insulated from the harsh living conditions of most workers.

The Second Sino-Japanese War, 1937–45

With the Japanese invasion of northern China in 1937, the Kuomintang modified its prioritization of women's familial roles and obligations in the New Life movement to accommodate a new effort to mobilize women for patriotic resistance in the public domain. To accomplish this, the Women's Advisory Committee of the New Life movement, chaired by Madame Chiang, was appointed the leading national agency for advising and training women leaders and coordinating programs for war work. Most of the committee members consisted of wives and daughters of trusted Kuomintang officials, professional women, and women missionaries from the West.[57] A women's committee was created in each province and chaired by the wife of a provincial governor.

In response to the urgency of wartime mobilization, the women's advisory committees came to perform similar functions as the government-sponsored women's organizations in imperial Japan. In order to serve their respective governments' nationalistic ends, government-affiliated women's organizations mobilized women to extend their caregiving roles from the domestic realm to the public arena. In addition to being educators of a nation's children at home, women were mobilized to provide moral support and medical care for wounded soldiers and to be caregivers for orphans. As on the home front of Japan proper and in colonial Taiwan, the provincial women's advisory committees in China mobilized women to assume the jobs of male farmhands and mill workers left vacant when men were sent to the frontlines. In both imperial Japan and Nationalist China, women were urged to instruct their children and the public to live a thrifty lifestyle, recycle and reuse discarded materials, and raise funds for medical supplies and the war effort.[58]

During the war, the Women's Advisory Committee mobilized Chinese women to raise funds for the creation of handicraft workshops and credit unions for disabled soldiers and war widows. They also made uniforms, comforters, and socks for soldiers. In her speeches, Madame Chiang defined a model mother as a valiant woman who would sacrifice her self-interest and the lives of her sons for the cause of national salvation against Japanese aggression. Rather than demanding women's rights from society, Chinese women were expected to achieve gender equality through active participation in the war effort. With national salvation as the top priority, the state subordinated women's individual rights and the interests of the family.[59]

Some women activists proposed to create autonomous grassroots organizations for the war effort, but the Kuomintang was suspicious of women's organizations independent of its direct control. Since the Kuomintang's suppression of radical mass movements in 1927, the women's movement under Madame Chiang's leadership during the New Life Movement had remained by and large an upper- and middle-class philanthropic movement in urban China. Due to its elitist orientation, efforts to organize women workers and rural peasants for war work remained limited in scope throughout the duration of the war.[60]

Chinese Nationalist Rule on Taiwan, 1945–2000

With the defeat of Japan in World War II, the Allies transferred the governance of Taiwan to the Kuomintang government. In 1945, Chinese Nationalist troops landed on Taiwan to claim the former Japanese colony. Due to the shared ethnic heritage of the Taiwanese and the mainlanders, the Taiwanese welcomed the Kuomintang troops and hoped that their fellow Chinese would fulfill their long-awaited wish for Taiwanese self-rule.

Yet, in 1945, contrary to the expectations of the Taiwanese elite, the Kuomintang government in Nanjing issued Rules and Regulations on the Organization of the Office of Chief Administrator at Taiwan Province (*Taiwansheng xingzheng zhangguan gongshu zuzhi tiaolie*). In essence, the rules concentrated the administrative, judicial, and military powers in the Office of Taiwan's Chief Administrator. Whereas the joint consultation system (*heyizhi*) of the Kuomintang-controlled provinces in mainland China enabled the executive and legislative branches of each provincial government to work with each other as separate branches of government, the newly promulgated rules precluded this possibility for Taiwan by conferring absolute power upon Taiwan's Chief Administrator.[61]

With the lack of separation of power between the administrative and legislative branches of government, most members of the Taiwanese elite felt that the Office of Taiwan's Chief Administrator and the Japanese colonial government were similar in their authoritarian character. Coupled with the difference between the joint consultation system of the provinces on mainland China and the unique institution of the Chief Administrator in Taiwan, many Taiwanese were convinced that the Kuomintang government intended to treat them as second-class citizens of China.[62]

This assumption was confirmed after the arrival of the Chief Administrator from the mainland. Appointed by the Chinese Nationalist government in Nanjing, the Chief Administrator, Ch'en Yi (1883–1950), treated the Taiwanese as conquered subjects. Upon his arrival, Ch'en ushered in a program for Taiwan's de-Japanization and re-Sinicization. Just as the Japanese governors-general banned Chinese-language publications in colonial Taiwan during the imperialization movement (1937–45), Ch'en's government banned Japanese books, magazines, and newspapers. In 1945, Mandarin Chinese replaced Japanese as the national language. In the following year, the Chief Administrator's office claimed that more than ten thousand books were banned from circulation.[63]

As most Japanese nationals were evacuated from Taiwan in 1945, many administrative and managerial positions in Taiwan's bureaucracies and industries were left vacant. This created a shortage of personnel that the Taiwanese elite had hoped to fill. Instead, these positions were mostly taken by relatives and friends of the Kuomintang officials from mainland China. The mainlander-dominated bureaucracy of the Chief Administrator excluded the Taiwanese on the grounds that they needed to rid themselves of their slavish education under Japanese colonial rule before they could be ready to serve the cause of Chinese nationalism.[64]

From 1945 through 1949, several social commentators from the mainland discussed their impressions of Japanese colonial education and Taiwanese social mores. Since 58 percent of Taiwanese were literate in Japanese in the early 1940s,[65] the commentators were impressed that many working-class Taiwanese women were able to communicate through writing. They also praised Taiwanese women for their work ethic, financial self-reliance, and participation in virtually all sectors of the Taiwanese economy—a rate of workforce participation and functional literacy higher than women on the mainland at the time. But one commentator was troubled by what he perceived as Taiwanese women's lack of courage to point out the mistakes of their superiors and their blind submission to the directives of authority figures.[66] These mixed reviews of Japanese colonial education differed from Hsieh Hsueh-hung's assertion that colonial Taiwan's population had already attained a modern cultural standard and the ability to govern themselves. Whereas Hsieh advocated Taiwan's independence during the Japanese colonial era, in 1945 she indicated that Taiwan had ample qualified individuals for self-governance within China. In other words, she argued that the Chinese Nationalist government should grant Taiwan a high degree of political autonomy.[67]

As the political debate continued, Ch'en's administration did little to prevent the Kuomintang officials and troops from exploiting the island's resources at the expense of the people's livelihood. The civil war between the Kuomintang and the communists on the mainland also caused rampant inflation on both sides of the Taiwan Strait. Consequently, hunger and discontent became widespread among the people. On February 28, 1947, the Taiwanese population rose up in mass protest against the government's corruption and the mainlanders' monopolization of political power. In the aftermath of the Kuomintang's military suppression of the popular uprising, it was estimated that between eighteen thousand and twenty-eight thousand civilians were massacred.[68] Among those killed or imprisoned were many of the island's intellectual elite.[69]

Two years later, in 1949, the Kuomintang government fled to Taiwan after losing the civil war on the mainland to the Chinese Communists. The mainlanders' exile community in Taiwan consisted of over 1.5 million troops, government bureaucrats, and other civilians. In the postwar era, the Chinese refugees who arrived in Taiwan with the Kuomintang regime after 1945 came to be known as mainlanders.[70] Conversely, the six million ethnic Chinese whose families had settled in Taiwan prior to the Japanese colonial era were classified as Taiwanese. In other words, the Taiwanese consisted of the population that had already settled in Taiwan prior to the arrival of the Kuomintang regime in 1945. Most of their forebears emigrated to the island from southeastern coastal China in the seventeenth century and thereafter.

To justify the mainlander minority's political domination over the Taiwanese majority, the Kuomintang continually insisted that it was the sole legitimate government of China. It instituted two layers of government on Taiwan in order to perpetuate this myth. The top layer consisted of the national government dominated by mainlander officials; the lower layer consisted of the Taiwan provincial government as well as county and municipal governments. With this political hierarchy, the mainlander leadership dominated the Taiwanese majority until the 1970s.[71]

In retrospect, Taiwanese and mainlanders' divergent identities can be attributed to differences in the two peoples' geographic and linguistic identities, historical experiences, the February 28th incident, and inequality in the Kuomintang regime's political hierarchy.[72] From 1947 to the late 1960s, the trauma of the February 28th massacre and the ensuing suppression of civil liberties in the period of White Terror contributed to the Taiwanese people's sense of political alienation vis-à-vis the Kuomintang government from the mainland. In fact, Taiwanese political dissidents referred to the Kuomintang as a regime from outside (*wailai zhengquan*).[73] Though most Taiwanese could trace their ethnic origin to mainland China, this alienation contributed to their ambivalence about their Chinese identity.[74] The Taiwanese duality of both sameness with and difference from mainland China has contributed to the Taiwanese people's unresolved national identity since the 1940s.[75]

From 1949 through the 1960s, the mainlander-dominated leadership envisioned its eventual return to the mainland. They viewed the island as a temporary military base for the campaign to recover mainland China from the Communist occupation. In order to defend the regime against Communist subversion, in 1948 and 1949 the Kuomintang enacted martial law and amendments to the ROC constitution known as the Temporary Provisions Effective during the Period of Mobilization for the Suppression of Communist Rebellion. Based on the Kuomintang's Leninist organizational structure, the temporary provisions and martial law brought the ROC government, the armed forces, and all public security forces under the centralized elitist leadership of the Kuomintang party dictatorship.[76] These legal provisions also suspended civil liberties stipulated in the constitution and thereby severely restricted freedom of speech, the press, and assembly. The Taiwan Garrison Command was given broad power to arrest political dissidents, try in military courts certain crimes committed by civilians, and censor publications. In addition, the legal provisions forbade the creation of new political parties and the staging of strikes and mass political rallies.[77]

To ensure the Kuomintang's dominance in Taiwanese society, its public security forces routinely arrested and imprisoned individuals suspected of espousing multiparty democracy, human rights, Taiwanese self-determination, or communism. According to one estimate, as many as ninety thousand individuals from both Taiwanese and mainlander backgrounds were arrested in the 1950s, and about half of them were executed.[78] The party-state's anti-communist crusade, including authoritarian police control, surveillance of the populace, and emphasis on loyalty to the national leader were reminiscent of the regime's fascist past during the Nanjing decade. Starting with the aftermath of the February 28th massacre in 1947 and continuing through the 1960s, the decades of hard authoritarian rule on Taiwan came to be known as the era of the White Terror (*baise kongbu*).[79]

In 1947 and 1948, members in the Kuomintang regime's parliamentary bodies, the Legislative Yuan and the National Assembly, were elected by their respective provinces in mainland China. After the Kuomintang regime's retreat to Taiwan in 1949, the mainlander legislators enjoyed lifelong tenures in the lame-duck parliamentary bodies. Under the Kuomintang's One China policy, the regime promised to hold the next nationwide election after the restoration of its rule in mainland China.[80] Under the Temporary Provisions of the Period of Communist Rebellion, President Chiang Kai-shek (1948–75) and his eldest son and successor, President Chiang Ching-kuo (1978–88), enjoyed extra-constitutional power as the Kuomintang's party chairs and heads of state during their tenures in office.

Due to the imbalance of power between the executive and the legislative branches of the Kuomintang government, the Legislative Yuan functioned mainly as a rubber stamp for the policy initiatives of the Executive Yuan. In the one-party state, the Central Standing Committee of the Kuomintang controlled most of the policy initiatives of the executive branch. Hence, the Kuomintang party-state's top-down policy making, the ineffectiveness of the Legislative Yuan to reflect Taiwan's public opinion, and the political culture of the White Terror all contributed to the insulation of the Kuomintang's policy decision making from Taiwanese public opinion.[81]

Ideology and Policies on Women

After the 1950s, the Kuomintang allocated most of its resources to economic development and military expenditure. Due to the silence and marginality of Taiwanese women's voices, the government only allocated a small share of its annual budget to building Taiwan's social welfare infrastructure.[82] Beginning in 1949, the Kuomintang policymakers developed a family-centered welfare ideology in Taiwan. They expected the family to be the primary socioeconomic unit for taking care of the elderly and the young. Consequently, many housewives took care of their in-laws and raised their children at home without receiving any social benefits from society or the state. In this way, the state did not have to earmark a large portion of its budget for nursing homes and childcare facilities.[83]

In contrast to the government's idealization of married women's domesticity, the Kuomintang encouraged young women to participate in the workforce prior to marriage.[84] Between 1966 and 1973, economic planners sought to transform Taiwan into an export-oriented industrial economy. The government utilized the inexpensive labor of unskilled and semi-skilled single women[85] in order to attract foreign investments from Japan and the West. With economic development as the government's top priority, it exploited married women's unpaid labor in the domestic sphere and single women's transient labor in the workforce.[86] From 1966 to 1973, women's participation in the labor force rose from 32.6 to 41.5 percent. As Taiwan emerged as a newly industrializing economy in the mid-1970s, 30 percent of all unskilled and semi-skilled workers in Taiwan's labor-intensive industries were female. In addition to factory workers, many women were employed in service-oriented positions that were traditionally regarded as female, such as barbers, waitresses, entertainers, clerical secretaries, and workers in banking and other service industries.[87]

In the mid-1960s and thereafter, the party-state's prioritization of economic growth over social welfare also provided justification for many business enterprises to lay off female employees when they married or had children. Although the Factory Law of the Nanjing decade stipulated paid maternity leave for working women before and after childbirth,[88] this legal provision was not consistently implemented by most private companies.[89] In cases where employers permitted married women to continue working, many women in low-paying service jobs and labor-intensive industries chose to quit their jobs upon the birth of their first child in their mid-20s. These women's decisions could be related to the lack of incentive and motivation to continue working in jobs with limited prospects for promotion, the Confucian ideology's ascription of caretaking roles to women, and a shortage of affordable childcare facilities.[90]

After their children attended elementary schools, some married women in their mid-30s would re-enter the workforce. Due to the absence of continuity in these women's employment history, they were paid less than their male counterparts. Although the Factory Law of 1929 stipulated that the same wages should be given to men and women who performed the same tasks, in the 1970s and 1980s Taiwanese women earned only two-thirds of their male colleagues' salaries in the same economic sectors.[91] When women workers reached their mid-50s, many would leave the workforce to take care of their husbands' elderly parents.[92]

To avert the problem of labor shortage in Taiwan's economy in the late 1970s, the government created mothers' classrooms (*mama jiaoshi*) in various local communities to train housewives on the skills required to manufacture consumer goods in what was called their living-room factories (*keting gongchang*). To implement this program, the government offered many households low-interest loans to purchase the mechanical equipment necessary for the manufacturing of handicrafts, garments, toys, and ornaments at home. Because homemakers who participated in this program were paid on a piece-rate basis, they were offered meager wages and were ineligible for health insurance coverage. Socially, a homemaker's piecework was seen as supplementary income for her family. As such, it was not accorded the same rights and recognition as regular factory work in the public domain. Based on the Confucian family-centered ideology, mothers' classrooms also taught homemakers the methods of family planning, the preparation of balanced nutritious meals for the family, ways of taking care of children and ailing parents-in-law, and communication skills for improving relationships among family members. In this way, the state, the family, and the industries contributed to homemakers' double burden and exploited homemakers' housework and underpaid piecework in the domestic realm.[93]

Married women's freedom to participate in the regular workforce outside the home was mitigated by the Kuomintang's conceptualization of women's gender roles.[94] As part of the Kuomintang's effort to preserve traditional Chinese culture in Taiwan, Confucianism was incorporated into the national literature curriculum (*guowen*) in Taiwan's high schools. Prior to the lifting of martial law in 1987, the National Institute of Compilation and Translation (*Guoli bianyuguan*) compiled and edited a standardized version of every textbook for Taiwan's national education system (*guomin jiaoyu*). In order to ensure state orthodoxy in the Kuomintang-controlled system, every teacher in Taiwan was required to teach materials from the standardized textbooks.[95]

In postwar Taiwan, the Kuomintang's Confucian conception of women's gender roles was in many ways a continuation of the New Life movement of the 1930s. Through the Kuomintang-controlled educational system and mass media, women were urged to play supportive and complementary roles vis-à-vis their male family members. As it was during the Nanjing decade, the educational system and the media repeatedly glorified married women's roles as virtuous wives and good mothers. On every Mother's Day, model mothers were selected in every major locality to be publicly rewarded and praised. These model mothers generally demonstrated that their children had achieved success through their maternal care and sacrifice.[96]

In the Kuomintang-controlled educational system, teachers fostered a Confucian family-centered ideology among the children.[97] The authoritarian regime viewed the nation as a family-state; just as the head of state was the patriarch of the nation, the father was the patriarch of a family.[98] As the head of the first family of the Republic of China on Taiwan (1949–75), Chiang Kai-shek was portrayed as the patriarch of the Chinese nation and the Generalissimo of the Kuomintang troops by the government-controlled media. Madame Chiang was depicted as the virtuous wife and helper of Chiang Kai-shek, as well as a good mother of the Chinese people.[99]

In both mainland China and postwar Taiwan, Madame Chiang's emphasis on women's fulfillment of their familial obligations and patriotic duties resembled some aspects of relational feminism in the West. During the Progressive Era (1890–1920), Madame Chiang spent her adolescent years in the United States. At the turn of the twentieth century, most American suffragists and women social activists were relational feminists. Because these progressive women visualized an extension of American homemakers' nurturing capabilities and housekeeping skills from the domestic realm into the society, women's historians labeled their relational feminism "social feminism."[100]

Similar to the relational strand of American feminism, Madame Chiang's family-centered ideology acknowledged men's and women's distinctive gender roles. It also validated the two genders' interdependence, complementary relationships, and mutual obligations in the family.[101] Madame Chiang urged Chinese women in Taiwan to manage their households (*qijia*) and be virtuous wives and good mothers at home. As a social feminist, she also urged all modern Chinese women to extend the love they felt for their families to their national community. In other words, a modern Chinese woman should love her nation as she would her family. To translate one's patriotism into action, she advocated that women should contribute their homemaking skills and nurturing capacity to enhance the patriotic cause of recovering the mainland from the communist occupation (*baoguo*).[102] At home, women should instruct their children (*jiaozi*) and urge their husbands to be loyal to the nation.[103] As occurred during the second Sino-Japanese War, Madame Chiang urged women in postwar Taiwan to extend their maternal love and homemaking skills to the national community by producing and mending military uniforms for the Chinese nation.[104]

As a self-styled women's leader, Madame Chiang perceived herself as the role model of Chinese womanhood. Not only did the mass media preserve her image as a devoted wife to Chiang Kai-shek, she was also a tireless volunteer outside her home. In the 1950s, this dual ideal of Chinese womanhood as a virtuous wife at home and a tireless volunteer for the nation was an unattainable goal for most women,[105] since most married women had several children to raise.[106] In the 1950s, Taiwan was just recovering from the war-torn economy. Many women had to work in the fields or family sideline businesses to make ends meet. By contrast, Madame Chiang, as the first lady of Nationalist China, had servants at home to enable her to volunteer outside the home.

As the leader of government-affiliated women's organizations in postwar Taiwan, Madame Chiang was vested with the political power to advocate the state sponsorship of women's social welfare programs. Yet, Madame Chiang was more interested in mobilizing women to support the Kuomintang troops and the party-state's anti-communist goals.[107] Consistent with Madame Chiang's priorities during the second Sino-Japanese War, the Kuomintang-affiliated women's organizations under her leadership prioritized women's participation in female-oriented volunteer work outside the home over the advocacy of women's individual rights and special interests in postwar Taiwan.[108]

The prioritization of national goals over women's rights and interests could be traced back to the nationalistic objectives of the Chinese intellectual elite at the turn of the twentieth century. In order to resist further intrusion from Japan and the West after China's defeat in the first Sino-Japanese War (1894–95), Chinese students in Japan appropriated the Japanese concept of *good wife, wise mother* (*ryosai kenbo*) to modernize the Confucian concept of *virtuous wife, good mother* (*xianqi liangmu*) in Chinese society. Inspired by the Japanese concept of a *wise mother,* Chinese intellectuals conceptualized a good mother in modern China as one who could transmit modern knowledge and the spirit of Chinese patriotism in the home. She would educate her children to become productive citizens who could enhance the nation's wealth and power.[109] This vision of modern Chinese motherhood would exert significant impact on the Kuomintang ideology on motherhood in and beyond the Nanjing decade (1927–37).

In the early twentieth century, the prevailing understanding of modern Chinese motherhood coexisted alongside many Chinese intellectuals' support for women's education and participation in the workforce. These intellectuals saw the improvement of women's status as a means of mobilizing resources for strengthening the nation's economic power to resist Western and Japanese imperialism.[110] The Kuomintang elite's conception of women's participation in activities outside the home as a means of enhancing its nationalistic objectives would remain unchanged when the government-affiliated women's organizations were created in postwar Taiwan. In order to strengthen the Kuomintang's military power for its recovery of mainland China, Madame Chiang advocated women's dual roles as active participants in the public domain and educators of future citizens at home. In other words, the Kuomintang did not conceive of the struggle for women's individual rights as a vital end in itself.[111]

Government-Affiliated Women's Organizations

Just as Chiang Kai-shek was in charge of national and military affairs, Madame Chiang was the leader of government-affiliated women's organizations in postwar Taiwan. As the Generalissimo was preparing his troops to fight back to the mainland (*fangong dalu*), Madame Chiang's women's organizations provided social services and moral support to his troops. Analogous to the traditional gender roles of a married couple, there was a division of labor between the masculine roles on the frontline and the feminine roles on the home front. In this sense, the government-affiliated women's organizations performed the auxiliary functions of the Kuomintang government's perpetual wartime mobilization. With this rationale for the existence of government-affiliated women's organizations, these organizations also served as the institutional means for Madame Chiang to carve out her power base in the patriarchal party-state.[112]

Upon Madame Chiang's arrival in Taiwan from the United States in 1950, she established and reorganized several government-affiliated women's organizations to mobilize women for the campaign to recover mainland China from the communists. As a continuation of her efforts in the New Life movement, she began her fundraising activities in postwar Taiwan for philanthropic projects, such as nurseries, orphanages, charities, and homes for the disabled and the elderly. Both the philanthropic projects and the government-affiliated women's organizations catered to the needs of the predominantly mainlander and male career military personnel and their dependents. In other words, women's eligibility for these social services was based primarily on their status as wives, daughters, and mothers of male military personnel. In postwar Taiwan, government-affiliated women's organizations assisted the families of the deceased soldiers who fought against Japan during the second Sino-Japanese War as well as families of martyrs who fought against the Chinese Communists.[113]

One of the women's organizations that provided social services to military families was the Taiwan Provincial Women's Association (*Taiwansheng funühui*—hereafter also referred to as the Provincial Women's Association). Established by Ch'en Yi's administration in 1946, Madame Chiang brought the Provincial Women's Association under her guidance in 1950 and assumed the title of its honorary president.[114]

Reminiscent of Madame Chiang's endorsement of women's dual roles in the New Life Movement, the Provincial Women's Association supported women's contribution to the national economy as well as their traditional gender roles at home. To foster women's domestic roles and promote family stability, the Association provided matchmaking services, mediated domestic disputes, sponsored radio shows on the resolution of family conflicts, and ran seminars and published essays on home economics and childcare. Married women were also reminded of their primary role as educators of children in the family.[115] Analogous to the public health campaigns in the New Life movement, the Provincial Women's Association conducted seminars and lectures to inform its members and the general public about the ways to practice personal hygiene and enhance environmental sanitation (*huanjing weisheng*). To promote the health of Taiwan's citizenry, the association reminded homemakers that food should be kept clean and fresh during and after preparation; that garbage should be disposed of properly in a timely manner; and that public restrooms should be kept clean. It also urged its members to bring these concepts of hygiene to the attention of local governments, so that they could be enforced among the local populace.[116]

In 1950, the Provincial Women's Association proposed the creation of childcare facilities in rural Taiwan. As members of the association toured the countryside in 1950, they noticed that women often carried their toddlers on their backs while they worked in rice paddies. The small children looked as if they were fainting in the summer heat. To solve this problem, members of the association created nursery schools in rural Taiwan that provided preschool education to rural children.[117] According to proponents of the rural childcare facilities, there were several reasons for creating nursery schools in rural Taiwan. First, the double burden of childcare and farm work should be alleviated for peasant women. Second, a strong and healthy race (*qiangzhong*) is a prerequisite for a strong nation (*qiangguo*). By providing proper childcare, nutrition, and educational experiences to preschoolers, these children would be well prepared to enter elementary schools. Ultimately, they argued, these children would make positive contributions to national development. Thus, in addition to alleviating peasant women's double burden, members of the Provincial Women's Association also conceived of nursery schools in rural Taiwan as an instrumental means for strengthening and enriching the nation.[118]

In order to create these daycare centers, the association solicited financial contributions from industrialists and business enterprises. The Social Welfare Department of the provincial government also allocated a limited budget for their establishment. In addition, the provincial government requested that the farmer's association (*nonghui*)[119] in each locality contribute a certain amount of money to this endeavor. Even with contributions from these sources, the financial resources remained short of the original goal. Consequently, the original plan of creating nursery schools for year-round daycare was replaced by a modified plan to provide childcare services only during the busy seasons of sowing and harvest. In addition to the lack of financial resources, the project faced a shortage of childcare professionals. To remedy the shortage, preschool teachers and instructors of home economics were hired to train female junior high graduates to be caregivers. Since most rural childcare services were only available during the peak periods of sowing and harvest, the caregivers were hired on a temporary basis. Due to the temporary nature of the job, it was difficult to find young women who would commit to it.[120]

Nevertheless, many rural villages established seasonal childcare services. Most of them were free of charge. Simple meals were provided for children in the mornings and afternoons. To alleviate peasant women's workload, children were given baths before they were sent home. Since most childcare services in rural Taiwan could ill afford to purchase fuel for heating, each morning the caretakers would fill up several large tin barrels with fresh water. By mid-afternoon, the water would be hot enough for the children to take a bath. In the 1950s, this method of solar heating was widely practiced in rural Taiwan.[121] Despite the practical necessity of these facilities, there was no evidence to suggest that Madame Chiang lent her prestige and influence to the fundraising campaigns for this endeavor.

After 1968 the Provincial Women's Association also worked to ensure that every female child in rural Taiwan obtained nine years of universal compulsory education. To promote the government's program for the creation of living-room factories, the association ran training seminars in embroidery, dressmaking, and other female-oriented vocational skills. To enable married women to work outside the home, the association offered career counseling, government-subsidized driving lessons, and recommended hired servants to working mothers. Moreover, legal counselors and volunteers assisted women in family crises and provided temporary shelters for distressed women.[122]

In comparison with the Kuomintang's training of women in handicraft skills and the promotion of women's literacy in mainland China, the Provincial Women's Association made more positive contributions to women's lives at the grassroots level in postwar Taiwan than the Kuomintang-affiliated women's organizations did in mainland China prior to 1949. This can be attributed to the relatively small size of Taiwan in contrast to the vast countryside in mainland China. Since most Kuomintang officials were from the upper- or middle-class elite in urban China, its policies and programs tended to have a more direct impact on the urban minority than on the rural majority of the Chinese population. Secondly, the Kuomintang devoted most of its human and financial resources to resisting Japanese aggression and to fighting communists in mainland China prior to 1949.[123] In postwar Taiwan, the regime enjoyed over five decades of economic growth and sociopolitical stability that enabled it to implement its policies toward women at the grassroots level.

Among the government-affiliated women's organizations in postwar Taiwan, the one that received the greatest attention from Madame Chiang was the Chinese Women's Anti-Aggression League (*Zhonghua funü fangong lianhehui*—hereafter referred to as the Women's League). Established with Madame Chiang's leadership in 1950, the Women's League created chapters in various cities, counties, and townships in Taiwan. In most instances, wives of local chief executives headed the chapters in their respective localities. By and large, members of the Women's League were government employees or female family members of military personnel.[124] The mission of the league was to mobilize women to provide social service to the troops and to engage in the anti-communist struggle. From Madame Chiang's perspective, Chinese Communists on the mainland were collaborators of Soviet expansionism. Thus, it was the Kuomintang's mission to liberate the Chinese people from their entrapment in the Iron Curtain. Members of the Women's League made weekly radio broadcasts to engage in psychological warfare against communist troops on the mainland. Their radio messages depicted socioeconomic progress for the ROC on Taiwan and urged troops across the Strait to defect and join the Kuomintang's anti-communist campaign.[125]

In contrast to the demoralized Kuomintang troops who lacked medical attention by qualified personnel during the Chinese Civil War on the mainland, the exiled regime in post–1949 Taiwan endeavored to revive the troops' morale and readiness. The Women's League raised funds and organized seminars to train several thousand of its members to be nurses and paramedics in emergency rescue on the frontlines and during air raids. The trainees were also taught the practical knowledge and skills of personal hygiene and public health. After their initial training, these nurses and paramedics provided healthcare services in military and civilian hospitals and government health agencies. Madame Chiang expected these paramedics and nurses to be mobilized to provide emergency care to wounded soldiers on the frontlines. To give them a sense of mission, Madame Chiang often compared their potential to the spirit of service and patriotism exhibited by Florence Nightingale. During the Crimean War (1853–56), Nightingale pioneered the nursing profession in Britain and organized nurses' corps to take care of wounded soldiers on the battlefield.[126]

To ensure the Kuomintang troops' loyalty to the regime, members of the Women's League were also trained to assist military personnel with their job searches. Modeled after the goals of the Woman's Advisory Committee during the second Sino-Japanese War (1937–45), members of the Women's League urged the public to donate apparel, food, radios, and other daily necessities for needy military personnel and their families. To console disabled soldiers and enhance the quality of their lives, the Women's League raised funds for the installment of their artificial limbs and eyes. It also maintained numerous orphanages for children of deceased soldiers.[127]

When thousands of military personnel retreated to Taiwan from the mainland in 1949, there was a shortage of housing. In 1956, Madame Chiang and the Women's League spearheaded a campaign to raise funds for the construction of new housing. In response, some private individuals donated their savings to housing construction. As Madame Chiang made numerous speeches for the fundraising effort, she also mobilized the Kuomintang's Central Committee and the Executive Yuan of the Chinese Nationalist government for the same endeavor. To generate enough resources, major industries and big businesses were pressured to contribute large sums of money. Tax revenues were also appropriated. The Taiwan provincial government and the Kuomintang's military establishment were assigned the task of building the houses. In other words, various branches of the Kuomintang government and major sectors of the Taiwanese economy were mobilized to contribute to the housing projects. Consequently, the projects had ample financial and human resources to build residential communities for military families.[128] Most residential communities had a clinic, recreational center, barbershop, grocery store, daycare center, and schools.[129]

Reminiscent of women's roles in mending and sewing military apparel on the mainland during the second Sino-Japanese War, members of the Women's League, the Provincial Women's Association, and the Women's Working Committee of the Kuomintang participated in the making of several million military uniforms in factories created for that purpose. Despite Madame Chiang's attempts to galvanize masses of women to volunteer for this endeavor, most women who worked periodically in these factories were women employees of various government agencies. In other words, the women's places of employment required them to report to the sewing factories periodically. Although the Kuomintang-controlled mass media portrayed these women as volunteers, most of them were actually there as a result of institutional mobilization. The fact that virtually all hands in the sewing factories were female also attested to the Kuomintang elite's assumption that sewing was a woman's job.[130]

The organization that played a leadership role in the Kuomintang's mobilization of women to make military uniforms was the Kuomintang Women's Working Committee (*Zhongyang funü gongzuohui*, hereafter also referred to as the Women's Working Committee). In 1953, the committee was established and chaired by Madame Chiang. A main function of the committee was to enforce and implement policies pertaining to women formulated by the

Kuomintang's Central Supervisory Council on Women's Work (*Zhongyang funü gongzuo zhidao huiyi*). As the supreme policy-making body for women's issues in the Kuomintang party-state, the council formulated policies to be implemented by the Women's Working Committee, the Women's League, and the Provincial Women's Association. This top-down directorial approach tended to compromise the institutional autonomy and independent policy initiative of the women's organizations. Consequently, all three organizations prioritized the implementation of Kuomintang policies over the resolution of women's problems.[131]

Organizationally, the Women's Working Committee was modeled after the Kuomintang Women's Department during the First United Front (1923–27). That is, it organized branch committees in Kuomintang headquarters of counties, cities, colleges, and state-owned industries in order to mobilize masses of women in various institutions and localities. Like the Women's Department in the 1920s, the strategy of the Women's Working Committee in postwar Taiwan included the training of cadres of women to be the organizational nucleus for the recruitment of more women to engage in party work.[132]

But unlike the Kuomintang's lack of political influence in the vast countryside of mainland China during the second Sino-Japanese War and the Chinese Civil War, the authoritarian party-state enjoyed decades of peace and stability in postwar Taiwan and was thus effective in mobilizing local branches of the Women's Working Committee to support Kuomintang candidates in provincial, county, and municipal elections in communities throughout Taiwan.[133] Under martial law, elections of national legislative bodies were postponed indefinitely pending the Kuomintang's recovery of mainland China. On the other hand, the authoritarian party-state sponsored popular elections on the provincial, county, and municipal levels to give the Taiwanese people an opportunity for electoral participation and thereby enhance their identification with the political process of the Chinese Nationalist state.[134] Since martial law forbade the creation of any genuine opposition party, the vast majority of the candidates in these local elections were Kuomintang-nominated candidates. To give an appearance of freedom in Taiwan and the international community, the Kuomintang also allowed a minority of independent candidates without party affiliations to run for local offices.[135]

The Women's Working Committee also provided political and leadership training to women and potential female candidates on the provincial, county, and municipal levels in order to strengthen Kuomintang members' identification with the party. In this way, the party was able to effectively recruit politically talented and ambitious Taiwanese women in each local community and provide them with both favorable exposure in state-controlled media and the necessary human and financial resources to win local elections. Consequently, the vast majority of women elected to political offices under the authoritarian regime were Kuomintang members.[136]

As a legacy of the Kuomintang's progressive social policies during the First United Front, the party platform in postwar Taiwan still included "protection of women's legal rights and social status, and creation of job opportunities for women."[137] In reality, economic planners created job opportunities for women without providing enough childcare facilities to enable working mothers' full participation outside the home. Reminiscent of the New Life movement in the 1930s, the three women's organizations had all endorsed the Kuomintang's notion of womanhood as good wives and mothers and as anti-communist Chinese patriots. In concert with the Kuomintang's emphasis on creating a strong and healthy citizenry for its military project of reclaiming mainland China, the Women's Working Committee offered female citizens in many local communities the necessary natal care and vaccinations for their children.[138] Both the government-affiliated women's organizations and the mass media inculcated in the popular consciousness the idea that the Kuomintang was the government that granted Taiwanese women their political and civil rights.[139] That is, in contrast to the disenfranchisement of Taiwanese women under Japanese colonial rule, the ROC Constitution of 1947 granted both universal suffrage and gender equality to female citizens on both sides of the Taiwan Strait.[140]

Because most Taiwanese women in the 1950s spoke Hoklo Taiwanese and Japanese rather than fluent Mandarin, mainlander women in the Women's League and the Women's Working Committee volunteered to tutor their Taiwanese counterparts in literacy classes for Mandarin Chinese. With a sense of mission and a paternalistic attitude, they believed that Japanese influences should be eliminated and that the Taiwanese should be reeducated to identify with Chinese nationalism. To this end, the Women's League ran teachers' training seminars to instruct their members in teaching Mandarin Chinese to Taiwanese women and Taiwanese soldiers in the armed forces.[141] In the 1950s, the top-down approach of the mainlander-dominated Women's League and Women's Working Committee was evident in their approaches to the creation of local chapters for each organization. As a legacy of the elitist approach to party organization from the First United Front, the headquarters of the Women's League and the Women's Working Committee sent their cadres to each city and town to establish local chapters.[142]

Prior to the creation of these organizations, the Provincial Women's Association was the first and only government-affiliated women's organization on the island. Since the early 1950s, the Kuomintang designated the Women's League and the Women's Working Committee as organizations on the national level. Conversely, the Provincial Women's Association was accorded a local provincial status. From the perspective of the Taiwanese women elite, the association was demoted from the sole women's organization to a subordinate institution. Since the chapters of the three women's organizations generally had similar programs and agendas in the same localities, competition for human and financial resources was inevitable. Through the ideological construction of the Chinese Communists as the common enemies of the Taiwanese and the mainlanders in Taiwan, Madame Chiang attempted to obscure and redirect tensions between the two groups. It was her hope that the mainlander and Taiwanese women would set aside their differences and unite under her leadership for the anti-communist campaign.[143]

As time went on, however, the Kuomintang leadership's dream of returning to mainland China gradually faded. Starting in the 1960s, the leadership began to invest more resources in upgrading Taiwan's industries and infrastructures based on the foundations laid during the Japanese colonial era. With Taiwan as an American ally during the Cold War, from 1951 through 1968 the U.S. government provided approximately 1.5 billion dollars in the form of grants to facilitate the island's economic development, encourage the privatization of state-owned industries, and support entrepreneurship. These grants accounted for over a third of the island's total capital investment and also provided the necessary capital for upgrading infrastructure and training technical specialists.[144] At the suggestion of American advisors, the Kuomintang instituted nine years of universal compulsory education in 1968.

From 1966 through 1973, Taiwan became a popular site for American- and Japanese-owned companies that took advantage of its literate and inexpensive female workforce in labor-intensive light industries, such as the production of textiles, garments, plastics, shoes, toys, and electronics.[145] The United States was the largest market for the island's exports, and Taiwan rapidly industrialized after the mid-1960s. As other developing countries' cheap labor began to compete fiercely with Taiwan in the mid-1970s, the Kuomintang government enacted a new industrial policy to encourage Taiwanese enterprises to shift from labor-intensive production (1966–73) to capital-intensive manufacturing and technologically oriented industries. Since the mid-1970s, an increasing number of women have worked in the capital-intensive industrial sectors, including the production of components for personal computers, semiconductors, and precision instruments.[146] As more young single women preferred to work in the newly emerging white-collar service sector rather than the blue-collar manufacturing sector, married women in the middle-aged cohort were recruited to avert the potential labor shortages on the factories' shop floors.[147]

The Emergence of Democratic Opposition and the Postwar Autonomous Women's Movement

In the 1970s, social stability and economic expansion contributed to Taiwan's emergence as a newly industrializing society and to the growth of its urban middle class. In response to the demand of the middle class for greater freedom of expression, the Kuomintang began to tolerate more sociopolitical debate within the parameters set by its one-party rule.[148] As a minor concession to Taiwanese civil society, the party-state, during the Supplementary Election of 1969, added a few seats to the national legislative bodies for elected representatives of Taiwan's constituencies. Three years later, in the Supplementary Election of 1972, several non-Kuomintang electoral candidates, led by a national legislator, Huang Hsin-chieh, and his political protégé, K'ang Ning-hsiang, used the term *Dangwai* (outside the party) to designate their democratic movement in opposition to the Kuomintang. Dissatisfied with one-party rule, these *Dangwai* politicians began to use their election platforms to criticize the government and demand further political liberalization. Through active participation in electoral campaigns, the opposition movement used elections to publicize their ideas for democratic reform, increase popular support for the opposition movement, and erode the Kuomintang's political monopoly over Taiwanese society. In this way, elections served as an important catalyst for Taiwan's democratization.[149]

In 1971, the Chinese Communist government of The People's Republic of China (PRC) replaced The Republic of China (ROC) on Taiwan as the government of China in the United Nations. Under diplomatic pressure from the international community, the Kuomintang government withdrew its membership from the United Nations. The loss of the Kuomintang's legitimacy and prestige in the international community emboldened dissident intellectuals in Taiwan to challenge the limits of political permissibility set by the authoritarian regime, including the publication of political journals and magazines challenging press control, censorship of speech, and restrictions on the freedom of assembly.[150]

By the mid-1970s, the *Dangwai* combined the strategies of both the intellectual and the political wings of the movement by publicizing dissident political views in journals and magazines and running organized campaigns of *Dangwai*'s electoral candidates.[151] While most of the *Dangwai* activists were Taiwanese, there were also some mainlander dissidents in their ranks. The *Dangwai* activists were united in their calls for the revocations of martial law and the legal provisions that forbade the creation of new political parties, the restoration of civil liberties as guaranteed by the 1947 ROC Constitution, and the release of political prisoners. The *Dangwai* also argued for the reduction of the government's military expenditures and an increase in its spending on social services for economically disadvantaged groups in society. It criticized the regime's overemphasis on economic development over environmental issues and social and ethnic justice.[152]

Beginning in 1977, a rift began to emerge within the *Dangwai* movement between the moderate faction of K'ang Ning-hsiang and a radical faction that comprised a younger cohort of activists. K'ang's faction preferred to work within the established political system by using electoral campaigns and the bully pulpits of *Dangwai*'s elected officials to pressure the authoritarian state to liberalize its political culture. Conversely, the radical faction placed greater emphasis on mass demonstrations and civil disobedience in an effort to attract the public's attention and to pressure the regime to accelerate its democratic reform.[153]

In retrospect, the rise of the Taiwanese middle class in the 1970s put pressure on the Kuomintang government to recruit more Taiwanese into the upper echelon of its bureaucracy.[154] In the 1970s and thereafter, class division gradually replaced the old ethnic division between the mainlanders and the Taiwanese as the primary distinction among Taiwan's population. Thus, the new sociopolitical forces within Taiwan and the Kuomintang's diplomatic setbacks all converged to force the authoritarian regime into making concessions to the emerging civil society. Gradually, the regime's tolerance of dissenting voices within the parameters of its soft authoritarian political culture created an opportunity for the emergence of autonomous social movements independent of the regime's direct control.[155]

In 1972, Hsiu-lien Annette Lu (Lu Hsiu-lien), a civil servant with a law degree from the United States, launched postwar Taiwan's autonomous women's movement.[156] Although a main objective of the autonomous women's movement was to challenge Kuomintang-sponsored Confucianism, the Kuomintang educational system's emphases on women's gender-specific familial obligations and contribution to the nation nonetheless exerted some influence on the views Lu expressed in *New Feminism* (*Xinnüxing zhuyi*). In other words, she was not entirely immune from the pervasive power of the Kuomintang propaganda's ideological indoctrination.[157]

Conclusion

In this chapter I have distinguished the autonomous women's movement from the government-affiliated women's organizations in postwar Taiwan. Among the government-affiliated women's organizations, members of the Provincial Women's Association created childcare facilities in Taiwan's rural communities. The association conceived of the rural childcare facilities as an instrumental means of strengthening and enriching the nation's future through the upbringing of healthy children. Whereas most beneficiaries of the movement to create rural daycare facilities were Taiwanese women, most beneficiaries of the state-subsidized housing were military families of mainlander background. The former's chronic shortage of funds in comparison to the latter attested to the gender and ethnic inequalities in a mainlander-dominated patriarchal authoritarian state from the 1950s through the 1960s.

Though the Kuomintang had endorsed women's participation in paid and voluntary work to contribute to the national economy and its anti-communist objective, it also prioritized married women's domestic roles over their participation in paid work outside the home. In the New Life movement and in postwar Taiwan, the Kuomintang's idealization of women's traditional gender roles inadvertently caused a double burden for working mothers. From the Nanjing decade to the period of Chinese Nationalist rule on Taiwan, most women activists of the government-affiliated women's organizations did not criticize the patriarchal aspects of the ROC civil codes. They also failed to undertake an in-depth analysis of the deeply entrenched ideological and institutional patriarchy that still persisted in the interpersonal relationships of the family and society.

In contrast, beginning in the 1970s the activists of the autonomous women's movement critiqued the patriarchal aspects of the civil codes and the Confucian patriarchal ideology that permeated different facets of Taiwanese life. In the 1970s, the activists of the autonomous movement belonged to a new generation that had come of age in postwar Taiwan. As members of the emerging middle class, they obtained higher education and gained access to professional careers in the 1960s and 1970s.[158] The integration of the mainlanders with the Taiwanese enabled social activists from both backgrounds to work together in Taiwan's autonomous women's movement.

3. Hsiu-lien Annette Lu: The Pioneering Stage of the Postwar Autonomous Women's Movement and the Democratic Opposition, 1972–79

On the occasion of International Women's Day in 1972, Lu Hsiu-lien (Hsiu-lien Annette Lu) made a speech at the law school of National Taiwan University that launched the autonomous women's movement in postwar Taiwan. This autonomous social movement emerged from the Taiwanese middle class within the context of the Kuomintang regime's limited tolerance of sociopolitical dissent from the early 1970s. Concurrently, the greater tolerance for dissent than had previously been shown by the regime enabled Lu to launch the pioneering stage of the autonomous women's movement from 1972 through 1977.[1]

Contrary to the Kuomintang-affiliated women's organizations discussed in chapter 2, the autonomous women's movement was independent of the Kuomintang's control. Historically, the origin of the autonomous women's movement was significant. It was the first social movement in postwar Taiwan to grow and flourish.[2] Lu's founding of the movement was motivated by her sense of urgency to call into question the prevalent male-centered values in Taiwanese society and was an expression of her struggle for gender equity and social justice.[3]

This chapter examines the impact of the Kuomintang's authoritarianism in shaping the elite-sustained character of the movement in postwar Taiwan. Contrasts between the autonomous movement in the 1970s and the Kuomintang-affiliated women's organizations are also analyzed. For the purpose of cross-cultural and historical comparison, I examine similarities and differences between Taiwan's elite-sustained autonomous women's movement with that of the United States.

This chapter also analyzes the content of *New Feminism* (*Xin nüxing zhuyi*), the definitive expression of Lu's feminist thought. In the 1970s, Taiwan's feminist community universally recognized *New Feminism* as the main text of Taiwan's feminist discourse. Written in 1973, its content was subsequently revised and republished in 1977 and 1986.[4] This chapter looks at Lu's selective incorporation of ideas from Western liberal feminism and Confucianism to formulate a feminist discourse within the Chinese cultural context of Taiwanese society. In examining the nature and extent of the Kuomintang political culture's influence on the formation of Taiwanese feminism in the 1970s, I analyze the arguments that Lu devised to negotiate and compromise with the authoritarian regime.[5]

In particular, I look into the ideological influences of Anglo-American women's rights advocates on Lu's formulation of her feminist views, including Mary Wollstonecraft, Margaret Mead, and Betty Friedan. The socialist ideas of American feminist Charlotte Perkins Gilman (1860–1935) also exerted considerable influence on Lu's conceptualization of socialized childcare and housework.[6] In 1976, Lu's Pioneer Press compiled a translated anthology of feminist essays from the Anglo-American tradition entitled *Cong nüren dao ren* (*From Being a Woman to Becoming a Human Being*). The writings of Wollstonecraft, Mead, and Gilman were in this translated anthology and it became a main source of Western feminist thought in Taiwan. With the translation of book two of Simone de Beauvoir's *The Second Sex* (1949) into Chinese, *the second sex* (*di er xing*) became the Taiwanese feminists' rallying cry for denoting women's status as second-class citizens.[7] In *New Feminism*, Lu quoted extensively from de Beauvoir to substantiate and strengthen her arguments.[8]

Additionally, I discuss the ways in which Western feminist theorists influenced Lu's ideas on women's identities, women's gender and social roles, employment, marriage and the family, cooperative home economics, and abortion rights. For the purpose of assessing Lu's effectiveness in introducing Western feminist intellectual traditions to her Taiwanese audience, I critique the historical accuracy of Lu's narrative in *New Feminism*. I also evaluate the ways in which the Kuomintang historiography affected Lu's narrative on the women's movement in pre–1949 China and contributes to her omission of information on Taiwan's autonomous women's movement in the 1920s. Before discussing the content of *New Feminism*, I discuss Lu's life experiences that culminated in her leadership role in the pioneering stage of the postwar movement, the problems and challenges she faced in a male-centered society in Taiwan, and her self-definition as a new woman (*xinnüxing*).

The Making of a New Woman: Annette Lu's Formative Years

In 1944, during the last years of the Japanese colonial era, Hsiu-lien Annette Lu was born in the city of Taoyuan in northern Taiwan. Her parents were Taiwanese merchants who owned a small family business. As a response to Lu's complaint to her parents that it was not her fault to be born a girl, they began to educate her as if she were a son and expected her to achieve academic excellence. At an early age, her father taught her oratorical skills.[9]

Throughout Lu's formative years, her elder brother was her role model. She set a goal of entering the School of Law at National Taiwan University after her brother was admitted to the program. With her persistent self-discipline and determination to succeed, Lu entered the judicial division of National Taiwan University's School of Law in 1963 with the highest score on the joint university and college entrance examination.[10] In 1968, Lu graduated first in her class at the University's Graduate School of Law.[11]

Through academic achievement, Lu transformed her aversion to her gender identity in male-centered society (*nanxing zhongxin de shehui*) into positive self-esteem that affirmed her womanhood. Throughout Lu's life, she has adhered to her goal of self-realization and has urged other women to do the same.[12] In a sense, Lu's commitment to women's education and self-realization were based on her personal experience. As a young woman, Lu was fond of a Taiwanese pen pal who studied law in France. Although they had never met in person, "the man's family had already checked her out and approved of her."[13] Soon thereafter, in 1969, Lu accepted a scholarship to study comparative law at the University of Illinois in Urbana-Champaign. They corresponded over the next few years to maintain their emotional ties. Finally, the two met in New York, and Lu came to the realization that the necessary chemistry to continue the romantic relationship was not there.[14]

This experience marked a turning point in Lu's life. It was then that she made the conscious decision to pursue her career ambitions and remain single. By living her life this way, she could retain her identity as an independent woman without having to share her life with a significant other.[15] Lu asserted that every person ought to have the right to pursue his or her ambitions and happiness. She stated, "Rather than expecting others to fulfill one's ideals, why not become the embodiment of one's own ideals!"[16]

In 1969, Lu became an eyewitness to the American Women's Liberation movement while studying in Urbana-Champaign. During her spare time, she collected information from university libraries about the movement and about women's organizations in the United States. Due to Lu's socially conservative upbringing under the Kuomintang regime, she opposed radical feminists' call for the liberation of women's sexuality.[17]

In 1971, Lu obtained her law degree. She returned to Taiwan to assume the position of section chief with the Commission of Laws and Regulations in the Executive Yuan of the Republic of China (ROC). In addition to her government job, Lu also accepted a visiting professorship at Taipei's Ming-ch'uan Women's College of Business in 1974 and offered courses on civil and commercial law. In the mid- and late-1970s, numerous students from the business college would serve as volunteers in the autonomous women's movement under Lu's leadership.[18]

Pioneering the Autonomous Women's Movement, 1972–77

In 1971, there was much discussion in the government about the possibility of setting a preferential quota for male admissions to certain majors in institutions of higher learning. As more women took the annual college entrance examination and scored higher each year, some feared that women would outnumber men in majors such as literature and history.[19] In defense of women's right to equal competition in the entrance examination, Lu challenged the traditional attitude of favoring men over women in an article published in the *United Daily News* (*Lianhe bao*). Lu argued that the growing number of women admitted to universities attested to the high quality of education in girls' high schools and female students' painstaking efforts in preparation for the examination. Not only did the Ministry of Education fail to encourage this positive development, it sought to violate the spirit of meritocracy, universality, and equality in the ROC Constitution of 1947, since the Constitution had stipulated that all citizens of the ROC should be given equal educational opportunities.[20]

Because some conservative educators argued for restrictions on female admissions on the grounds that a woman's place was at home, Lu cited Margaret Mead's research findings in the three Melanesian societies of New Guinea to refute the idea that gender roles were biologically predetermined. Since the women of these societies were assertive and active outside their homes, Lu suggested that the traditional gender roles of Taiwan might not be socially acceptable elsewhere.

Lu was convinced that men and women with similar educational and life experiences had the same potential for achieving excellence in their occupational endeavors. Based on trends in university admissions during the early 1970s, Lu emphasized that women's intellectual abilities were by no means inferior to those of men. Hence, it was their right to enjoy the same access to all branches of learning in higher education. Lu asserted that gender roles should thus be modified and adjusted to meet the new societal needs of modernity. In her view, men and women should be fully educated to contribute to all sectors of the economy and enhance the collective wealth and power (*fuqiang*) of the island's people.[21] With the publication of her article in one of Taiwan's most widely circulated newspapers, Lu made a powerful demand for gender equality in postwar Taiwan. As a result of this article and the Legislative Yuan's opposition to the Ministry of Education's gender-biased perspective, the proposal to create a preferential quota for male students in certain majors was revoked.[22]

In the following year, Lu gave a speech on International Women's Day to launch the women's movement at the Law School of National Taiwan University. In the same year, Chung Chao-man, a Ph.D. student at the University of California in San Diego, murdered his wife and escaped back to Taiwan to evade prosecution. Taking advantage of the Taiwanese public's admiration for overseas scholars and the sexual double standard in Taiwanese society, the murder suspect claimed that he killed his wife out of rage, after suspecting that she was committing adultery. Many in Taiwan sympathized with him for punishing an unfaithful wife.[23]

Deeply disturbed by this development, Lu decided to expose the sickness of the male-centered society. She wrote an article entitled, "Which is More Important, Chastity or Life?" (Zhencao yu shengming shuzhong), and published it in the *China Times* (*Zhongguo shibao*). In it, Lu attacked the sexual double standard. She asked her audience whether the public would extend as much sympathy and forgiveness to the murderer if Chung's wife were the one that killed her unfaithful husband.[24] Lu reminded her audience that life was more important than chastity, and whoever believed that a woman's chastity was more important than her life was an adherent of the outdated Confucian rites (*lijiao*).[25] Lu further reminded her readers that Chung had no right to take his wife's life. She then demanded a fair trial to bring the suspect to justice.[26]

Lu's article brought out the inhumanity of certain traditional Chinese values and prompted much public discussion. As a result, Lu became the leading commentator of women's issues in Taiwan's public discourse.[27] Due to the readership's enthusiastic response, *China Times* invited her to be a columnist. The article also attracted numerous supporters and volunteers to her feminist cause.[28] Many individuals who agreed with Lu's woman-centered perspective wrote letters either to the newspapers or to her personally to express their support for social justice and women's rights.[29]

Conversely, some individuals who opposed Lu's perspective wrote anonymous letters to attack her character,[30] while others accused her of borrowing Western ideas to destroy traditional Chinese family values. Still others wrote unsigned letters with derogatory sexual terms and disrespectful comments. In order to put a stop to these personal attacks, Lu made photocopies of the original letters and published them in the front section of her book *Counting the Pioneering Footsteps* (*Shuyishu tuohuang de jiaobu*). No one wrote letters to insult her with obscene language again.[31]

As the leader of the autonomous women's movement in the 1970s, Lu was mindful of the residual effect of the Kuomintang's White Terror. During the 1970s, Taiwan's political culture under martial law was still more authoritarian than that of the United States during the second Red Scare in the 1950s. Nonetheless, American feminists in the 1950s and their Taiwanese counterparts in the 1970s faced similar problems and challenges in a conservative anti-feminist political environment. Because the socially conservative public opinion and political climate were not conducive to mobilizing a broadly based movement with thousands of members for mass protests, each movement organized a small but committed group of feminist elite to sustain their survival.[32]

With Taiwan under martial law from 1949 through 1987, the Legislative Yuan of the ROC merely served as a rubber stamp for policies drafted by the Kuomintang's Central Committee. The unsuitability of the Legislative Yuan as a channel for public opinion and the Kuomintang's hostility toward sociopolitical agitation[33] all contributed to the absence of direct legislative lobbying by Taiwanese feminists' in the 1970s. This was in stark contrast to American liberal feminists' active involvement in legislative lobbying, including participation in congressional hearings, gathering signatures for legislative petitions, and corresponding with members of Congress.[34] Comparatively, this difference attests to the centrality of political culture in shaping the strategies of feminist activists.

In the 1970s, Taiwanese feminist activists' attempts to renegotiate women's status with the authoritarian state ran into many obstacles. In 1972, Lu and thirty other women's rights supporters filed an application for the creation of the Contemporary Women's Association (*Shidai nüxing xiehui*). After nearly ten months of waiting, the Social Welfare Department of the Taipei city government rejected the application on the grounds that the agenda of the association was similar to that of the Taiwan Provincial Women's Association (*Funühui*).[35] Indeed, there were some similarities in the agendas of the Kuomintang-sponsored Taiwan Provincial Women's Association and the independent Contemporary Women's Association. Both organizations' goals were to promote women's career advancement and welfare. To this end, both associations professed to provide assistance for women who sought legal counseling, advice for careers, and assistance in personal or family problems.[36]

On the other hand, the Provincial Women's Association propagated certain ideologies that Lu and her feminist associates sought to modify. Whereas the Provincial Women's Association idealized women's roles as virtuous wives and kind mothers (*xianqi liangmu*), the program of the Contemporary Women's Association under Lu's initiative did not emphasize traditional women's roles in the family and the society. Lu believed that women could engage in more productive activities to contribute to the nation's development than mending military uniforms. As mentioned in chapter 2, the Provincial Women's Association served as an institutional means for the Kuomintang to mobilize Taiwanese women for their auxiliary roles in the military establishment's campaign to recover the mainland from the Communist occupation.[37]

Because the Provincial Women's Association was affiliated with the Kuomintang regime, it had sufficient financial subsidies from the Taiwan Provincial Government to create chapters in virtually every city and town in Taiwan. Conversely, the independence of the autonomous women's movement from the sponsorship of the authoritarian regime rendered it ineligible for the government's financial resources. Most of its financial resources were derived from fundraising activities and private donations. Due to these financial constraints, most of the movement's activities were limited to Taiwan's major urban centers, most notably Taipei and Kaohsiung.[38]

As the leader of an autonomous women's movement, Lu did not draft the agendas of the Contemporary Women's Association with the intention of recovering mainland China. Lu's indigenous orientation was evident in her emphasis on the urgency of transferring the talents and creative energy of nearly two million housewives to the public domain where they could contribute to Taiwan's economy. Lu saw the Contemporary Women's Association as encouraging the awakening of women's gender consciousness and the advocacy of women's self-realization in Taiwanese society. One of the main purposes of establishing the association was to mobilize its human and financial resources for the dissemination of Lu's feminist thought through word of mouth, lectures, and published materials.[39]

In order to circumvent the party-state's restrictions on the creation of non-governmental organizations, Lu decided to create a gathering place and business venture in Taipei where feminist activists could exchange ideas, co-ordinate activities, and generate funds for the movement. In 1972, Lu named the coffee shop Home of the Pioneers (*Tuohuangzhe zhi jia*). From its initial conceptualization to the day it first opened, more than twenty individuals contributed funds and volunteered for the endeavor. In the ensuing months, many volunteers worked in the kitchen and served drinks and refreshments to generate revenue. Most of the volunteers were Lu's students and colleagues from Taipei's Min-ch'uan Women's College of Business, Lu's friends who either taught or studied at the law school of National Taiwan University and other academic institutions in the Taipei area, and supporters of Lu's feminist stance. The last category included individuals from urban middle-class backgrounds, such as students, housewives, and professional men and women.[40]

Many activists and financial contributors of the movement offered Lu assistance on the condition that their identities remain secret. In the politi-cal climate of martial law, this anonymous approach of working behind the scenes could minimize the Kuomintang's surveillance of and interference in one's daily life. Conversely, Lu's leadership roles in the movement as its principal theorist, fundraiser, and organizer, and her high visibility in the news media, exposed her to governmental surveillance. For example, the Kuomintang wiretapped her telephone conversations.[41] According to Lu, one financial contributor who became the manager of the Home of the Pioneers was actually an undercover agent sent by the Kuomintang's Investigation Bureau to sabotage the project and serve as a government informant. This, coupled with some poor management decisions, resulted in the disappear-ance of a significant sum of the Home of the Pioneers' assets. In other words, it was operating on a deficit. In 1973, Lu made the decision to close down the business.[42]

In the following year, at the age of thirty, Lu was diagnosed with thyroid cancer. After surgery, she was able to bring her illness under control with medication.[43] As the leader of the autonomous women's movement, Lu put her emphasis on raising the Taiwanese public's awareness of the societal need for gender equality and changing the cultural values and belief systems of the socially conservative Taiwanese public.[44] Due to Lu's emphasis on ideological transformation, it is conceivable that her feminist strategy was influenced by the cultural-intellectual approach. Traditionally, Chinese intellectuals considered the transformation of cultural values and belief systems as pre-conditions for other changes in society. This mode of thinking was termed *the cultural-intellectual approach.*[45]

In the early 1970s, Lu collected statistical data and legal documents published by the ROC government to analyze the gender inequalities in men's
and women's economic opportunities and the ROC's family laws. Through
her writing she called attention to the need to revise gender-biased family
laws and penal codes. To forge a consensus among legal scholars and feminist
activists, Lu invited the publisher of *Falu shijie* (*Juridical World*), a monthly
on jurisprudence, to coordinate a roundtable discussion in 1975.[46] The participants included several attorneys, professors of jurisprudence, a newspaper
columnist, feminist activists, and a legislator. Their consensus called for the
transformation of a married couple's joint property into separate individual
property, the relaxation of divorce restrictions, the elimination of paternal
monopoly over child custody, and the legalization of abortion.[47] Despite
the absence of feminist activists' direct lobbying in the Legislative Yuan, it
was Lu's hope that the consensus of the legal and feminist communities and
a pro-feminist public opinion could exert pressure on the government to
eliminate the gender-biased civil and penal codes.[48]

Lu's compilation of gender-biased family laws and statistical data to illustrate gender inequality underscored the need for an autonomous women's
movement in Taiwan. In her attempt to urge the Taiwanese public not to
fall behind international trends, Lu cited the United Nations' designation of
1975 as International Women's Year and the vitality of the American Women's
Liberation movement as additional reasons for an autonomous movement
in Taiwan.[49] To propagate her ideas, Lu made speeches on college campuses,
organized panel discussions, and wrote articles for the major newspapers in
Taiwan. Lu's newspaper articles convinced many intellectuals of the urgent
need for social reform.[50] Among the intellectuals who joined Lu's call were
Ku Yen-lin and Lee Yuan-chen,[51] both of whom would later play a pivotal
role in launching the feminist magazine, *Awakening*, during the 1980s.[52]

In 1975, Lu accepted a grant from the American-based Asia Foundation
to visit women's organizations in the United States, Japan, and South Korea.
While Lu was touring college campuses in different regions of the United
States, she gave talks on her book, *New Feminism*, to American students
and faculty. To raise funds for the women's movement back home, Lu sold
hundreds of copies of *New Feminism* to immigrant communities and graduate students from Taiwan. In the same year, the feminist organizers of the
world conference of International Women's Year in Mexico City invited Lu
to attend. The Mexican government denied her a visa after the delegation of
the People's Republic of China (PRC) voiced their objection to having "the
renegade province of Taiwan" represented at the conference.[53]

Upon Lu's return to Taiwan she resigned from her government position to be a full-time feminist activist. With the money she raised in the United States, financial contributions from the Asia Foundation, and private donations in Taiwan, in 1976 Lu established a twenty-four hour hotline at the southern port city of Kaohsiung. The hotline dealt with cases of sexual assault and domestic violence and offered counseling to female victims.[54] Because Taiwanese society in the 1970s still expected women to guard their chastity at all costs, the vast majority of rape victims did not report such incidents to the police. Consequently, the male perpetrators were able to walk free with impunity. Even in instances where female victims reported incidents to the police, the male-centered law enforcement agencies and the legal system tended to demand unreasonable proof from the victims. As a result, few rapists were convicted. The hotline was thus intended to create a legitimate channel for female victims of sexual assault to break their silence and obtain counseling. Lu also hoped that perpetrators of rape could be brought to justice.[55]

Prior to the creation of the hotline, Lu befriended a couple in Kaohsiung's Christian community who enabled her to set up the hotline in the office space of Kaohsiung's Christian social service center. Another friend, the editor of the Kaohsiung-based newspaper, *Taiwan Times* (*Taiwan shibao*), publicized the hotline.[56] These personal relationships (*guanxi*) enabled Lu to launch the hotline and make it successful. More than one hundred women volunteered to assist Lu in the endeavor.[57] Among them, sixty-eight were chosen to offer medical care and legal and psychological counseling to victims of sexual assault and desertion. To ensure victims' ease in sharing their traumatic experiences, all counselors on the telephone lines were women. Likewise, most medical doctors and lawyers who counseled the victims were affiliated with the hotline. Lu and her volunteers also solicited support from policewomen in Kaohsiung's police department to investigate cases of sexual assault.[58]

Due to the high-profile nature of the hotline in Taiwan's second largest city, some conservatives in governmental circles began to criticize it for publicizing sexual violence against women in Taiwanese society. They speculated that the Chinese Communists across the Strait would use these negative images to wage an international propaganda campaign against the Kuomintang on Taiwan. Consequently, the Social Welfare Department of the Kaohsiung municipal government demanded that the hotline expand the scope of its service to tackle all problems concerning women. That is, in addition to providing assistance to female victims of sexual assault, desertion, and domestic violence, the hotline should also assist women with general problems in marriage and the family, as well as providing general medical advice and career counseling. To minimize possible state interference in the hotline's operation, Lu acceded to the municipal government's request.[59]

As a result of the hotline's positive reception by Kaohsiung's residents, Lu decided to create another hotline in Taipei to assist female victims of assault and desertion as well as women workers who migrated from rural Taiwan to work in Taipei. In addition to receiving hundreds of calls from troubled women from all walks of life, several Kuomintang officials' wives called the hotline with their marital problems without revealing their identities. Meanwhile, an undercover Kuomintang agent at the Taipei hotline harassed the female volunteers. Two years after the founding of the Taipei hotline, Lu had no other alternative but to terminate the service. Despite this setback, its counterpart in Kaohsiung remained in service from the mid-1970s through the 1980s.[60]

In the mid-1970s, Lu created a women's reference center in Taipei to recruit high-school student volunteers to conduct a citywide survey on housewives' married lives and women's problems. The results showed that many women were dissatisfied in their relationships with their husbands, but financial dependence, gender-biased family laws, and societal and familial expectations left them with few options but to stay in unhappy marriages. Based on the data collected in the survey, Lu, with the support of her feminist associates and the mass media, publicized the results and organized public forums and seminars to discuss issues of marriage and sex. Ultimately, this information reached ten thousand participants nationwide.[61]

While the survey encouraged public discussions of sexuality and marital problems, the martial-law regime imposed censorship on virtually all printed materials published in Taiwan. In 1974, Lu's publisher halted the sales and distribution of New Feminism after an overseas Chinese writer falsely accused the book of advocating sexual promiscuity. According to Lu, she made the strategic decision not to discuss the sensitive subjects of sexual relationships outside the marital context. Despite her deliberate omission, in 1976 the Ministry of the Interior refused to grant Lu a copyright.[62]

After Lu's publisher refused to sell New Feminism, she and several other women writers and translators[63] established the Pioneer Press (Tuohuangzhe chubanshe) to publish several of Lu's works and translate Western feminist writings. Since the Kuomintang was less stringent in its rules and regulations for the creation of publishing houses than for the establishment of non-governmental civic organizations,[64] the creation of the press provided a base for feminist activists to gather and coordinate their activities.[65]

On International Women's Day in 1976, Lu and her feminist associate at the press, Lo Lo-chia,[66] organized a workshop on "women outside the kitchen" and an open-air men's cooking contest to encourage male participation in housework. With extensive media coverage of both events, the activists demonstrated that the kitchen should not be solely a woman's domain. These activities were a direct challenge to the traditional norm of expecting Confucian gentlemen (*junzi*) to stay away from the kitchen.[67] In the same year, the press published *Their Blood and Sweat, Their Tears.* In contrast to the urban middle-class orientation of Lu's *New Feminism, Their Blood and Sweat, Their Tears* discussed the daily lives and problems of prostitutes and of women in the rural peasantry and the urban working class. Since the book exposed the darker side of Taiwanese life, the Kuomintang government banned its circulation on the grounds that it fomented social disorder.[68] By 1977, the press encountered many of the same problems as the Home of the Pioneers. It struggled with a shortage of funds and infiltration by government informants. Although no evidence suggests overt factional divisions within the autonomous women's movement, subtle tensions did exist beneath the surface. Several activists stated that they left the movement because Lu had taken their sacrifice for granted and did not acknowledge their contributions. Lu disagreed with their perspective and contended that the movement had never suffered from a shortage of volunteers.[69] Faced with these challenges and obstacles, Lu decided to close down the press and attend Harvard Law School.

In retrospect, several factors could explain the Kuomintang's suspicion of the autonomous women's movement in the 1970s. First, as a one-party authoritarian regime, the Kuomintang looked with suspicion upon any social agitation that might upset the sociopolitical status quo. Second, the Kuomintang-affiliated women's organizations wanted to minimize the potential competition from a women's group that had ideologies and goals different from their own. Lastly, the Kuomintang was originally from mainland China. Since Lu was a native Taiwanese and a non-party member who attempted to create a non-governmental women's organization, her activities were under the surveillance of the Investigation Bureau of the Ministry of Justice. The tension between the Kuomintang and the autonomous women's movement was exacerbated by the latter's attempt to test the boundary of permissibility for social dissent.[70]

New Feminism

One of Lu's challenges to the authoritarian patriarchal culture was her conceptualization of the *new woman.* As indicated above, Lu published the first edition of *New Feminism* (*Xinnüxing zhuyi*) in 1974. In Nationalist China prior to 1949, both *nüquan zhuyi* (women's rights principle) and *xinnüxing* (new woman) were terms commonly used among progressive Chinese intellectuals. In her book, Lu created the term *xinnüxing zhuyi* (new woman's principle; new feminism) to supersede *nüquan zhuyi* in order to transcend the narrow focus on demanding women's rights (*nüquan*) from men. Lu claimed that *xinnüxing zhuyi* conveyed her vision for women's ideological transformation into new women. She also stated that the ideological transformations of both new women and new men (*xinnanxing*) were crucial for the emergence of a new gender-egalitarian ethos characterized by cooperation and mutual respect between human beings.[71]

Women's Individual Identity

Inspired by the liberal concept of individual rights from the West, Lu stated that every person's goal in life ought to be the preservation of self-identity and dignity. He or she should not be a means for others to achieve their goals.[72] Mary Wollstonecraft influenced Lu's belief that "everyone [should] be prepared to be an independent person before he or she identifies his or her gender. Let everyone be treated equally, regardless of sex."[73]

To oppose the traditional Chinese prejudice against women and girls, Lu asserted that new feminism was a modern and rational ideology that valued universal human rights. Since children have no control over whether they are born of a particular sex, she argued, it is utterly unfair and inhumane to treat children unequally based on their gender identities. Likewise, an individual should not be discriminated against based on the socioeconomic situations into which he or she is born.[74]

In *New Feminism,* Lu appropriated Simone de Beauvoir's term *the second sex* (*di er xing*) to denote women's status as second-class citizens in Taiwanese society.[75] Historically, men were entitled to the rights and privileges of human beings. Rather than accord women the same dignity and rights, they were generally considered a sub-class. Consistent with de Beauvoir's conception of the common humanity of women and men, Lu's *New Feminism* underscored that as human beings first and foremost, both genders ought to enjoy equal rights.[76]

Women's Gender and Social Roles

Not only did Lu emphasize gender equality (*nannü pingdeng*), she also wrote extensively on women's gender roles. Based on Margaret Mead's findings in *Sex and Temperament in Three Primitive Societies,* Lu criticized the assumption that gender roles were biologically predetermined. She endorsed Mead's contention that socialization was the main determinant of gender-specific behavioral patterns. Lu argued that both male and female individuals were born with unique temperaments and behavioral traits that were not linked to their sex. Yet, in boys, Western and Chinese societies suppressed socially ascribed female traits and accentuated the socially ascribed male traits. The same societies suppressed socially defined male traits and accentuated the socially defined female traits in girls. To persuade her Taiwanese audience that socio-cultural conditioning rather than innate biological difference shaped men's and women's gender roles, Lu summarized Mead's research findings from three distinctive societies in New Guinea during the 1930s.[77]

Among the three, Lu stated that both males and females of the Arapesh society had personalities, temperaments, and behavioral patterns that were considered feminine and passive by traditional Chinese and Western standards. Conversely, both males and females of the Mundugumor society were socialized to acquire aggressive temperaments and behavioral patterns from childhood. Thus, both sexes had personalities considered masculine by Chinese and Western standards. Tchambuli males, however, were socialized to be passive, while women were socialized to acquire dominant personalities. The gender-role differentiation in Tchambuli society could be seen as an inversion of traditional gender roles in Chinese and Western societies.[78]

With this summary, Lu tried to undermine her Chinese readers' assumption that traditional gender roles were absolute and culturally universal in different times and places. She suggested that the socially acceptable gender roles in Taiwan might not be acceptable in other societies, like the three in New Guinea. The striking differences in the three New Guinea societies' conceptualization of gender also demonstrated the relativity of the social construction of gender in different cultural contexts.[79]

To accommodate Taiwan's conservative sociopolitical climate in the 1970s, Lu did not object to gender differentiation along the lines of biological sex. Lu asserted that women's social and biological differences from men should not preclude their right to demand equal participation in public life. Lu argued that gender equity is not a synonym for sameness. Hence, women had the right to preserve their differences from men and to achieve equity at the same time.[80]

Lu compared the two genders to a flower in full bloom that needs green leaves to complement it. The beauty of both the flower and the leaves cannot be fully manifested without both complementing each other. In other words, masculine attributes and beauty should complement gentle and sweet feminine temperaments. Based on Lu's analogy, it is possible that her conceptualization of gender distinctions was influenced by the concept of *yin* and *yang* in traditional Chinese cosmology. Just as Lu conceptualized the two genders as complementary opposites that were not absolute dichotomies, *yin* and *yang* are two contrasting and complementary parts that are integrated into a harmonious rounded whole. Similar to Lu's view of gender difference as relative rather than absolute, *yin* and *yang* generally are not conceived of as two absolute extremes. Rather, they interpenetrate each other in a state of flux. Lu asserted that like the *yin* and *yang*, biological differences between men and women are not total and absolute, but partial and relative.[81] Unlike the Confucian interpretation of the masculine *yang* as the dominant half over the feminine *yin*,[82] Lu reinterpreted and modernized Confucianism to depict a married couple as two equal and complementary partners who peacefully coexist in a relationship of mutual respect, compromise, and mutual assistance.[83] In so doing, Lu formulated the relational strand of new feminism.

Because Lu was influenced by the Confucian concept of familial obligation, her conceptualization of individual freedom never went as far as that of de Beauvoir. As a French existentialist, de Beauvoir believed that an individual should have the freedom to explore and define his or her own future and test various possibilities free from familial constraints or socially imposed values.[84] In contrast, Lu viewed the fulfillment of an individual's familial and societal responsibilities as a condition for preserving individual rights.[85] Lu suggested that one's individual freedom should be counterbalanced by fulfillment of specific obligations in family and in society.

We can see her emphasis on the importance of fulfilling societal and familial obligations in her famous quote, "One should behave in accordance with who one is (*shisheme, xiangsheme*)." In this context, "who one is" refers to a person's familial and societal roles.[86] In Confucianism, the term *rectification of names* (*zhengming*) denotes a person's proper conduct and fulfillment of obligations in accordance with his or her socially ascribed roles and positions in the family and in society.[87] In accordance with the Confucian vision of interpersonal relationships, Lu posited that a public servant should be loyal to his or her superior and fulfill the responsibilities assigned to one's job. Similarly, a wife should fulfill the obligations associated with her roles in relationship to her husband.[88]

Lu's *New Feminism* was thus clearly influenced by the Confucian notion of the rectification of names. On the other hand, she explicitly called for the elimination of gender bias in Confucianism and the prevalent double standard in the treatment of men and women. Like her Taiwanese feminist counterparts in the 1920s, Lu criticized the Confucian admonitions that only women should be chaste (*pianmian zhencao*); of continuing the family line through male offspring (*chuanzong jiedai*); of respecting men and demeaning women (*nanzun nübei*); and that men's domain is outside the home, whereas women's domain is inside the home (*nanzhuwai nüzhunei*).[89]

Employment

In regard to advocating women's equal participation in paid work outside the home, Lu stated that the kitchen could no longer satisfy women's aspirations for realizing their full potential. Similar to Betty Friedan's perspective in *The Feminine Mystique*, Lu believed that housewives' latent energy and creative talents constituted an untapped reserve that could contribute to a productive workforce, and, by extension, to socioeconomic progress.[90] Lu also posited that the relationship between individuals and society is reciprocal, and that women's right to work should be regarded as the fulfillment of their social obligation in the public domain. Since society invested ample resources to educate female students, she argued, women should take advantage of the knowledge and skill they acquired to contribute to society. Lu encouraged every woman to choose an occupation on the grounds that it was good for her self-development, the financial needs of her family, and the progress of society.[91]

Like their American counterparts, Taiwanese women in the 1970s were socialized to work in less prestigious and lower-paying jobs, despite the fact that no scientific evidence suggested a correlation between gender identity and intelligence. Like Margaret Mead, Lu asserted that the societal and occupational roles that men and women play in the public arena ought not be based on gender distinctions. That is, women's potential and occupational aspirations in the public domain should not be stifled by societal pressure to conform to socially ascribed gender roles.[92] To overcome occupational segregation along gender lines, both Mead and Lu advocated that women should have the freedom to participate fully in any paid work in traditionally male-dominated professions. Lu's notion of individual variation based on a person's unique talents and interests rather than gender distinction was derived from Mead's perspective. Both asserted that each individual's unique aptitudes and interests should be the main determinants of his or her roles and occupations.[93]

Inspired by the liberal individualist feminism of the American Women's Liberation movement, Lu advocated that men and women receive equal pay for performing the same jobs and be given equal opportunities for hiring and promotion. In the United States, Betty Friedan called for women's self-realization in the public sphere.[94] In Taiwan, Lu asserted that it is incumbent on every woman to translate new feminism into action for the pursuit of self-determination (*zijue*) and self-empowerment (*ziqiang*). As women began actively participating in all walks of life, Lu believed that each woman "would no longer be a shadow of history, [but] an individual who creates history." As the female portion of the human race contributes to all societal endeavors, our human experience would no longer be called "his-story," it would be termed the "human story."[95]

To promote men's support for women's employment outside the home, Lu cited de Beauvoir's contention that a financially independent wife could liberate her husband from shouldering the burden of being the sole breadwinner of the family. By forcing women to be men's dependents, she suggested, men had inadvertently enslaved themselves.[96] Knowing that most men would not want to find themselves in women's state of dependency, Lu reminded Taiwanese men of a Confucian adage: "Do not impose on others what you yourself do not desire" (*Jisuobuyu, wushiyuren*).[97] Lu believed that a self-confident man would not feel threatened by his wife's freedom and personal achievement.[98]

Marriage, Family, and Cooperative Home Economics

In addition to Lu's belief in husbands' and wives' contributions to household economy, she asserted that a durable marriage should be based on the premise that the couple would honor the marital agreement to remain monogamous. Despite the ROC penal code's stipulation that an adulterer was subject to a year's imprisonment or less, Taiwanese society tolerated a married man's decision to keep mistresses or pay prostitutes. As a consequence of this sexual double standard, an unhappy marriage often survived through a chaste wife's fatalistic acceptance of her husband's adulterous behavior.[99]

In an effort to eliminate this double standard of expecting only women to be chaste (*pianmian zhencao*), Lu reminded her audience that a husband with extramarital affairs ought not to expect fidelity from his wife. Once again, Lu evoked the Confucian adage: "Do not impose on others what you yourself do not desire." Based on this ethic of mutual respect and reciprocity in human relationships, Lu reminded her male audience that inasmuch as a husband did not wish his wife to betray his trust, he should not betray her trust. If a husband were to demand fidelity from his wife, the wife also had the same right to demand faithfulness from her husband. Lu called for the replacement of this sexual double standard with a single standard of sexual morality for men and women.[100]

Obviously, Lu's perspective on sexual morality had a strong tinge of puritanism. In her view, many people in the West were engaging in loveless sexual relationships before marriage. For the single men and women of Taiwan, she recommended love before marriage and sexual activity only within the marital context. Like her Taiwanese feminist counterparts in the 1920s, Lu believed that marriage is a carnal and spiritual union between two equal individuals who share a genuine relationship characterized by compatibility, mutual respect, and reciprocity.[101] Yet, Lu suggested that if the love between a couple was to develop into a sexual relationship prior to marriage, others should tolerate it without passing value judgments.[102]

In regard to marriage, Lu posited that the traditional Chinese practice of expecting the bridegroom to offer payment to the bride's family for betrothal (*pinjin*) should cease. She felt that the *pinjin* system was based on the traditional assumption that a daughter was her parents' wasted investment. Once she was married off, she became the means for her husband's family to produce a male heir. Thus, the old saying goes, "a daughter married off is spilled water outside the family door." In this patrilocal and patrilineal context, *pinjin* was the bridegroom's monetary compensation for the bride's family in appreciation for raising the daughter for his family.[103]

Despite the persistence of the *pinjin* system in Taiwan during the 1970s, Lu regarded it as an outdated practice incompatible with modern marriage. Consistent with the Taiwanese feminists' argument in the 1920s, Lu contended that a modern couple should consist of two equal individuals who entered the marriage based on their own volition. Inasmuch as a human being's value cannot be quantified with money, it is dehumanizing to treat the bride as a commodity to be exchanged between two families.[104]

Just as a woman had the right to make a personal choice to marry, Lu also asserted that a woman has the right to remain single. As a woman committed to self-realization, Lu chose to fulfill her ambitions in the public domain rather than sharing her life.[105] In a society in which unmarried older women were often ridiculed and denigrated, Lu's status as a single woman and her feminist perspective posed a challenge to Taiwan's social norms. In *New Feminism,* she demanded that single women be accorded the same social recognition and respect as married women. Like Friedan, Lu stated that erotic love and marriage were not the only means for women to achieve happiness and self-fulfillment.[106]

Lu cited de Beauvoir's assertion that Western societies socialized girls to believe in erotic love and marriage as the sole purpose of their existence. Conversely, boys were taught that love and marriage were enriching aspects of their lives rather than their entire existence. Lu agreed with de Beauvoir, and indicated that society had done an injustice to women by socializing them to be dependent upon men's love and financial support. If a husband were to desert his wife, the wife would be left alone without the job experience and independent spirit needed for economic self-reliance.[107]

To foster women's independent spirit, Lu argued that marriage is a personal lifestyle choice and a basic human right for men and women. Contrary to a common misconception in Taiwan, Lu stated that marriage should not be considered a familial obligation. Rather than using women's bodies as instrumental means for producing male heirs, Lu contended that the traditional Chinese argument that one's failure to produce a male heir was the greatest offense against one's parents should be seen as an outdated idea in the modern age.[108]

In Lu's words, a man's use of his wife to carry on the family line is just as misguided as a woman's attempt to fish for a golden turtle (diao jingui). As a Chinese saying, "to fish for a golden turtle" refers to a single woman's quest for a husband with lots of earning potential to provide her with financial security. In other words, she marries up to acquire her husband's socioeconomic status. Lu urged women to forsake the traditional expectation of finding a husband more educated and older than she for the purpose of securing a permanent meal ticket. Like Friedan, Lu encouraged married women to participate in paid work outside the home to broaden their horizons and be recognized based on their own merits in society.[109]

In order to lighten married women's workload in the home, Lu suggested that both husband and wife contribute to family finances and participate in household affairs. She urged husbands and fathers to be attentive to their children's development and education. Just as a husband should be capable of cooking his own meals,[110] a wife should strive for her own financial independence. The attempt to blur the distinctions of gender roles notwithstanding, Lu did not call for the complete elimination of gender distinctions in the family. In her attempt to compromise with the family-centered ideology of Kuomintang-sponsored Confucianism, Lu emphasized mothers' and wives' primary roles in managing the household (qijia) and educating children (jiaozi).[111] She suggested that a wife should shoulder more household responsibilities than her husband until a society in the future would be ready for a married couple to share housework equally.[112]

According to Lu, her partial acceptance of wives' and mothers' gender roles in marriage and the family and her inclusion of women's "feminine nature" in New Feminism were strategic decisions to minimize the authoritarian regime's objection and secure the socially conservative public's acceptance of her feminism.[113] While she incorporated certain Confucian concepts, such as women's gender-specific obligations in familial relationships, into New

Feminism, she also envisioned gender equality and women's self-realization in the public domain. This demonstrated her attempt to synthesize certain aspects of normative Confucian values with liberal individualist feminism from the West.[114] In Lu's own words, a new woman is one capable of holding a pen as well as pots and pans; she would be an excellent intellectual as well as a good homemaker.[115]

In separating women's gender-specific familial roles from their gender-neutral public roles,[116] Lu did not critically evaluate the personal conflict that could result from the double burden of attempting to fulfill both obligations capably. Since Lu recommended that married women spend more time and energy in household management than their husbands, it was difficult to expect them to compete equally with men in the public arena. Yet Lu expected women to strive for professional excellence.[117] In her attempt to selectively incorporate aspects of Confucian family-centered ideology with Western individualism, Lu inadvertently reinforced working women's double burden. This contradiction also showed that Confucianism and Western individualism were incompatible ideologies.

In contrast to Lu's partial acceptance of familial gender roles, de Beauvoir was critical of marriage and the family as bourgeois institutions that expected women to shoulder most domestic responsibilities. As a Marxist existentialist, de Beauvoir stated that many working mothers had to compromise the quality of their job performance and thus their career advancement. In the 1940s, de Beauvoir argued that women's situation would not allow them the liberty to become self-actualizing human beings. To enable women's full participation in the public domain, the capitalist socioeconomic structure needed to be radically transformed to create a socialist society conducive to gender equality. The socialist state would create facilities to provide adequate childcare and train professional housekeepers to perform household tasks for working women. With ample time and energy to focus on their paid jobs, working mothers would be empowered to fully realize their career potential.[118]

Contrary to de Beauvoir's belief in the creation of a socialist society as the precondition for gender equality, Lu envisioned the possibility of achieving gender equality in a welfare state (*fuliguo*) within the existing social structure of Taiwan's capitalist economy. This included the legislation of a Woman's Welfare Law to hold society responsible for sharing the profit losses from working women's maternity leaves. The law would also prohibit employers from discriminating against or dismissing women employees during and after their maternity leaves.[119] Although the notion of a Woman's Welfare Law in a welfare state was a socialist-inspired idea, Lu never used the term "socialism" (*shehui zhuyi*). Conceivably, she was mindful of the danger of state censorship within the political context of the martial law regime's anti-Communist ideology.

However, influenced by both de Beauvoir and Charlotte Perkins Gilman, Lu appropriated several socialist tenets for the alleviation of working women's domestic burden, including the professionalization of housework, the establishment of childcare facilities, the creation of public dining halls in each community, and the transfer of certain household responsibilities from the family to society. [120] Instead of acknowledging the socialist origin of these ideas, Lu coined a politically neutral term, *cooperative home economics* (*hezuo jiazheng*).[121] Coupled with the increasing availability of time-saving appliances in Taiwan, it was Lu's hope that more married women could actively participate in the workforce.[122]

Abortion Rights

In addition to supporting women's participation in the workforce, Lu also advocated women's abortion rights. In 1973, Lu concurred with the United States Supreme Court's decision affirming women's right to choose whether to have an abortion. In Taiwan, abortion was illegal prior to the Legislative Yuan's passage of the Eugenic Law for the Protection of Health (*Yousheng baojianfa*) in 1984. According to the ROC penal code of 1945, a pregnant woman who aborted a fetus would receive a maximum penalty of six months in prison or pay a maximum fine of 100 yuan. The person who aborted the fetus for a pregnant woman would receive a maximum penalty of two years in prison. In situations where the pregnant woman's health was endangered by the pregnancy, however, the woman and her abortion provider were exempt from prosecution.[123]

This exemption notwithstanding, the rationale behind the anti-abortion penal code of 1945 was the preservation of the fetus's life, the pregnant woman's health, and the ROC's population. To refute these anti-abortion arguments, Lu cited the stipulation of the ROC civil code number 6. It stated that a person's eligibility to possess human rights began at birth and ended with death. However, civil code no. 7 contradicted this by stipulating that a fetus should be regarded as a person already born. His or her personal interest should be protected under the law.[124]

To counter the argument that a fetus should have the same rights as a person already born, Lu stated that a fertilized egg is attached to the wall of a pregnant woman's uterus and relies on the woman's nutrients for its growth and survival. If the woman were deficient in certain hormones, the condition could cause a miscarriage. Since a fetus does not possess the conditions and capabilities of a complete human being, it is more reasonable to regard it as a part of a pregnant woman's body. Hence, a fetus does not have the right to enjoy the same legal protection as a person already born. To strengthen her argument, Lu quoted the saying of an American obstetrician, Dr. Barbara Roberts, who contended that "[a]nti-abortion laws give fetuses rights that living people don't enjoy. No human's right to life includes the use of another human being's body and life support systems against that individual."[125]

To disprove the anti-abortionists' contention that abortion would harm a pregnant woman's health, Lu argued that illegal abortions were far more hazardous. Twenty percent of women in Taiwan had at least one illegal abortion in their lifetime, and the desperation to obtain an abortion often meant that pregnant women had to seek abortion providers with dubious credentials and ill-equipped facilities. Conversely, the legalization of abortion could enable the state and the medical community to set safety standards for abortion procedures.[126]

In response to the anti-abortionists' contention that abortion would lower the ROC's population, Lu argued that Taiwan's annual rice production could barely feed the island's population in 1976. If population growth were not adequately curbed, Taiwan's overpopulation could negate the island's economic growth. Based on her insight after touring small Western European countries in 1970, Lu contended that the quality of a nation's citizenry is more important than the size of its population.[127] Lu argued that the legalization of abortion was consistent with the Kuomintang government's family planning program within which abortion should be performed as the last resort to terminate an unwanted pregnancy after the failure of birth control methods.[128]

To demonstrate that abortion had not always been illegal in the Anglo-American tradition, Lu mentioned that an English court, in 1327, ruled that aborting a fetus should not be regarded as murder or a punishable crime. Yet, with the British Parliament's passage of the Lord Ellenborough Act in 1830, abortion became an illegal offense. With this legal precedent, many states in the United States passed legislation prohibiting abortion. Finally, with the cases of *Roe v. Wade* and *Doe v. Bolton,* the United States Supreme Court ruled that the anti-abortion laws of Texas and Georgia were unconstitutional. Lu quoted the United States Supreme Court's ruling: "The right of privacy is broad enough to encompass a woman's decision [on] whether or not to terminate her pregnancy."[129] Concurring with liberal feminists in the United States, Lu argued that a woman ought to have the right and the freedom to make decisions for her own body and receive the appropriate medical care for the abortion procedure.[130]

Historical Narratives in New Feminism

In *New Feminism,* Lu included a section entitled "A Brief History of the International Women's Movement" for the purpose of introducing the intellectual tradition of Western liberal feminism to her Taiwanese audience. She understandably identified *A Vindication of the Rights of Woman* by Mary Wollstonecraft (1792), *A Doll's House* by Henrik Ibsen (1879), and the feminist treatise of John Stuart Mill as important works that laid the ideological foundation for the international women's movement.[131] Lu also cited the publication of Betty Friedan's *The Feminine Mystique* in 1963 as the driving force behind the reemergence of the American women's movement and the creation of the National Organization for Women in the postwar era. Along with *The Feminine Mystique* as a work of liberal feminism, Lu also traced the origins of the Marxist strand of American feminism to the New Left.[132]

Moreover, Lu created the English-language phrase *depolarization of sex roles* to denote the concept of androgyny in the writings of radical American feminists.[133] According to Hester Eisenstein, radical feminism was transformed from a discourse on androgyny in the early 1970s to a woman-centered perspective by the mid-1970s. Since the mid-1970s, the emerging woman-centered analysis included the concept of *woman-identified woman* in lesbianism, the critique of the cultural meaning of mothering, and the validation of women's distinctive psychological experience as potential sources for women's self-empowerment.[134] Because Lu completed *New Feminism* in 1973, it was impossible for her to have included this new development. She did not update or incorporate the woman-centered analysis of American radical feminism in the 1977 edition either.[135]

In addition to Lu's concise summary of the diverse strands of American feminism in the 1960s and 1970s, *New Feminism* presented a synopsis of the Kuomintang's interpretation of the Chinese women's movement on mainland China prior to 1949. Based on the Kuomintang's repertoire of historical writings, Lu acknowledged Chinese intellectuals' efforts to unbind women's feet and promote women's education in the late nineteenth century as a means to strengthen the Chinese nation against Western imperialism. Lu also praised the martyrdom of the Chinese woman revolutionary, Qiu Jin (1875–1907), for her heroic attempt to overthrow the Qing dynasty (1644–1911). Moreover, she praised the Chinese suffragists' militant protest against the Chinese Senate's failure to include a gender-equality clause in the newly founded ROC's temporary legal provisions in 1911.[136]

In *New Feminism,* Lu acknowledged the May Fourth intellectuals' contributions to gender equality and women's rights in the New Culture movement (1915–23). In an anti-communist political climate, it was impossible for Lu to acknowledge the ideological influence of Marxism-Leninism on May Fourth intellectuals' conceptualization of women's status after the creation of the Chinese Communist Party in 1921. Nor did she mention the cooperation between Chinese Nationalists (Kuomintang) and Chinese Communists during the First United Front that led to the Kuomintang's passage of several resolutions for the promotion of women's rights in 1926. Instead, Lu attributed the passage of resolutions on women's rights solely to the achievements of the Kuomintang's northern expedition in 1926. In regard to the Kuomintang's promulgation of civil codes in 1931, Lu objectively assessed both the gender-biased and gender-egalitarian aspects of the ROC civil codes. Lastly, she introduced to her Taiwanese audience the legal provisions for gender equality and women's suffrage in the ROC Constitution of 1947.[137]

After the Kuomintang government fled to Taiwan in 1949, the state-sponsored historical narrative discussed women's experiences in Nationalist China on the mainland prior to 1949 and women's experiences in post–1949 Taiwan under Chinese Nationalist rule. Its omission of women's distinctive experiences in colonial Taiwan presented the distorted impression that Chinese women on both sides of the Taiwan Strait shared the same historical experience prior to 1945. In line with Kuomintang historiography, Lu's *New Feminism* presented no narrative of Taiwan's autonomous women's movement under Japanese colonial rule. It is conceivable that Lu chose to omit the island's colonial history under Japanese rule in order to render her historical narrative acceptable to the Kuomintang authorities.

In retrospect, Kuomintang historiography contributed to Lu's omission of the Chinese Communist Party's efforts to improve women's status in mainland China. Likewise, the martial law regime's restrictions on the study and teaching of Taiwanese history during the Japanese colonial era also played a part in Lu's exclusion of women's experiences prior to 1945. These omissions attest to the powerful impact of Kuomintang historiography in shaping Lu's historical narratives.

Taiwanese National Identity and the Democratic Opposition

In 1977, Lu left Taiwan to pursue another Master's degree in jurisprudence at Harvard Law School. She completed her study the following year. Her political consciousness grew when she came across numerous books on Taiwanese history at the university's Yen-ching Library. She was troubled by her

Taiwanese compatriots' lack of knowledge about Taiwan's historical past.[138] During her studies she also became aware of the United States' decision to sever its diplomatic ties with the ROC government on Taiwan and normalize its diplomatic relationship with the People's Republic of China (PRC) on the mainland. Prior to this dramatic shift in U.S.-ROC relations, Lu's writings about Taiwanese feminism showed her willingness to compromise with the Kuomintang regime. In response to Taiwan's diplomatic crisis in 1978, Lu radicalized her stance against the authoritarian government.

Based on the data she gathered on Taiwan's diplomatic status vis-à-vis the United States and the PRC and her perusal of numerous books on Taiwan's past, Lu wrote a short narrative history of Taiwan from the Taiwanese perspective.[139] Published in 1979, *Taiwan's Past and Future* (*Taiwan de guoqu yu weilai*) asserted that the Taiwanese were by and large a Han Chinese people that had established an immigrant society on Taiwan beginning in the late sixteenth century. In addition to the Malayo-Polynesian indigenes, the Han Chinese immigrants' pioneering spirit, the Dutch colonization in the seventeenth century, and the Japanese colonization in the early half of twentieth century were all historical experiences that distinguished the island from mainland China.[140]

Regardless of Taiwan's distinctive history, Lu argued that the divisions and prejudices between the Taiwanese and the mainlanders in postwar Taiwan should cease. To conceptualize a common immigrant experience among the Taiwanese and the mainlanders, she asserted that the mainlanders were later immigrants from China, whereas the Taiwanese were early immigrants. Whether one is an early immigrant, a later immigrant, or a Malayo-Polynesian, she argued, a person is Taiwanese as long as he or she identifies with Taiwan, lives in Taiwan, and shares a common destiny with the island's future. Within the political context of the Kuomintang's restrictions on the research and teaching of Taiwanese history, Lu demanded that all Taiwanese have the right to learn about their historical past.[141]

In regard to Taiwan's political future, Lu asserted that, for Taiwan's security and survival, the ROC government on Taiwan should peacefully coexist with the PRC government on the mainland as two sovereign states.[142] In the late 1970s, her belief was contrary to the Kuomintang's official policy, which still insisted that it was the sole legitimate government on both sides of the Taiwan Strait. Due to the Kuomintang's press censorship, Taiwan's news media did not report on the impending shift in the United States' diplomatic relationships vis-à-vis Taiwan and the PRC prior to the Carter administration's announcement in December 1978.

At this critical juncture in Taiwan's history, Lu felt that the Taiwanese people had the right to know what was about to happen to them. She made the decision to return to Taiwan and stand for election to a seat in the national assembly. Upon her return, Lu joined the *Dangwai* Campaign Assistance Group. Founded by Huang Hsin-chieh, the group offered assistance to co-ordinate *Dangwai* candidates' election campaigns and also devised strategies for improving their performance in the elections to be held in December.[143] News of the cessation of the United States' ties with the ROC on Taiwan was officially announced in December. In response to this diplomatic crisis, the Kuomintang postponed the elections indefinitely.

As the leader of a moderate faction in the *Dangwai,* K'ang Ning-hsiang chose not to contest the cancellation of the election. Instead, he urged other *Dangwai* activists to unite behind the Kuomintang government at the moment of national crisis. This position alienated him from the majority of *Dangwai* activists, who perceived the cancellation as a convenient excuse for the Kuomintang to avoid the electoral challenge of *Dangwai* candidates. Radicals, such as Lu Hsiu-lien, rallied behind the leadership of Huang Hsin-chieh and opted for the radical faction's strategy of mass action to protest the Kuomintang's action.[144]

As an effort to circumvent the Kuomintang government's prohibition against the formation of new political parties, Huang led the *Dangwai* radicals to create the Formosa Magazine Publishing House (*Meilidao zazhishe*) in 1979. Lu joined the staff of the publishing house as its deputy director. With the de-legitimization of the Kuomintang in the international community, the founders of the magazine chose to name their publication *Formosa* (beautiful island) in order to denote Taiwan's distinctive island identity vis-à-vis China. Because Formosa was the name that Portuguese explorers gave to Taiwan in the sixteenth century, its non-Chinese origin also posed an implicit challenge to the Kuomintang's claim that Taiwan was a part of China. In order to optimize the magazine's circulation and coordinate political activities, *Formosa* staffers established branch offices in twelve major cities throughout Taiwan. The magazine raised the public's awareness of the Taiwanese people's right to determine the island's political future and also suggested the need to hold an island-wide legislative election to unseat the senior legislators elected in mainland China prior to 1949. By its fourth issue, the magazine reached a circulation of one hundred thousand copies and had become the second most widely read magazine on the island second only to Taiwan's *TV Guide*.[145]

On December 10, 1979, *Formosa* staffers organized a mass rally in Kaohsiung to celebrate the anniversary of the Universal Declaration of Human Rights. While the rally organizers were committed to the principle of non-violent demonstrations, the public security forces surrounded the demonstrators to prevent more citizens from joining the crowd and to stop participants from marching down the street or leaving the site. Violence soon broke out between the demonstrators and the police. This incident provided authorities with a pretext to arrest the organizers of the march. Among the eight *Formosa* staffers arrested were Huang Hsin-chieh and Lu Hsiu-lien. The interrogators used sleep deprivation to extract fabricated confessions from the political prisoners. The following year, the eight *Formosa* staffers were court-martialed and sentenced to long prison terms.[146] Lu was given a twelve-year prison sentence for sedition. The regime charged Lu with inciting the riot that ensued after she made a speech for Taiwan's self-determination, when "in fact she had urged non-violence upon the crowd."[147] Meanwhile, Amnesty International adopted the jailed leaders as prisoners of conscience.

In retrospect, the imprisonment of the *Formosa* staffers was only a temporary setback for the *Dangwai* movement. In response to pressures for democratization within Taiwan and abroad, the postponed election was finally held in 1980. Several family members and defense attorneys for the *Formosa* staffers ran for public office and garnered many sympathy votes to win seats in national legislative bodies. Many citizens also cast their votes to protest the courts-martial. Significantly, the election of 1980 launched the political careers of several defense attorneys of the *Formosa* staffers, most notably that of Chen Shui-bian, the president of Taiwan from 2000 through 2008.[148]

In 1982, the women's movement was reinvigorated when Lu's feminist associates organized the Awakening Magazine Publishing House (*Funü xinzhi*). In contrast to Lu's political involvement in the *Dangwai* movement in 1978 and 1979, most of her feminist associates in the 1970s and 1980s did not join the *Dangwai* to oppose the government. As the feminist activists struggled to maintain their independence from Kuomintang control, they hoped that their neutrality would minimize the regime's interference in their feminist activities. Because most Taiwanese women were apolitical in the 1970s and 1980s, feminist activists used political neutrality as a strategy for attracting more women to their cause. In fact, Lu was a politically neutral leader of the autonomous women's movement from 1972 through 1977. It was not until 1978 that Lu made the decision to join the *Dangwai*—a year after she closed down Pioneer Press.[149]

Conclusion

As we have seen in this chapter, Annette Lu formulated her feminist views within an authoritarian political context. Under her leadership, the autonomous women's movement was capable of maintaining its independence from the authoritarian government's control. Yet, it had to work creatively within the political boundaries set by the martial law regime. Lu's moderate feminism should be seen as her attempt to walk the fine line between her need for social protest against injustice and her need to compromise her feminism with the conservative sociopolitical climate.[150] Mindful of the Kuomintang's anti-communist ideology, Lu also did not explicitly challenge the capitalist economic system. Due to the Kuomintang ideology's Confucian patriarchal orientation,[151] the only way the government would tolerate Lu's new feminism was for her to concede to certain traditional gender roles in the institutions of marriage and the family. Nonetheless, Lu explicitly criticized the gender inequality in Taiwan's Confucian-inspired family-centered ideology.[152] Thus, Lu was as much a progressive-minded feminist reformer who critiqued the patriarchal aspects of Confucianism as she was a cultural product of the Kuomintang's Confucian-oriented educational system.[153]

Looking at the history of Taiwanese feminist discourses in a larger perspective, the issues of concern between the autonomous women's movements in the 1920s and 1970s were remarkably similar. Despite the discontinuity of colonial Taiwan's autonomous movement (1920–31), feminist activists in both the 1920s and 1970s were similarly critical of gender-biased Confucian concepts and its oppression of women. With some variations, the autonomous women's movements of both periods advocated gender equality in educational opportunities and political and economic participation, as well as women's autonomy in marriage and the family.[154]

In both the 1920s and 1970s, liberal feminists in Taiwan conceived of feminism as a modern and rational ideology that valued human rights and human dignity as well as the common humanity and equality of women and men. Like Taiwanese feminists in the 1920s, Lu contended that society had done an injustice to women by socializing them as dependents of men's financial support.[155] In the 1920s and 1970s, liberal feminists regarded economic independence as the way for a woman to free herself from the control of others and become the master of her own destiny. In both decades, liberal feminists envisioned a reciprocal relationship between an individual and her family and society. Just as society conferred rights to an individual, the individual should also contribute to society and fulfill her familial responsibilities. Liberal feminists in both periods believed that a woman's paid work outside the home could contribute to her financial self-reliance, her family's finances, and Taiwan's socioeconomic progress.[156] In order to give women a voice in the political process, social and political activists in colonial Taiwan advocated universal suffrage. In 1947, the ROC Constitution granted women the right to the franchise. Since women's suffrage had already been attained in postwar Taiwan, Lu urged women to run for political office and become lawmakers.[157]

Lu's poem titled "The Song of New Women" (*Xin nüxing zhi ge*) illustrates the feminist aspirations in the 1920s, the 1970s, and thereafter:

> Regardless of our educational background, occupation, or age, we are
>   New Women.
> We are responsible, assertive, and independent.
> We love our nation, our family, and ourselves.
> We do not ask for special privileges, nor do we accept oppression.
> We beautify ourselves with knowledge.
> We enthusiastically contribute to the society—sciences, arts, and politics.
> We participate in all endeavors.
> Let us lift up the sky and stand firm on the ground (*dingtian lidi*).
> Let us be independent and indomitable beings.[158]

In retrospect, Lu's greatest contributions during the pioneering period of the autonomous women's movement were the formulation and dissemination of feminist ideas among Taiwan's urban middle class. After Lu was imprisoned in 1979 for her leadership role in the democracy movement, some members of her audience, along with feminist activists from the 1970s, provided the financial and human resources necessary to sustain the autonomous women's movement into the 1980s.[159]

4. Lee Yuan-chen and *Awakening,* 1982–89

In 1982, one of Lu Hsiu-lien's feminist associates in the 1970s, Lee Yuan-chen, emerged as a leading figure in Taiwan's autonomous women's movement.[1] In the same year, Lee and other feminists (*nüxing zhuyi zhe*) founded *Awakening* (*Funü xinzhi*), a monthly magazine for feminist intellectuals and activists. In this chapter, I refer to the women who regularly contributed essays to the magazine as the Awakening feminists. I analyze Lee's *Awakening* essays from the monthly's initial publication in 1982 to 1989, the year that Lee stepped down from her position as the chairperson of the Awakening Foundation's board of trustees. I discuss these essays, together with her book *Women's Forward March* (*Funü kaibuzou*), in order to analyze the ways in which various strands of Western feminism influenced her ideas. According to Lee, Margaret Mead's liberal individualism, Simone de Beauvoir's Marxist existentialism, and Jean Baker Miller's[2] radical feminist concept of woman-centered culture all exerted considerable influence over her formulation of feminist thought in the 1980s.[3]

This chapter also examines the Awakening feminists' contributions to the autonomous women's movement in the same period. In particular, I discuss their first attempt at legislative lobbying for the legalization of abortion. The changes and continuities of the movement's strategies and discourses from the pioneering stage in the 1970s to the awakening stage in the 1980s are also analyzed. Among the Awakening feminists, Lee Yuan-chen's role as a leader of the women's movement was central to its growth in the 1980s and thereafter.

Lee Yuan-chen and the Awakening Feminists

Born in 1946 in the city of Kunming,[4] Lee Yuan-chen was the eldest child of a family with a tradition of military service in the Kuomintang navy. In 1949, her family moved to Taiwan when the Kuomintang transferred its government to the island. In 1964, Lee was admitted to the undergraduate program of the Chinese literature department at National Taiwan University; she received her bachelor's degree there in 1968 and her master's degree in Chinese literature in 1970.[5]

Soon thereafter, she assumed a teaching position at Tamkang University in Taipei and married a classmate. As a self-avowed "modern couple," Lee and her husband had the mutual understanding that they would have an egalitarian relationship. For the first two years, the young couple was happily married. After the birth of their daughter, however, Lee's husband insisted on moving in with his parents. As a daughter-in-law who was expected to play her traditional roles, Lee felt stifled by the hierarchical relationships in her husband's family.[6] In 1973, Lee divorced her husband.

Because the ROC family law granted child custody to the husband, Lee personally experienced the injustice of the judicial system. With much emotional anguish, Lee left Taiwan in 1974 to study drama in the theater department at the University of Oregon. Meanwhile, she also acquainted herself with various strands of feminism in the American Women's movement. For two years, she experienced a new life in a new culture.

During this time, she went through a period of profound soul-searching and self-reflection in order to decide whether to stay in the United States. The decision to return to Taiwan in 1976 was a turning point in her life. She had left Taiwan with the emotional scars of her divorce still fresh. She now returned to the land that had nurtured her since childhood with a new sense of purpose to contribute to the island's future. Upon her return, she resumed her teaching position at Tamkang University and joined the intellectual circle of native soil literature (*xiangtu wenxue*)[7] and the democracy movement.[8]

Due to the male-dominated power structure of Taiwan's democracy movement, the professed ideals of liberty, justice, and equality did not necessarily translate into male activists' equal treatment of and respect for women activists. The marginalization of women activists convinced Lee that gender inequality would persist in a democratic Taiwan without a separate movement to promote women's rights and status. Her personal experiences in the democracy movement, in her marriage, and in her petition for child custody all contributed to her commitment to the struggle for gender equality.[9]

After Lee's return to Taiwan and her subsequent involvement in the women's movement, the democracy movement, and the native soil literary movement, she developed a strong identification with Taiwan and considered herself a Taiwanese woman of mainlander heritage. In the late 1970s, Lee befriended Lu Hsiu-lien and became an active participant in several panel discussions sponsored by the Pioneer Press. After Lu was imprisoned for her political activities in the democracy movement, Lee and her feminist associates established the Awakening Publishing House (*Funü xinzhi* zazhishe) in 1982 to promote gender equity.[10]

During the 1980s, Lee reaffirmed Lu Hsiu-lien's conviction that feminism (*nüxing zhuyi*) was essentially a human rights ideology. As a liberal feminist committed to women's self-reliance, Lee stated that the goals of *Awakening* were to promote women's self-development and potential. That is, the magazine intended to help women develop the ability and resourcefulness to take personal responsibility for their economic and emotional independence.[11]

Prior to the lifting of martial law in 1987, the Awakening Publishing House was the only non-government affiliated women's group in Taiwan that explicitly challenged gender hierarchy and advocated gender equality in the 1980s. The magazine was the single most important feminist monthly and as such it dominated Taiwan's feminist discourse.[12] Just as feminist intellectuals in the late 1970s used Lu's Pioneer Press as the organizational base for their activities, the Awakening Publishing House became the rallying point of feminist activities in Taiwan during the 1980s. The magazine's dominant leadership role in Taiwan's feminist community would not diminish until the early 1990s.[13]

In the opening statement of the first issue, the feminist activists attributed most women's over-reliance on marriage to the outdated socialization of girls at home and in society. Inasmuch as many women were taught to rely on their husbands rather than on themselves, they did not take full advantage of the educational and occupational opportunities available to them. This explanation of women's dependent situation corresponded with the views expressed by Lu Hsiu-lien. The Awakening feminists believed that it was only through women's heightened awareness of their inferior status that they would begin to motivate themselves for collective action to challenge the status quo and struggle for their own rights.[14]

As it was with Lu's cultural-intellectual approach in the 1970s, the Awakening feminists considered the transformation of cultural values and belief systems an essential prerequisite for societal changes.[15] Like their pioneering counterparts in the 1970s, the Awakening feminists wrote articles and organized lectures and panel discussions to offer possible solutions for resolving the problem of gender inequality. The discussion sessions enabled participants to communicate and share their diverse perspectives with each other as well as enrich their knowledge of women's issues. Moreover, they heightened the Taiwanese public's awareness of specific women's issues after the mass media covered the events. In the 1980s, the Awakening feminists enjoyed considerable success in influencing the editorial policies of major newspapers and magazines, which resulted in more coverage and analyses of important women's issues.[16]

To attract the attention of the mass media and raise women's gender consciousness, on every International Women's Day, the publishing house coordinated activities that featured panel discussions and lectures on a variety of topics, including a cultural critique of the objectification of women's bodies in commercial advertising, the need to revise gender-biased civil and penal codes, homemakers' potential roles in the public arena, and dialogues between the sexes, among others.[17]

Lee Yuan-chen on Gender Relations, Homemakers' Potential, and Motherhood

Similar to Lu's vision in the 1970s, the Awakening feminists advocated the creation of a gender-egalitarian society where men and women could peacefully coexist in the spirit of mutual cooperation. In order to enhance communications and mutual understanding between the sexes, *Awakening* sponsored panel discussions and workshops to promote dialogue. For instance, men and women had joint dialogues on the negative effects of socially-imposed gender roles. It was hoped that the media's coverage of the discussions would encourage conversations between the sexes in every household and in society at large.[18]

Women vastly outnumbered men at the *Awakening*-sponsored seminars. According to Lee Yuan-chen, men's absence attested to their perception of the issues pertaining to marriage and family as female-oriented small affairs (*xiaoshi*) undeserving of their attention. Since marital and familial relationships existed in the domestic context, most men in Taiwan regarded the improvement of these relationships as the woman's responsibility.[19]

Conversely, men considered issues concerning international relations, national defense, politics, and economics in the public domain as male-oriented major affairs (*dashi*). Despite the equal importance of both types of issues to humanity's existence and survival, Lee contended that the male-dominated culture's prioritization of *dashi* in the public domain over *xiaoshi* in the domestic realm had done humanity a great disservice. Whereas modern women were beginning to participate in *dashi,* many men still felt that getting involved in *xiaoshi* was beneath their dignity.[20]

Like Jean Baker Miller's insights about American society, Lee observed that a woman typically invested more time and effort in her marital relationship than her husband. Consequently, she could be disappointed if her spouse were incapable of returning the same affection. From both Lee's and Miller's perspectives, emotional expression is an essential part of every human being's daily existence. They suggested that patriarchal society's denial of men's expression of their vulnerability is indicative of its inhumanity and that the suppression of boys' emotional expression does great harm to their emotional development. Thus, while men are accorded a dominant status in patriarchal society, they have had to suppress part of their humanity to retain their masculinity.[21]

Lee contended that men's and women's lack of commonality and inability to communicate effectively with each other were contributing factors to the prevalence of unhappy marriages in Taiwanese society. From her point of view, emphasis on the opposite sex's external appeal rather than the exploration of each other's inner qualities was a major cause of a married couple's emotional estrangement. She saw the crucial need to improve Taiwanese males' ability to verbally express their inner emotions as the first step to enhance genuine dialogue between men and women in relationships. In order to test each other's compatibility, Lee advised every young couple to put effort into getting to know each other's inner emotional qualities through effective communication. If men and women could develop mutual respect and genuine friendship, Lee believed that the sexual objectification of the opposite sex and instances of sexual harassment, sexual assault, and domestic violence could be significantly reduced.[22]

In the context of Taiwan's transition from traditionalism to modernity, many wives and children were beginning to demand more rights and greater autonomy in the family. Yet, in the authoritarian patriarchal culture, a father generally expected his power, needs, and opinions to supersede those of the mother and children. Whereas parents in traditional Chinese society tended to treat their children as personal possessions, Lee, imbued with the Western notion of individual rights, urged parents to respect children's dignity and autonomy.[23] The inequality along gender and generational lines made it difficult for family members to communicate effectively in an atmosphere of mutual respect.

In addition to advocating for the rights of women and children, Lee Yuan-chen urged middle-class housewives to break away from their isolation at home and contribute their creative energies to community service in the public domain. As traditional extended families were replaced by urban nuclear families, Lee spoke to an urgent need to create a new sense of community among strangers and neighbors in residential areas. She suggested that housewives meet regularly in their apartment complexes to establish friendships and devise ways to solve problems together and assist one another. Lee urged homemakers to take turns supervising preschool children in the neighborhood so as to free each other for either part-time paid work or volunteer work in the community.[24] From a cross-cultural perspective, Lee's vision of extending homemakers' nurturing roles from the private sphere to the public sphere was analogous to American feminists' concept of "social housekeeping" during the Progressive Era (1890–1920).

On International Women's Day in 1985, *Awakening* and Taipei's YWCA co-sponsored seminars to address homemakers' self-development and potential. Participants discussed relationships with husbands and children, homemakers' rights and responsibilities as consumers, housewives' self-expectation, information and strategies for improving women's mental and physical health, and possibilities for reentering the workforce.[25] These topics were based on the consensus reached in 1983 between Awakening feminists and homemakers who responded to Lee's articulation of their potential roles in the public arena. Just as Lu Hsiu-lien argued in *New Feminism,* Lee and her *Awakening* associates urged housewives to participate in civic activities and paid work in the public domain. They hoped that homemakers could improve the quality of their lives, develop self-confidence, and contribute to the society. From group discussions with homemakers, the Awakening feminists learned that job training and greater availability of childcare were crucial for homemakers' reentry into the workforce. Inspired by the designation of 1985 as the year of housewives' self-development and potential, three hundred housewives collectively issued a press release calling for the government and the business community to provide flexible work schedules for homemakers who chose to enter the workforce.[26]

To facilitate homemakers' participation in the workforce, Lee Yuan-chen posited that childrearing ought to be a distributive responsibility of both parents, their places of employment, and society, just as Jean Baker Miller had argued. Both Miller and Lee considered the development of gender-specific personalities and maternal love as consequences of social conditioning rather than the outcome of natural instinct.[27] Instead of defining childrearing as primarily a mother's responsibility, Lee, like Miller, advocated that the government and employers provide daycare facilities to working couples. Further, Lee urged the Taiwanese government to protect mothers' working rights rather than tacitly permit private companies to dismiss their female employees upon the births of their children. She wanted the government to acknowledge that women were creating new members of society's future workforce. Like Lu Hsiu-lien, Lee advocated socialized childcare in the public domain, which would allow working mothers to enhance their professional potential in the market economy.[28]

After the revocation of martial law and the easing of the Kuomintang's anti-leftist campaign, Lee praised the state-sponsored childcare benefits and the legislative achievements of Sweden. Based on the Swedish model, Lee argued that the Legislative Yuan should enact a law that would permit both parents to take a one-year leave of absence after a child is born. Parents would have the option of taking care of the infant and managing household affairs full time until the child reached one year of age and were then admitted to a daycare center. This way, a new mother would not have to give up her job or suffer the consequence of a double burden. Lee posited that a maternity and paternity leave bill and adequate daycare centers could enable a working mother to pursue her career goals, contribute to family finances, and remain a productive member of society.[29]

In addition to promoting the notion that both parents should be equally responsible for childcare, Lee also advocated fundamental changes in the working environment. Influenced by Miller, Lee suggested that a manager should take the input of subordinates into consideration in his or her decision-making process. As was true in the United States, the majority of Taiwanese managers, administrators, innovators, and decision makers in positions of power and leadership were males. Most of the caregivers and providers of clerical services in auxiliary roles and subordinate positions were females. Although most of the decisions made by male leaders could not be effectively carried out without the supportive effort of female subordinates, Lee contended that the latter's importance tended to be undervalued. That is, society generally gave credit to the male leader for a successful project. Like Miller, Lee argued that the over-evaluation of the male leader's contribution tended to perpetuate gender inequality in a hierarchical organizational structure. Inasmuch as both leaders and subordinates were equally crucial for the proper functioning of any organization, both Lee and Miller envisioned an egalitarian culture in the future that would give equal respect and recognition to the contributions of both leaders and subordinates.[30]

Lee then used the example of Taiwan's democratization to illustrate the possibility of power-sharing between leaders and subordinates. Under martial law, the policies and performances of political leaders were by and large insulated from the popular demands of ordinary citizens. But as Taiwan democratized, electoral candidates were increasingly obligated to respond to ordinary citizens' demands and were also held accountable for their campaign promises in exchange for the voters' support.[31] Likewise, Lee posited that a leader should acknowledge his or her subordinates' contributions to a project and promote a culture of cooperation and collective decision making in the organization. Instead of expecting women to assimilate into the male culture, with its emphases on struggle and competition to achieve power and control over others, Lee suggested that men should learn from women's traditional emphases on cooperation, peace, and the promotion of mutual benefits.[32] As a result, the male-dominated culture's focus on competition and power struggle in an authoritarian and hierarchical environment would be replaced by a more democratic and egalitarian culture.[33]

To foster a more gender-egalitarian society, Lee suggested that men and women should adopt the positive aspects of both genders' cultures and integrate them into daily life. It was her hope that the rigid dichotomy of socially imposed gender roles could be gradually broken down. While men should learn from the strengths of women's culture, the male cultural characteristics that Lee considered worth emulating were assertiveness and self-reliance.[34]

In her vision of a gender-egalitarian society, Lee, like Margaret Mead, believed that an individual's unique personality, talents, interests, and choices should determine his or her occupational role. No individual would be socially pressured to assume a role or an occupation based on his or her gender identity. Every man and woman could freely aspire to become a leader, an inventor, a secretarial clerk, or a caregiver. Whereas Lu Hsiu-lien urged married women to fulfill the obligations ascribed to their gender roles in the familial context, Lee envisioned freedom for men and women to express their individuality without having to conform to socially defined gender roles. Lee posited that society should respect a couple's decision to let the husband be a full-time father at home, as his wife assumed the role of the sole breadwinner of the family.[35]

Lee envisioned a democratic and pluralistic society that would grant every individual the flexibility and freedom to determine his or her life plans and lifestyle choices.[36] In this sense, Lee's vision of democracy (*minzhu*) was not restricted to the narrow concepts of universal suffrage and the individual right to political participation and constitutional protection. As an advocate of women's self-determination, her broadened definition of *minzhu* also encompassed an individual's right to engage in the existential quest for self-realization.[37]

Lee's definition of self-realization included the freedom to choose one's occupation and to strive for excellence in that professional endeavor. In terms of a woman's personal life, self-realization consisted of the freedom to choose whether to remain single or to marry, to decide whether to have children, and to determine the number of children one would have.[38] Contrary to Lu Hsiu-lien's conception of motherhood solely within the context of marriage, Lee suggested that single women who chose motherhood could consider adoption or artificial insemination. However, she cautioned that only single women who were emotionally and financially ready should take on this long-term responsibility.[39]

In order to safeguard the rights and dignity of single mothers and their children, Lee called for the elimination of the stigma associated with illegitimacy. She connected the social stigmatization of an unwed mother and her child to the unwed mother's supposed failure to integrate into the patriarchal legal system prior to giving birth to the child. Since patriarchal society disapproved of women's sexual activity and motherhood outside the context of marriage, unwed mothers' children were deemed illegitimate. In a traditional Chinese patrilocal household, a married woman generally looked upon producing a son as an obligation she must fulfill to her husband and his parents in order to achieve a higher status in the family. With the nuclear family as the new norm among young couples in urban Taiwan, Lee urged married women to empower themselves to make personal choices about motherhood. As a liberal feminist committed to women's individual rights, Lee insisted that a woman should assert her reproductive choice in her relationship with her husband. Influenced by Simone de Beauvoir, Lee posited that becoming a mother should be a personal choice rather than a biological destiny or an obligation to others. In this way, a woman would take responsibility for the choice that she made and be a loving mother to her children.[40]

The Eugenic Law for the Protection of Health

In 1984, the passage of the Eugenic Bill for the Protection of Health greatly enhanced women's reproductive choices. That year, *Awakening* became the vanguard of non-governmental affiliated groups petitioning for the bill's passage in the Legislative Yuan. Drafted by the Kuomintang government's Department of Public Health in 1971, the Eugenic Law (*Yousheng baojianfa*) was approved by the Executive Yuan in 1982 and sent to the Legislative Yuan for further deliberation. In 1984, the Legislative Yuan passed the bill and legalized abortion in Taiwan.[41]

The Eugenic Law for the Protection of Health states that a pregnant woman is exempted from prosecution for abortion: (1) if she or her spouse has a hereditary or a contagious disease, (2) if the fetus were severely handicapped, (3) if the pregnancy were caused by rape or incest, (4) if the pregnancy endangers the woman's life, or (5) if the pregnancy negatively affects the woman's mental health or family life, on the condition that the woman acquires the consent of her husband to obtain an abortion.[42] If the female were a legal minor, she would need the signature of a legal guardian. In other words, only the fifth situation requires a woman to acquire the consent of her husband or a legal guardian to obtain a legal abortion. A woman could choose to have an abortion without the consent of either her husband or a legal guarantor in the first four cases.[43]

During deliberations over the bill, fifty legislators opposed its last provision. They contended that the exemption of women from prosecution for abortion on the grounds of the negative effect on their mental health or family life amounted to de facto legalization of unlimited abortion. Further, they argued that the legalization of abortion would increase instances of sexual promiscuity in society. To convince the socially conservative Legislative Yuan that the Eugenic Law should be passed in its entirety, Awakening feminists argued that there is no evidence to suggest that legalizing abortion causes an increase in sexual promiscuity. They argued that selective, legalized abortion could protect women's health and save women's lives from unregulated illegal abortions. Legalized abortion could also control population growth and thereby ensure social stability. Since Taiwan had the second highest population density in the world, the Awakening feminists, as a matter of strategy, appealed to the Kuomintang's family planning campaign as a rationale for passage of the legislation. To ensure the socially conservative legislators' support for the Eugenic Law, the Awakening feminists emphasized passage of the legislation for the good of the entire society rather than based on a woman's individual right to control her own body.[44]

In the 1970s, Lu Hsiu-lien contended that the legalization of abortion was essential for protecting a woman's right to control her own body.[45] As proponents of women's rights, some feminists had misgivings about the clause in the law that stipulated the need for the husband's consent to abort a fetus. Lee Yuan-chen was troubled by the state's power to limit the number of obstetricians permitted to perform legal abortions. Nevertheless, the effectiveness of the Awakening feminists' petition to facilitate passage of the law demonstrated a pragmatic approach for which they compromised their ideological purity in order to achieve actual gains for women.[46]

Conclusion

In the 1970s and 1980s, feminist activists' ideological compromise with the authoritarian regime was a common strategy to ensure both the movement's survival and attainment of the movement's goals.[47] Comparatively, Lu Hsiu-lien's new feminism of the 1970s and Lee Yuan-chen's liberal feminism in the 1980s were human rights ideologies committed to the development of women's potential. Both activists encouraged women to be resourceful and take personal responsibility for their financial and emotional independence.[48]

In the 1980s, Lee Yuan-chen's conceptions of motherhood and gender relations were influenced by the feminist discourses of Miller, Mead, and de Beauvoir. Similar to the perspectives of these Western theorists, Lee considered the development of gender-specific personalities and nurturing skills the consequences of social conditioning rather than biological instinct.[49] Lee, like Lu Hsiu-lien, adopted the notion that socialized childcare in a capitalist economy would enhance gender equality in society. As a win-win proposition for a woman, her family, and the society, socialized childcare could enable a working mother to be financially independent and contribute to family income as a productive member of the nation's economy.[50]

As a legacy of Lu Hsiu-lien's liberal feminist tradition from the 1970s, in the 1980s the Awakening feminists persistently advocated the revision of gender-biased civil and penal codes. Despite the Awakening feminists' commitment to the notion that maternity should be a personal choice, they strategically appealed to the Kuomintang government's birth control campaign as a rationale for the passage of abortion legislation.[51] In 1984, the legalization of abortion under martial law set the historical precedent for the passage of other pro-women legislation in the post–martial law era.

5. The Autonomous Women's Movement and Feminist Discourse in the Post–Martial Law Era

After the revocation of martial law in 1987, Taiwan's democratization facilitated the diversification of feminist discourses and the creation of non-governmental women's organizations. Rather than providing a comprehensive analysis of all such organizations during the period, this chapter will focus selectively on organizations that address specific women's issues.

In contrast to feminists' prior need to compromise with conservatives, activists threw off their self-censorship after martial law ended. Hence, I will compare the post–martial law feminist discourses and organizational strategies with their earlier counterparts in the authoritarian political culture. I will also analyze the ways in which ideas in liberal feminism, relational feminism, Marxist feminism, and radical feminism influenced these discourses in post-martial law Taiwan. Furthermore, I will demonstrate that prior to the lifting of martial law, there were certain incipient developments in the early 1980s that contributed to the emergence of non-governmental women's organizations after 1987.

The Homemakers' Union and Foundation for Environmental Protection

On International Women's Day in 1983, Lee Yuan-chen, a leader in Taiwan's feminist community, urged middle-class housewives to extend their love and concern for family to the community and the larger society.[1] Consequently, homemakers' networks and directories were established in the greater Taipei area. As Taiwan's politics began to liberalize in 1987, these networks served as the organizational foundation for the creation of the Homemakers' Union for Environmental Protection (*Zhufu lianmeng huanjing baohu jijinhui*). Spearheaded by the Executive Secretary of *New Environment* magazine, Hsu Shen-shu, the Homemakers' Union was established in 1987 as the women's auxiliary of the *New Environment* magazine and foundation.[2]

Troubled by Taiwan's worsening environment during the years of rapid industrialization after the mid-1960s, members of the Homemakers' Union were mostly mothers in their thirties and forties who organized study groups to familiarize themselves with ways to improve Taiwan's environment and family life. Like relational feminists in the Japanese colonial era, members of the Homemakers' Union conceptualized women's self-development within their familial roles as mothers and wives.[3] On a weekly basis, members of the Homemakers' Union gathered to learn about modern child psychology, effective communication strategies, proper nutrition, and approaches for protecting consumers' rights and the environment through changes in habits of consumption.[4]

Moreover, the Homemakers' Union provided housewives with a circle of friends and a support network that empowered and trained them to become community activists. As Taiwan's primary consumers, members of the Homemakers' Union considered themselves to be best suited for the propagation of environmental consciousness to their children and the public, including the need for and methods of recycling, the creative use of discarded materials, and ways to reduce wasteful use of water and electricity. Moreover, the union published pamphlets and submitted articles to newspapers. By 1990, it had achieved considerable success in the promotion of environmental education in elementary schools.[5]

In addition to urging municipal governments to allocate human and financial resources for the recycling of used paper, plastics, and glass containers, the Homemakers' Union also popularized the idea of mass producing durable nylon shopping bags that could be washed, brought to grocery stores, and reused. Instead of placing purchased goods and groceries in new plastic bags that could only be used once and then discarded, a durable nylon shopping bag eliminated the problem of bringing excess bags home after each trip to the grocery store. Based on the ideal of being environmentally conscious consumers, this approach created less rubbish to recycle.[6]

For environmental conservation, the Homemakers' Union opposed deforestation and the construction of golf courses. The union, the Awakening

Foundation, and thirty-four other non-governmental organizations cosigned the 1988 Declaration in Opposition to the Building of the Fourth Nuclear Power Plant to address the health hazards associated with nuclear waste and prevent a nuclear incident on the densely populated, earthquake-prone island. In a public health campaign, the homemakers opposed the dumping of imported cigarettes as they educated the public about the harmful effects of second-hand smoke.[7]

As proponents of educational reform, many housewives endorsed *Awakening*'s 1988 call for the revision of gender-biased content in elementary and middle school textbooks. To provide a sound institutional structure and raise more funds for the housewives' various social causes, on International Women's Day in 1989 the Homemakers' Union achieved its organizational independence from the New Environment Foundation and was transformed into its own foundation.[8] By 2006, it reported approximately a thousand members from the cities of Taipei and Taichung.

Juvenile Prostitution

In the context of Taiwan's political liberalization in January 1987, *Awakening* and several non-governmental women's organizations formed a coalition with the Taiwan Presbyterian Church, the Taiwan Human Rights Association, and organizations of indigenous peoples to stage a public demonstration against juvenile prostitution.[9] In the 1970s and 1980s, many crime syndicates persuaded the parents of adolescent girls from Malayo-Polynesian backgrounds to sell their daughters to work as maids. Demographically, Malayo-Polynesian indigenes comprised less than two percent of Taiwan's population, yet more than 20 percent of Taiwan's prostitutes. Since many resided in economically depressed mountainous regions of Taiwan, they were often recruited as domestics for urban middle-class households. Many were forced into prostitution upon their arrival in the cities. In Taiwan, juveniles represented 34 percent of all Taiwanese prostitutes in 1992. The approximate number ranged from sixty-five thousand to one hundred thousand girls.[10]

To safeguard the teenage prostitutes' human rights, the coalition of protesters called for government intervention to stop organized crime's sales of legal minors in the sex trade. According to Ku Yen-lin, this marked the first public demonstration on behalf of women and girls in postwar Taiwan. The protest sparked an island-wide movement that attracted ample media coverage and thereby put pressure on police authorities to take action.[11]

A month after the revocation of martial law, several Awakening feminists joined women lawyers, physicians, and scholars to establish the Taiwan

Women's Rescue Association (*Taiwan funü jiuyuan xiehui*). With donations from supporters, the Rescue Association accumulated enough money to organize a foundation in 1988. It was renamed the Taipei Women's Rescue Foundation.[12] Most of the Rescue Foundation's members were middle-class professionals from the ethnic Chinese majority. Like the Chinese gentry scholars of the traditional past, members of the Rescue Foundation perceived themselves as the moral-intellectual elite that should offer assistance to the less fortunate members of the society.[13]

To raise the Taiwanese public's awareness of juvenile prostitution, the Rescue Foundation submitted articles to newspapers and staged public demonstrations with several other non-governmental organizations. In cooperation with social workers and the Rainbow Project of the Taiwan Presbyterian Church, the Rescue Foundation sent volunteers to indigenous communities to educate parents about the potential dangers of selling their daughters into prostitution.[14]

In 1987, women attorneys in the Rescue Foundation demanded that the district courts issue search warrants against illegal brothels that housed juvenile prostitutes. In 1989, the Rescue Foundation, the Awakening Foundation, and the Homemakers' Union lobbied successfully for the passage of the Juvenile Social Welfare Law. To protect adolescents, the law forbade the presence of juveniles in red-light districts. If a law enforcement authority took a juvenile prostitute into custody, a social worker was to interview her and investigate the case. Based on the findings of the investigation, all adults responsible for the crime—the brothel that illegally employed the juvenile and the agent who bought and recruited her—were to be prosecuted. If a juvenile prostitute was between the ages of sixteen and eighteen, the police authority was to refer her to the municipal government's social welfare bureau. The social welfare bureau was to have responsibility for referring the prostitute to job training and rehabilitation centers.[15]

Despite passage of the law, most law enforcement agencies treated prostitutes of sixteen years of age or over as adults rather than legal minors. As illegal prostitutes, they were detained as adults rather than referred to social welfare bureaus as juveniles. Based on penal codes 221 and 227 of the Republic of China (ROC), male customers of underage prostitutes were to be charged with rape and sentenced to a year or more of imprisonment. Because the organized syndicates that owned the illegal brothels often bribed law enforcement officers, the male-centered law enforcement agencies rarely prosecuted the brothels or their male customers.[16]

In order to eliminate the sexual double standard of law enforcement, the Rescue Foundation's lawyers tried to persuade the rescued prostitutes to press charges against their customers, the illegal brothels, and the agents who bought them. The Foundation offered the girls free legal counsel and defended them in court to bring the perpetrators to justice. It also set up a hotline to help the victims of forced prostitution escape and to offer assistance to victims of sexual assault. In 1990, the Rescue Foundation established a halfway house to offer legal, medical, and psychological counseling to the rescued prostitutes. As a result of their advocacy and that of their allies, the Kuomintang government publicized the Juvenile Prostitution Prevention Law (*Ertong ji shaonian xingjiaoyi fangzhi tiaoli*) in 1995. In cooperation with job training programs in governmental agencies and non-governmental organizations, including the Garden of Hope Foundation,[17] the Rescue Foundation provided the necessary support that enabled some prostitutes to change their occupations.[18]

The *Awakening* Magazine, Foundation, and Associations

Because the feminist activists of the *Awakening* group were quite effective in drawing the public's attention to the plight of young prostitutes, the women's movement attracted many new volunteers and female college students to the cause. The Awakening feminists sustained their publication and activities primarily with volunteer work and private donations. As a result of the public demonstration in January of 1987, *Awakening* attracted more financial donors from all walks of life. In November 1987, four months after the revocation of martial law, the feminists transformed the Awakening Magazine Publishing House into a foundation.[19]

The mission of the Awakening Foundation (Funü xinzhi jijinhui) was to increase its financial resources and provide an institutional structure for the continuity of the women's movement.[20] As a foundation, Awakening consisted of a Board of Trustees and an Executive Office. The trustees selected fifteen to eighteen unpaid board members to serve two-year terms. The Board then selected six to seven salaried employees to work in the Executive Office. As an elite-sustained organization without a mass membership, the Awakening Foundation focused on the dissemination of feminist ideas and its nonpartisan legislative lobbying for pro-woman legislation.[21]

In recognition of the Foundation's inability to mobilize masses of women at the grassroots level, beginning in 1994 the Awakening Foundation recruited volunteers and raised funds to establish Awakening Associations in several major cities. Unlike the elite-sustained organizational model of the Foundation that centered its resources and decision making in Taipei, the Associations launched mass membership drives in various localities.[22]

Whereas the trustees appointed the Awakening Foundation's personnel, the processes of personnel selection and decision making were more egalitarian in the associations. With a mass membership, each association's members elected officers in their respective cities.[23] Institutionally, the Awakening Foundation and the Awakening Associations in Taipei and Kaohsiung are three separate organizations. Periodically, officers, board members, and staffs of these three organizations would get together to exchange ideas and share experiences.[24]

In 1995, the Awakening Foundation terminated the monthly publication of the magazine and replaced it with a quarterly journal entitled *Saodong* (*Stir*). In contrast to the magazine's traditional emphasis on reporting news pertaining to women and the feminist movements in Taiwan and abroad, *Saodong* provided an open forum for the feminist community to debate controversial women's issues from diverse perspectives.[25]

In addition to the transformation of the *Awakening* magazine into *Saodong*, the Awakening Foundation mobilized activists to lobby in the Legislative Yuan and to educate the public about various legislative bills affecting women. They hoped that favorable public opinion would put pressure on legislators to pass specific pro-women legislation. Awakening Foundation members perceived themselves as part of an ideological vanguard whose mission was to educate the public about women's issues and the need for legislative reforms.[26] This attested to the continuity of the cultural-intellectual approach in the autonomous women's movement. That is, activists were committed to the notion that transformations in people's knowledge and beliefs about women's issues were preconditions for other changes.

To educate the public, *Awakening* introduced the legislative bills concerning women's rights to its urban middle-class readership. As public opinion on various sociopolitical issues became more diverse and contentious, the feminist discourse in *Awakening* also became more pluralistic. As a politically neutral and nonpartisan publication, *Awakening* nevertheless encouraged women to vote in elections in order to have women's voices heard.[27] In the mid-1990s, the Awakening Association of Taipei launched training seminars on public speaking and leadership training to prepare female electoral candidates for political campaigns.[28]

With more sociopolitical space in which to express their views, feminists in the post–martial law era were relatively less compromising with traditional gender roles than Lu Hsiu-lien was during the 1970s. In 1988, Awakening feminists conducted a comprehensive textual analysis of gender-role stereotyping in elementary and junior-high textbooks and critiqued gender-biases in the Kuomintang's national education system.[29] By exposing gender bias and authoritarian tendencies in textbooks, Awakening feminists hoped that the Taiwanese public would join hands with the women's movement to exert pressure on the Ministry of Education to revise the textbooks' content.[30]

In 1988, Lee Yuan-chen critiqued Taiwan's authoritarian educational system as a major hindrance to children's critical thinking and freedom of expression. Lee stated that Chinese culture had been authoritarian and ideologically monistic for most of its history. Within the Chinese cultural context, Taiwan's educational system emphasized state orthodoxy and ideological indoctrination and conformity with Confucian patriarchal social norms at the expense of sociopolitical tolerance, creative thinking, and diversity. She argued that these tendencies were not conducive to educating the young to adapt to the realities of a modern democratic society. For instance, the textbooks anachronistically depicted men and women as conforming to traditionally ascribed gender roles: women were primarily depicted as good mothers and wives who handled all the household responsibilities. As a consequence, many male students grew up expecting their wives to do all the housework, despite women's full-time employment outside the home. Lee demanded that social studies textbooks emphasize the sharing of housework by men and women. In this way, children of both genders would be taught from an early age to consider housework a responsibility.[31]

Lee advocated that the textbooks' contents should include professional women's contributions to various occupational endeavors. Then, male students could learn to respect their female colleagues and female students would have professional role models. Lee imagined an educational experience that would foster the freedom to express one's individual personality. To this end, she believed, the Ministry of Education should offer seminars for teachers to transform their gender-biased attitudes and their traditional acceptance of authoritarian indoctrination.[32]

After nearly a decade of advocacy by a coalition of feminist activists, educational reformers, and parents' groups, in 1996 the National Institute of Compilation and Translation ended nearly five decades of monopolizing the development and editing of elementary school textbooks. In the spirit of democratic pluralism, the Taiwanese government welcomed various commercial presses to compile and publish new textbooks. In addition, elementary school teachers were given greater autonomy to choose textbooks that promoted gender equity. [33] In the 1997 edition of middle school textbooks entitled *Renshi Taiwan* (*Getting to Know Taiwan*), the book on society devoted a section to the post-war Taiwan's autonomous women's movement.

Based on the proposed draft bill written by a coalition of non-governmental civic organizations, the Awakening Foundation, and educational reformers, the Legislative Yuan passed the Gender Equity Education Act in 2004. The law stipulated that a gender-balanced curriculum should be integrated into students' learning experiences from kindergarten through twelfth grade, and every university in Taiwan should offer courses in gender studies. The law prohibited discrimination against pregnant women and girls within the school system and prejudicial treatment based on a person's sexual orientation. Also, the Act stipulated the creation of a Gender Equity Education Committee in the Ministry of Education and in every city and county government as well as in every school and university in Taiwan. At least half of all members in each committee were required to be women. At every level, the Gender Equity Education Committee was placed in charge of formulating and implementing policies and coordinating curriculum based on the principle of gender equity. Each school-based committee was also vested with the power and responsibility to investigate cases of sexual assault and harassment and to recommend appropriate punishment for offenders based on legal provisions. In addition to the creation of these committees, the Act stipulated the establishment of a Faculty Evaluation Committee and a Grievance Review Committee in every school and university in Taiwan. Each of these committees was required to have at least one-third of its members of either gender.[34] After nearly four years of lobbying, research, and legal consultation with experts, the passage of the Gender Equity Education Act was undoubtedly one of the greatest achievements of the Awakening Foundation.[35]

The Blossoming of Women's Studies

In line with their goal of promoting gender equity in the educational system, in 1985 the Awakening feminists supported the creation of Taiwan's first Women's Research Program (WRP) in the Population Studies Center of National Taiwan University (NTU). The WRP was created with a grant from the American-based Asia Foundation. Among the four pioneers of the interdisciplinary program, Nora Lan-hung Chiang and Elaine Tsui were faculty members of NTU. In order to participate in the coordination of the program, both Ku Yen-lin of National Chiaotung University and Chou Bih-er of National Tsinghua University had to commute periodically from the city of Hsinchu to NTU in Taipei. For the past two decades, several thousand students, scholars, and visitors from abroad have visited the library at the NTU Center for Population Studies to conduct research on gender issues in Taiwan.[36]

Since 1989, the WRP has published the *Newsletter of Women's Studies* (Funü yanjiu tongxun).[37] In 1990 the WRP also launched the publication of the *Journal of Women and Gender Research* (Funü yu xingbie yanjiu).[38] To facilitate research about women, the WRP compiled and published abstracts of published monographs in both Chinese and English in *Abstracts of Research on Women in Taiwan* (Taiwan funü yanjiu wenxian zhaiyao).

Whereas the WRP at the National Taiwan University was the pioneer of gender and women's studies, the departments of sociology and anthropology at National Tsinghua University (NTHU) launched the Research Program on Gender and Society (RPGS) in 1989. To promote interdisciplinary teaching and research about women in Taiwan, Chou Bih-er, the program's founder and first coordinator, designed a curriculum that focused on the studies of sexuality and gender relations in social institutions and the family. As an institutionally independent gender studies program on campus, faculty members of RPGS also supervised masters' theses on gender and women's studies.[39] In 1995, the RPGS launched the *Bulletin of Book Reviews in Gender Studies* (*Liangxing shuping tongxun*).

From 1985 through 1992, the research methodology of gender studies emphasized quantitative analysis of statistical data about women in Taiwan. Male-dominated social science departments in Taiwan's universities preferred this approach, which expected researchers to be detached from the subjects of their studies to ensure objectivity. Consequently, most researchers did not apply feminist theories in their analyses of gender inequality in Taiwanese society, nor did women's studies researchers utilize qualitative research methods that would allow female subjects' voices to be heard from a woman-centered perspective.[40]

According to Ku Yen-lin, the founder of both *Awakening* and WRP, the researchers at WRP and RPGS should have done more to promote the study and application of feminist theories to enrich the autonomous women's movement. She believed that studying Taiwanese women's lives and issues without a critical feminist perspective vis-à-vis the patriarchal society would not enhance Taiwanese women's status.[41] Ku's feminist associate, Lee Yuan-chen, also voiced her concern about the academic detachment of the WRP from the feminist perspective of the Taiwanese women's movement.

In response to the feminist community's call for greater mutual cooperation between women's studies researchers and the women's movement in the early 1990s, an increasing number of faculty members in WRP and RPGS incorporated feminist perspectives into the critical analysis of gender inequality in their research projects. The WRP faculty from various departments also co-taught a gender relations course to raise college students' awareness of gender issues.[42] Thus, the WRP contributed to the autonomous movement's goal of raising consciousness of gender inequality in Taiwanese society. By 1997, the WRP faculty at National Taiwan University had developed a certificate program on women and gender studies.

In addition to the development of gender studies curricula, from 1988 through 1990 female students on several college campuses organized women's studies clubs (*nüyanshe*). Club members studied Western feminist theories and discussed their applicability in Taiwanese society and in their daily lives. In 1991, a nationwide alliance of women's studies clubs on Taiwan's college campuses was established to facilitate the sharing of knowledge and information and the coordination of campus campaigns for common causes.[43]

According to Chang Chuan-fen, a leader of the women's studies club on the NTU campus, the emergence of women's studies clubs on college campuses was a direct result of the work of student dissidents in the democracy movement in the 1980s. Similar to women activists' experiences of gender discrimination in the American Civil Rights and New Left movements during the 1960s, many founders of women's studies clubs on Taiwan's college campuses were activists in male-dominated campus democracy movements during the 1980s. Just as their American counterparts broke away from the male-dominated New Left and Civil Rights movements to become radical feminists in the late 1960s, the female student activists' marginal status in Taiwan's male-centered democracy movement also raised their awareness of gender inequities.[44]

In 1992, student activists in the women's studies club and faculty at National Tsinghua University's (NTHU) Research Program on Gender and Society (RPGS) were actively involved in an anti-sexual harassment campaign on campus. The incident began when a male student in NTHU's library repeatedly harassed women students. To support the female victims, the activist wing of the women's studies club held consciousness-raising sessions in the university's dormitories and invited the faculty members of RPGS to participate. In response to the campus incident, RPGS developed the *Handbook on the Prevention of Campus Sexual Harassment*.[45]

A year later, feminist faculty on various college campuses created the Taiwanese Feminist Scholars Association (*Nüxuehui*) as an island-wide support network of women's studies scholars. The association's mission is to facilitate information-sharing among women's studies scholars, promote the women's movement on college campuses, and enhance feminist scholars' capacity to raise public and governmental awareness of the need to safeguard women's rights.[46] Many scholars of the *Nüxuehui* integrate feminist perspectives into their critical analysis of social problems in university research centers for gender, women, and sexuality. Gender and women's studies courses are offered on many college campuses in contemporary Taiwan because of the effort of *Nüxuehui* members.

Philosophically, both the Feminist Scholars Association and campus women's studies clubs promoted the unity of feminist scholarship and activism. That is, they felt that feminist scholarship should enhance social activism.[47] To translate this vision into action, the association published the *White Paper on Taiwanese Women's Position* in 1995. Through the mass media's dissemination of information from the book and oral presentations on college campuses and in governmental agencies, the feminist scholars offered their recommendations for policy reforms on a wide variety of issues.[48]

In the same year as the publication of the white paper, Ho Ch'un-jui (Josephine Ho), the pioneer feminist of Taiwan's sexual liberation movement and a faculty member of English language and literature at the National Central University, established the Center for the Study of Gender and Sexualities (*Xingbie yanjiushi*). In addition to publishing research findings about the sexuality of heterosexuals, gays, lesbians, bisexuals, and transgender populations, the Center also supports the rights of sexual minorities. Since 2000, several Taiwanese universities have established M.A. programs for gender studies.[49] With the passage of the Gender Equity Education Act in 2004, all universities in Taiwan are mandated to offer gender studies courses at the undergraduate level.

Warm Life Association for Divorced Women

One of the women's organizations that advocated gender equity in Taiwan's educational system was the Warm Life Association (*Wanqing xiehui*). Established in 1984 by a group of Awakening feminists to offer emotional support to divorced women, it was first known as the "Give-a-Hand Club." In 1986, it changed its name to the Warm Life Association. In response to popular demand, the association set up chapters in several major cities and counties throughout the island.[50]

In a family-centered culture, divorced women had to cope with discrimination in Taiwanese society. Most women were socialized to believe that marriage was the most important component of their lives, and those with broken marriages often accepted the social stigma attached to their supposed failures. This contributed to low self-esteem and feelings of hopelessness. In order to validate divorced women's sense of self-worth, the association organized support groups to provide a context in which divorced women could share their traumatic experiences and discuss ways to improve the quality of their lives. Because many members experienced repeated physical and emotional abuse, most of them sought emotional support in the association for at least five years. Similar to the mission of Awakening, the ultimate goal of the Warm Life Association was to empower divorced women to achieve emotional and financial independence.[51]

In the process of severing emotional and financial ties with their husbands and parents-in-law, some members of the Warm Life Association re-established close ties with their natal families. When parents provided their daughters with critical emotional and financial support during the trauma of divorce, many divorced women who later achieved financial autonomy reciprocated in kind by providing emotional and financial support to their elderly parents. As a result, many divorced women bolstered their status as daughters of their natal families. As relational feminists within the Chinese familial context, these divorced women learned to liberate themselves from the traumatic relationships they had endured with their ex-husbands and to re-establish interdependent relationships with their natal families. Unlike the high prevalence of remarriage in the West, most members of the Warm Life Association chose not to remarry. In order to shelter their children from the potential complications of a stepfamily, most divorced women in the association were content with the strong emotional ties they had cultivated with their children and their natal families.[52]

The Movement to Amend Family Laws

Divorced women who lost property and child custody to their former husbands sought emotional support and referrals for legal counsel from the association to deal with their traumatic losses. To overcome gender bias in the laws concerning child custody and matrimonial property, the Warm Life Association and the Awakening Foundation jointly launched the Movement to Amend the Family Laws (*minfa qinshu pian*) in 1990.[53] In June 1990, the Grand Council of Justices ruled that all members of the Legislative Yuan elected in mainland China in 1947 should retire by the end of 1991. This ruling raised new hopes that a newly elected legislature that represented Taiwan's constituencies would be more responsive to women's demands for the revision of family laws. Contrary to the absence of legislative lobbying as a strategy of the autonomous women's movement in the authoritarian political context of the 1970s, legislative lobbying now became an essential component of the Warm Life Association and Awakening feminists' strategy in the post-martial law era.[54]

Both organizations solicited the legal assistance of the Taipei Attorneys'

Federation to draft an amendment to family laws. After three years of research and consultation they held a joint hearing to familiarize the public and legislators with the finalized draft of their proposed amendment. The authors of the draft amendment called for the revision of the ROC family laws.[55]

Since their promulgation in mainland China in the 1930s, the family laws stipulated that a husband had the legal right to manage or dispose of his wife's property without her consent. On the other hand, they required that a wife obtain her husband's permission to sell her own property. If there was a disagreement between a married couple concerning a major issue pertaining to their child, the husband had the right to act unilaterally on the child's behalf.[56]

In accordance with the law pertaining to domicile, a married woman was obliged to reside at the locality of her husband's choice. Yet, no equivalent stipulation obliged a husband to do the same for his wife. If the wife failed to reside with her husband, he could divorce her for neglecting her wifely duty. Insofar as the wife was considered to be the party at fault, she was deemed ineligible for alimony. A divorce of mutual consent could, on the other hand, be easily obtained, but if one party objected, the court required the party filing for divorce to present medical evidence of physical abuse or proof of adultery. Unlike most divorce laws in the West, legal separation between a married couple was not considered a legitimate prerequisite for divorce.[57]

In 1993, the Awakening Foundation and the Warm Life Association recruited and trained women activists from all walks of life to solicit the public's support for their amendment. The activists traveled throughout Taiwan to speak in public meetings and gather signatures for the cause.[58] The following year, a coalition of non-governmental women's organizations petitioned the Grand Council of Justices (*Dafaguan huiyi*) at the Judicial Yuan to rule on the constitutionality of Civil Code no. 1089. The Justices ruled that the priority given to a husband to exercise power over his children without his wife's consent was unconstitutional and inconsistent with the Gender Equality Clause of the ROC Constitution.[59]

In addition to this legal victory, the activists persuaded Taiwan's three major political parties[60] to cosign the draft amendment to the family laws. On International Women's Day in 1995, the draft amendment was presented to the Legislative Yuan for deliberation. The Awakening Foundation and the Warm Life Association organized an observation team and a lobby to oversee the legislative process. Based on the draft amendment, the Legislative Yuan incrementally revised portions of the family laws. In 1996, the preference for fathers in child custody matters was abolished and replaced by a stipulation allowing the court to award child custody to whichever parent could best care for the legal minor. Unless the parent without custody was abusive, he or she would be granted visitation rights. In the revised code concerning domicile, a married couple should jointly reach an agreement on their place of residence.[61]

In 2002, the Legislative Yuan passed the portion of the family law that pertains to a married couple's property. The revised code abolished joint ownership of property between husband and wife and stipulated that husband or wife shall each manage, use, benefit from, and dispose of his or her own property. In other words, all the property registered under a wife's name belongs to the wife. The husband is not allowed to manage or sell the property without her consent. In addition to the living expenses of a family, the married couple should negotiate and agree upon a set amount of money for each person to freely use or to have at their disposal.[62]

Women lawyers of the Modern Women's Foundation in Taipei (*Taibeishi xiandai funü jijinhui*)[63] also authored and lobbied for the passage of the Domestic Violence Prevention Act (*Jiating baoli fangzhifa*). Enforced as of 1999, the act protects battered women in the family. It stipulates that courts have the power to issue injunctions to bar assailants in domestic violence cases from entering their own homes. Courts were also granted the authority to order assailants to pay for the victims' medical and living expenses. After the central government promulgated the new legislation, the previously silent victims of domestic violence began to seek legal protection from public authorities. From June 1999 through January 2001, the courts handled more than sixteen thousand cases of domestic violence and issued more than ten thousand injunctions.[64] The increasing visibility of battered women's plight was made possible by the nascent democratic culture's tolerance for the public discussion of family problems.

From 1999 through 2005, the Awakening Foundation invited several legal experts of family laws to formulate a draft bill for the family due process laws (*jiashi shijianfa*). The draft bill proposes that a system of family courts be established in every jurisdiction in Taiwan to resolve legal issues pertaining to financial and legal disputes among family members and between married or divorced couples. Codification of family due process laws could expedite the legal proceedings for determining such contentious issues as a divorced couple's respective rights and responsibilities regarding visitation and child support. The Awakening Foundation activists also hope that all laws pertaining to familial relationships will eventually be revised to accord the same status and rights to same-sex couples as to heterosexual marriages. This would include same-sex couples' right to marry and adopt children.[65]

Woman-Identified Woman, X-Centric, and the First Lesbian Organization

Within the context of Taiwan's democratization, lesbianism and the concept of woman-identified woman emerged from invisibility and silence to become a strand of radical feminism within the feminist community. In 1989, *Wai ji-aodu* was established as a consciousness-raising and study group for a handful of women college students from Taipei's universities. In Mandarin Chinese, *Wai jiaodu* literally means "askew angle." Since the male-dominated culture tended to see a woman's perspective as unorthodox and skewed, members of *Wai jiaodu* chose this name for their group to wage a cultural rebellion against male definitions of womanhood and thereby validate women-centered perspectives.[66]

Wai jiaodu members also created the English name "X-centric" for their study group. According to Sun Ruei-suei, a founder and coordinator of Wai jiaodu, "X-Centric" was the abbreviation for "eliminating the dominant center." Like their radical feminist counterparts in the United States, X-Centric members sought to de-center and deconstruct the hierarchical model of leadership in traditional organizations and replace it with an egalitarian organizational model without a center of power.[67]

In order to promote women's solidarity, members called themselves X-Centric sisters (*wai jiemei*). The membership consisted of female students from several universities in Taipei, graduate students returned from abroad, professionals from all walks of life, and urban industrial workers. To provide young women with an emotional refuge from the male-dominated hierarchical society, X-Centric sisters aspired to treat all its members as equals in a relaxed and informal setting. As a women's support group, members shared their intimate feelings and learned from each other's ways of dealing with daily problems. Some of the personal experiences discussed and shared among the X-Centric sisters were mother-daughter relationships, various types of violence and injustice against women, and sexual experiences.[68]

In the study group, X-Centric sisters periodically viewed and critiqued women-centered films and read feminist writings. In order to familiarize themselves with women's bodies, films on women's reproductive organs were also shown. These films and writings served as catalysts for generating discussions about various women's issues within the context of gender inequality in Taiwanese society.[69] Because some X-Centric sisters were also members of Awakening Foundation, many members of both Awakening and X-Centric read the Radicalesbians' position paper entitled "Woman-Identified Woman."[70]

According to the Radicalesbians, a true woman is one who internalizes the ideology of male supremacy and the male definition of womanhood. Her primary loyalty and commitment is to her husband rather than to other women. Rather than empowering her sisters, she competes with other women for male approval and affection. By identifying with her husband's ego rather than her own, the true woman gains social status through her husband. With her psychology of dependence on men, she also engenders hatred of the powerless self. She gains validation and approval from the male-defined society by compromising her selfhood and her dignity to be a male-identified true woman.[71]

A true woman internalizes the heterosexist values of the patriarchal society and shuns lesbians in fear of society's disapproval and ostracism. Thus, with the stigmatization of the word "lesbian," patriarchal society succeeds in dividing women's collective power, thereby ensuring the perpetuation of both gender inequality and heterosexism. Contrary to a male-identified true woman, a woman-identified woman emphasizes the primacy of identifying with and loving other women. Rather than competing with women for the approval and attention of male authorities, she validates her own self-esteem, defines her own identity, and empowers her sisters. Regardless of her sexual orientation, a woman-identified woman believes in the importance of committing to women's interests and rights in the social, political, and economic realms. She is aware of the interlocking and mutually reinforcing relationship between patriarchy and heterosexism. Hence, she knows that gender equality cannot be fully achieved without the elimination of heterosexism and homophobia.[72]

After reading "Woman-Identified Woman," a member of the Awakening Foundation, Hu Shu-wen, contended that the labels *straight* and *lesbian* were rigid categories imposed on women by a patriarchal heterosexual society to divide what it deemed "true women" from "sexually deviant women."[73] In the 1990s, *woman-identified woman (nüren rentong nüren)* became a political identity and a key concept of women's solidarity for many members of the Awakening Foundation and the X-Centric sisters.

In addition to "Woman-Identified Woman," the writings of Audre Lorde (1934–92) evoked a great deal of passion and enthusiasm among the X-Centric sisters. In the early 1990s, the X-Centric sisters read the original English text of Lorde's "Use of the Erotic, the Erotic is Power."[74] In the essay, Lorde posited that the freedom to exert one's inner erotic energy could ensure a woman's emotional and sexual satisfaction and thereby enhance her creative energy at work and in all other aspects of her life. Lorde differentiated lust from eroticism. Lust, in her view, is the objectification and use of another person's body to gratify one's senses. In contrast, eroticism is the sharing of one's erotic energy and experience with a person one cares about. Because erotic desire is part of every woman's inner self, patriarchal society's repression of a woman's freedom to express her sexuality is equivalent to the denial of an essential aspect of her humanity. Lorde considered the verbal sharing of erotic experiences among women and the erotic relationships between women as a means to strengthen the bonds of sisterhood.[75]

Lorde's thought-provoking statements inspired the X-Centric sisters to examine sexual repression in their own lives. They concurred with Lorde's assertion that the negative energy a woman used to restrain her sexuality within socially imposed norms ought to be redirected to achieve the freedom of erotic and sexual expressions on one's own terms.[76] As a black lesbian, Lorde's personal journey from emotional repression and silence to emotional and verbal assertiveness was particularly instructive to the X-Centric sisters given the context of Taiwan's democratization.[77] For nearly four decades, martial law had created a culture of silence among the Taiwanese populace. Parents would admonish their children to keep controversial opinions to themselves, so as not to invite undesirable reactions from the government. As Taiwan democratized in the early 1990s, lesbians and heterosexual sisters in X-Centric shared their diverse views on their erotic and sexual experiences. Since there was a wide range of sexual orientations and ideologies, there were some tensions and misunderstandings that elicited dialogue among the members.[78] Like Lorde, the X-Centric sisters saw their differences as opportunities to enrich their discourse, enhance their mutual understanding, and strengthen their bonds of sisterhood.[79]

Within the context of Taiwan's culture of silence, Lorde's essay entitled "The Use of Anger" had a transformational impact on many X-Centric sisters' lives. Initially, Lorde remained silent about her experiences living in society as a black lesbian. After she was recommended for surgery to remove a malignant tumor, she came to the realization that time might be running out for her to speak out. Rather than being intimidated by the possible disapproval of society, Lorde began to openly express her anger about the injustices inflicted upon disadvantaged and marginalized women in society.[80]

Inspired by Lorde's stance that the expression of anger was an assertion of one's inner power and energy, X-Centric became a support group in which women with personal problems or grievances could freely vent their anger and frustrations. In this women's subculture, members let their guard down to freely express their authentic feelings without the fear of social disapproval or value judgment. For example, a heterosexual woman in X-Centric shared the experience of the anger her lesbian friends directed toward her. This confrontation led to a personal transformation for her. She became more sensitive to and aware of lesbian issues and concerns after the emotional confrontation. Without the powerful effect of anger, she might not have taken her friends' grievances seriously. Thus, if strong emotions were channeled in constructive ways, anger and other forms of emotional expression could promote dialogue and mutual understanding, deepen relationships, and enable individuals to undergo transformation. After each gathering, many members walked away with a deep sense of sisterly love and empowerment.[81]

Committed to the notion that the personal is political, a graduate student in X-Centric voiced her objection to the male-dominated academic community's over-reliance on objective and impersonal approaches to conducting research in the social sciences. Another sister stated that she was discouraged from expressing her emotions in her interpersonal interactions at the university. In other words, it was an uphill battle for a handful of woman-identified women to transform the deeply entrenched social norms in larger society.[82] The X-Centric sisters often used the title of Audre Lorde's book, *Sister Outsider* (*Bianyuan jiemei*), to denote the marginal status of their woman-centered perspective in Taiwanese society.

Despite its commitment to the concept of *woman-identified woman*, X-Centric was still a predominantly heterosexual women's organization. In 1990, several lesbian activists in X-Centric and the Awakening Foundation formed the first lesbian organization in Taiwan, Between Us (*Women zhi jian*), to address issues confronting the lesbian community. The new members also discussed writings that validated their sexual orientation.[83]

In both Between Us and X-Centric, members read "Compulsory Heterosexuality and Lesbian Existence" by Adrienne Rich (b. 1929). After reading the original English text, they by and large concurred with Rich's analysis of the compulsory nature of heterosexuality. Rich posits that heterosexuality is a socially imposed mechanism to control every woman's sexual behavior, divide women's collective power, and perpetuate heterosexism and patriarchy via legal, religious, economic, and familial institutions. Since women are socialized to believe that heterosexuality is the only normal form of sexual behavior, their cooperation ensures the perpetuation of patriarchal families and heterosexuality. In both X-Centric and Between Us, members also familiarized themselves with Rich's concept of a lesbian continuum in every woman's life—in other words, every woman has experienced certain aspects of lesbian existence at some points in her life and every woman was born with some lesbian tendencies, regardless of whether she has been sexually involved with another woman. Hence, every woman should have the potential to become erotically involved with another woman. Rich also broadened the lesbian continuum to include heterosexual women who identified with women and rejected male domination.[84]

By contending that the line between a lesbian and a heterosexual existence is not as clearly drawn as the socially imposed heterosexual norm implies, Rich de-stigmatizes lesbianism and creates the possibility of uniting women's collective power across diverse sexual orientations. In her validation of lesbians' sexual identity, Rich empowered feminist activists from diverse sexual orientations to collectively wage a struggle against patriarchy and heterosexism. From the perspective of Between Us, the creation of Taiwan's first lesbian organization would challenge the invisibility of lesbian existence in Taiwanese society and force heterosexual feminists to confront their lack of understanding of lesbianism.[85]

As of 1990, Between Us provided a space where lesbians could gather to develop friendships and seek emotional support in a homophobic society. The members also discussed various strategies for coming out in their relationships with family members, close friends, and colleagues. The organization provided a space for lesbians to express their emotions and opinions freely. To provide yet another forum for lesbians, Between Us launched a bimonthly newsletter, Girlfriends (Nüpengyou), in 1994. Contributors to the newsletter freely shared their erotic experiences with their sister members in the lesbian community. In contrast to relational feminism's conception of a heterosexual couple as the basic unit of society, lesbian feminism validated the primacy of erotic bonds between women.[86]

Based on the organizational model of Between Us, many college campuses throughout Taiwan created gay and lesbian student organizations. They welcomed heterosexual supporters to join them in their critique of the homophobic society. With the alliance of gay and lesbian movements,[87] a bookstore and a hotline were set up in Taipei to provide information and counseling services to both communities. In recent years, student organizations and Between Us demanded gays' and lesbians' right to work without discrimination and the legalization of same-sex unions. In addition to the call for legislative reform, activists organized observation teams to question electoral candidates' stances on gay and lesbian rights and challenged the blind spots of the heterosexual society. In so doing, they transformed the gay and lesbian movement into a human rights movement.[88]

In 1995, Awakening published several issues that confronted the organization's prior silence on lesbian issues. As the foremother of other non-governmental women's organizations, by the mid-1990s the Awakening Foundation was faced with an increasing ideological rift between liberal feminists and their radical counterparts. Since the establishment of Awakening in 1982,

liberal feminists sought to promote gender equality within the existing sociopolitical and legal systems. In contrast, many young radical activists came
in contact with American radical feminist literature during Taiwan's democratization in the 1990s. Several radical feminists critiqued heterosexuality as
a patriarchal institution that controlled and divided women both physically
and emotionally. From their perspective, gender equality could never be fully
achieved without understanding the negative impact of heterosexuality on
women's solidarity.[89]

Like their feminist counterparts in the United States during the 1970s,
many liberal feminists in the Awakening Foundation were reluctant to challenge the institution of heterosexuality. Several Awakening feminists quietly
donated money to lesbian organizations behind the scenes. This prompted a
lesbian activist, Yu-hsuan A-chih, to characterize the relationship as one between a mother and her illegitimate daughter. She stated that the Awakening
Foundation has yet to break the silence of White Terror in the organization.[90]
From the perspective of an X-Centric member, Ku Ming-chun, the Awakening Foundation needed to overcome its homophobia and heterosexism before
its lesbian members would come out.[91]

Regardless of the willingness of the foundation and the lesbian community
to cosign each other's petitions, most Awakening feminists prioritized the
revision of family laws over lesbian issues. They claimed that the amendment
of family laws had already achieved a broad consensus in Taiwanese society.
Thus, it made more sense to ensure gender equality in family laws first. Once
the first phase was achieved, the Awakening Foundation would be able to
direct more resources to the struggle for lesbian rights. Because the revision
of family laws was primarily a heterosexual women's issue, many lesbian
members of the foundation felt that lesbians' struggle against discrimination was a more urgent priority. Consequently, some left the organization to
devote their full resources to Between Us.[92]

This division between lesbian and heterosexual feminists prompted Lee
Yuan-chen to urge the latter to be more inclusive of lesbian perspectives.
According to Lee, a dominant majority often found it convenient to oppress
and marginalize minority groups in order to maintain its privilege and power.
As the dominant majority in a movement that struggled against injustice,
heterosexual feminists, she argued, should respect the rights and opinions of
the lesbian minority in the movement.[93] In 2003, in response to the advocacy
of the activists in the gay and lesbian communities, President Chen Shui-bian
supported the Executive Yuan's proposed bill to legalize same-sex marriages
in Taiwan as part of the Human Rights Basic Law. Since then, progress on
the deliberation of the bill has been stalled in the Legislative Yuan. A sur-

vey conducted by the National Union of Taiwan Women's Associations and the Constitutional Reform Alliance found that three out of four adults in Taiwan considered same-sex relationships socially acceptable. Despite the majority opinion, no tangible legislative reform has been achieved to meet the demands of gay and lesbian communities.

Sexual Harassment, Sexual Liberation, and the Controversy over Licensed Prostitution

Since the 1990s, feminist scholars, campus women's studies clubs, and Taiwan's feminist community have been united in their opposition to sexual harassment. In order to assert their rights, some victims of sexual harassment decided to file lawsuits based on the legal provisions in the ROC penal code no. 228. The code stipulates that any superior convicted of using his power to rape or direct lewd and obscene conduct toward a subordinate shall be sentenced to no more than five years of imprisonment.[94] Without the specification of sexual harassment as a type of lewd and obscene conduct, most judges in Taiwan's judicial system acquitted male defendants on the grounds of insufficient physical evidence and the lack of eyewitnesses.[95]

To keep their jobs, most eyewitnesses of sexual harassment cases would not testify against their male superiors. Meanwhile, a male defendant could mobilize his wife, friends, and colleagues to defend his moral character in court and during press conferences. Through the mass media, a male defendant could often turn the tide of public opinion against the female plaintiff. In the 1990s, the profit-driven mass media scrutinized female plaintiffs' sexual history and private life for public consumption. Essentially, the mass media allied itself with male defendants and their supporters, casting doubt on the female plaintiffs' moral character. Moreover, male defendants reserved the right to file libel suits against the female plaintiffs. With the threat of libel suits and a slim chance of winning their cases, most female victims felt that they had virtually no alternative except to suffer in silence.[96]

As of the mid-1990s, the Ministry of Education had not formulated a clear policy on sexual harassment in institutions of higher learning. Consequently, the Ministry was ineffectual in its response to female students' complaints. To express their collective frustration about the indifference of the Ministry and the judicial system, campus women's studies clubs, the Feminist Scholars Association, and the Awakening Foundation staged a demonstration against sexual harassment on May 22, 1994. They demanded that the Ministry of Education formulate and implement a campus educational program on the prevention of sexual harassment. Moreover, they wanted the government to formulate and enforce a Sexual Harassment Prevention Act.[97] In order to forcefully convey women's rage and their demands, Ho Ch'un-jui (Josephine Ho)[98] composed a five-character poem that rhymed at the end of each verse to serve as the slogan of the demonstration. In English translation, it reads:

> I want sexual climax.
> I do not want sexual harassment.
> If you harass me again,
> I will use the scissors.[99]

Ho's poem signifies a woman's assertive demands of what she wants and does not want for her body. It also demonstrates that a woman has the right to defend herself against any unwanted intrusion of her body. On the day after the protest, the demonstrators were surprised to find that most newspapers emphasized the phrase "I want sexual climax" rather than the message of anti-sexual harassment. While many feminist activists lamented that the mass media selectively emphasized women's demand for sexual liberation over women's resistance against sexual harassment, Ho saw the media's emphasis as an opportunity to integrate women's sexual liberation into the public discourse.[100]

Four months after the demonstration, Ho published *The Gallant Woman* (*Haoshuang nüren*) to offer her perspective on women's sexual liberation. Whereas sexual liberation was a taboo subject excluded from public discourse under martial law, the nascent democracy enabled Ho's perspective to dominate Taiwan's feminist discourse in 1994 and thereafter.[101] In *The Gallant Woman*, Ho posits that enjoyment of good sex is every woman's basic human right. Like Audre Lorde, Ho contends that patriarchal society's repression of women's freedom to express their sexuality is equivalent to the denial of an essential aspect of humanity. In Taiwanese society, parents, the national education system, and the medical establishment all instilled feelings of guilt about sexual activities outside the marital context in the minds of adolescent girls. They were told that pre-marital sex could cause them to contract sexually transmitted diseases.[102]

Although families and society also warned men and boys about the perceived dangers of contracting venereal diseases, Ho observed that the proliferation of pornographic films and literature in the post-martial law era encouraged male sexual escapades. Since adult men had greater purchasing power than women, the commercialization of sexual products and literature by and large were geared toward male consumers. Whereas men benefited from the proliferation of sexual expression in the mass media, the quality of women's sexual experiences remained low.[103]

According to Ho, society's failure to acknowledge women's need for sexual satisfaction was indicative of gender inequality in sexual relationships. Based on the traditional patriarchal ideology, women's bodies were seen as passive instruments for reproduction and the means for fulfilling men's sexual needs. In contrast, Ho advocated women's right to reclaim their own bodies and determine their own sexual behaviors. Metaphorically, Ho compared a woman's freedom of sexual expression to a buffet. In Mandarin Chinese, the term *buffet* consists of three characters that denote a help-yourself meal (*zi-zhu-can*). In order to enjoy a buffet, a person has the option of choosing from a variety of dishes. Just as one's tastes and preferences for certain foods determine personal choices for creating a buffet, Ho envisioned a woman's freedom to determine the ways to use her body for the fulfillment of her sexual needs. As long as a woman reached an amicable agreement with her sexual partner on the rules of the relationship, she contended that neither individuals nor society has the right to infringe upon her right to control her own body and determine her own sexuality. According to Ho, determining one's sexual behavior consisted of the right to choose with whom she would engage in sexual activity, the number of sexual partners she would have, and the ways to enhance the quality of her sexual experiences. Hence, the metaphor of a buffet signified a woman's sexual self-determination.[104]

In order to validate women's diverse sexual experiences, Ho borrowed extensively from the theory of an American feminist, Gayle Rubin. According to Rubin, patriarchal heterosexist society created a hierarchy of sexual behaviors. In this hierarchy, the sexual activities between a heterosexual couple in a monogamous marriage for the purpose of procreation were accorded the highest social esteem. Conversely, virtually all other sexual activities outside the marital context were deemed less desirable. Through individuals' socialization into the hierarchical system, married couples with children often felt superior to married couples without offspring. Likewise, some married couples felt justified in passing value judgments on unmarried sexual partners. Monogamous couples frowned upon individuals with multiple sexual partners, while some heterosexual couples considered same-sex couples as sexually deviant.[105]

Like Rubin, Ho suggests that dismantling of the hierarchy of sexual behaviors is a precondition for liberating women's sexuality. She suggested that once all sexual behaviors are considered socially acceptable, every woman will be able to freely explore her sexual possibilities and define her sexuality on her own terms.[106] In a broad sense, Ho's vision of a pluralistic society that accepts women's diverse sexual behaviors and lifestyles is a logical extension of Lee Yuan-chen's vision of social tolerance for diverse lifestyles. In 1988, a year after the lifting of martial law, Lee envisioned a democratic and plu-ralistic society that would respect every individual's freedom to determine his or her lifestyle. In the same year, Lee critiqued the Chinese authoritarian culture's indoctrination of children to behave in accordance with socially imposed gender roles. According to Lee, this monistic approach to social-izing children stifled their freedom of self-development and the cultivation of human potential.[107]

By 1994, Ho extended the Taiwanese feminist critique of patriarchal soci-ety's imposition of gender roles to a new critique of the societal imposition of the monistic mode of sexual behavior as embodied in the institution of monogamous heterosexual marriage. In other words, Ho's new discourse on sexual freedom can be seen as a logical extension of Lee's call for liberation from the social constraints of gender roles and hence for the freedom to determine one's lifestyle.

Most students in campus women's studies clubs greeted positively Ho's rad-ical feminist perspective on sexual liberation. In the Sexual Liberation move-ment, members of women's studies clubs were the transmitters of the sexual liberation ideology from campus communities to the larger society.[108] On the first anniversary of the anti-sexual harassment demonstration, members of women's studies clubs from several college campuses staged a rally with the theme of "Uniting Women, Pioneering Eroticism." In order to counter the popular assumption that sexuality is a private matter unsuitable for public discussion, student activists reminded the Taiwanese public that patriarchal ideology had a long history of repressing women's sexuality by propagating the cult of female chastity in public arenas. To dismantle patriarchal control over women's bodies and sexual behaviors, organizers of the rally politicized women's sexuality and thus heightened the Taiwanese public's awareness of the need for women's sexual liberation.[109]

Because Ho's perspective on sexual liberation exerted significant influence on some college students, several social commentators and medical doctors considered her a socially irresponsible educator who misled youngsters into living a promiscuous life. From their perspective, Ho's message would cause the spread of sexually transmitted diseases and an increase in unwanted preg-nancies.[110] In response, Ho asserted that the freedom to choose the practice of safe sex, rather than compulsory abstinence, should be the solution to controlling the spread of venereal diseases and preventing unwanted preg-nancies. Contrary to her critics' overemphasis on the possibility that sexual liberation would lead individuals to take on multiple sexual partners, Ho stated that the primary goal of sexual liberation was to improve the quality of women's sexual experiences. Thus, the quality of a sexual relationship is more important than the number of sexual partners.[111]

In addition to criticism from social conservatives, labor activists contended that only the economically privileged women of the upper and middle classes had the leisure to enjoy sex. With a subsistence lifestyle and heavy household burdens, they suggested that it is unrealistic to expect working-class women to experience the same sexual satisfaction as upper- and middle-class women.[112] In response to this class analysis, proponents of sexual liberation acknowledged that upper- and middle-class women did have more leisure and resources to enjoy sex. But the advocates also argued that women of all classes should be more assertive in articulating their demands to their sexual partners. If working-class women were to remain silent and passive in their sexual relationships, they would not be empowered to assert their rights and demands for better wages and working conditions in the public domain. Thus, they suggested that there was a correlation between gender inequality in sexual relationships and inequality in the workplace.[113]

In addition to the public discourse generated by Ho's call for women's sexual liberation, the controversy over whether licensed prostitution should be banned also generated heated debate within Taiwan's feminist community. Historically, licensed prostitution enabled the Japanese colonial government to tax and regulate the sex industry as well as to contain the spread of venereal diseases. Because some parents in dire economic circumstances would either sell or indenture their daughters to brothel owners in colonial Taiwan, most intellectuals in the 1920s advocated the abolition of licensed prostitution to free sex workers from the abuses of brothel owners and from sexual exploitation by the male clientele.[114] In postwar Taiwan, the issue reemerged in 1996 when the Taipei Women's Rescue Foundation petitioned the municipal government to abolish licensed prostitution. The following year, the Taipei municipal government of Mayor Chen Shui-bian, in concurrence with the vote of the municipal legislature, announced the abolition of licensed prostitution.[115]

Several days prior to the ban, more than a hundred licensed sex workers marched to the municipal government demanding a two-year grace period. To conceal their identities, the prostitutes covered their faces as they marched down the streets of Taipei. On September 2, 1997, the Licensed Prostitutes' Association for Self-Salvation was established. A coalition of pink-collar workers, the Women Workers' Solidarity, and the Awakening Foundation[116] voiced its support for the petition in order to show solidarity with their proletarian sisters. In response to the demonstration, Taipei's feminist community participated in a highly publicized panel discussion on whether to abolish licensed prostitution. During the emotionally charged debate, opponents of licensed prostitution were pitted against the supporters of the sex workers.[117]

According to Yun Fan, the majority of abolitionists were thirty-five years of age or older. They were mostly middle-class housewives and female professionals with family responsibilities.[118] Consistent with the moralistic arguments of the Taipei Women's Rescue Foundation against juvenile prostitution, the abolitionists argued that the sex industry was a dehumanizing occupation that exploited women's bodies to satisfy men's sexual needs. In order to restore the sex workers' self-respect and human dignity, they argued that licensed prostitution should be abolished. They also advocated for the social welfare bureau of Taipei's municipal government to provide the prostitutes with adequate job training to enable them to change their professions.[119] Comparatively, this line of argument is reminiscent of many Taiwanese colonial intellectuals' call for the abolition of licensed prostitution in the 1920s.

In 1997, the feminist community had achieved a broad consensus in their opposition to legal minors' involvement in sex industries. Yet there was no consensus as to whether prostitution should be legal for women over the age of eighteen who willingly entered the profession. In contrast to most abolitionists' older age profile and puritanical stance, many supporters of licensed prostitution were young feminist activists and students in campus women's studies clubs who supported the sexual liberation ideology.[120]

To dismantle the patriarchal hierarchy of sexual behaviors that legitimized certain sexual acts and stigmatized others, sexual liberationists contended that the social designation of prostitution as a sexual taboo should be eliminated. In their view, if the prostitutes freely choose to use their bodies for earning a living, the government and society have no right to infringe upon their freedom. Rather, society should respect their profession instead of depriving them of their means of subsistence. In the mayoral election of 1998, the licensed prostitutes and their supporters politicized the issue and opposed Mayor Chen Shui-bian's candidacy. The repeated protests of licensed prostitutes elicited the sympathy for their plight among many Taipei residents and became one of the factors that contributed to the victory of Chen's opponent, Ma Ying-jeou. Since the proponents of licensed prostitution backed Ma's candidacy, he introduced a bill to grant a two-year grace period to the sex workers. As a consequence of lobbying by licensed prostitutes and their supporters, the municipal legislature passed the bill granting the grace period. When prostitution became illegal after the grace period had expired, most prostitutes continued working underground.[121] Social scientists who study the sex industry in Taiwan believe it is unlikely to disappear in the near future, as long as the capitalist economy offers lower wages to unskilled female laborers than the incomes they can earn from the sex industry.[122]

On a brighter note, after more than a decade of feminist advocacy and the joint effort of female legislators across all party lines, the Legislative Yuan, in 2005, passed the Sexual Harassment Prevention Act (*Xingsaorao fangzhifa*). It defined actions such as molesting, kissing by force, bribing for sexual services, or intimidating people for sexual purposes in a public place as sexual harassment.[123] The legislation stipulates that every level of the government should establish an arbitration system that can provide an alternative method for victims of sexual harassment to report an incident without having to meet the sex offender in court.[124]

The Alliance of Patriarchy and Capitalism in the Era of Globalization

Marxist feminism became an explicit category of analysis in Taiwan's feminist discourse. In 1988, Awakening feminists analyzed the interlocking relationship between patriarchy and capitalism in the oppression of women workers in Taiwan. According to Ts'ao Ai-lan,[125] women workers were a major bulwark of Taiwan's industrialization in the 1960s and 1970s. Whereas many rural families expected their sons to continue with their education, they encouraged their daughters to take up factory work upon graduation from junior high schools. Not only did most parents value sons over daughters, Taiwanese industries also supported the patriarchal ideology. Prior to passage of the Gender Equality in Employment Act (2001), many factory managers expected women workers to leave their jobs and become full-time homemakers upon the birth of their first child. Consequently, industrialists would not have to grant the women pensions or pay raises based on their seniority. Meanwhile, unpaid housewives raised children to carry on the patriarchal family line and to replenish the workforce of the capitalist economy.[126]

With a constant supply of temporary women workers from the Taiwanese countryside, most industries paid women workers only two-thirds the wages earned by their male counterparts for performing the same tasks. This wage disparity persisted, despite the stipulation of equal pay for equal work in the revised Basic Labor Standard Law of 1990.[127] Just as there is inequality between a higher-paid male worker and a lower-paid female worker, there is also a disparity between a wage-earning husband and an unpaid homemaker within the interlocking system of patriarchy and capitalism. A woman worker's lower economic status vis-à-vis a male worker in the public sector is correlated with the failure of patriarchy and capitalism to acknowledge the economic value of a housewife's labor in the domestic realm.[128]

Since the 1960s, a significant number of workers in Taiwan's labor-intensive light industries have been women. In response to the global recession of 1991, many factory owners transferred their labor-intensive industries to Southeast Asia and mainland China, where labor was cheaper than in Taiwan. Based on patriarchal ideology, the industrialists rationalized their dismissal of women workers on the grounds that a woman's place was in the home. Just as women were socialized to be more obedient than their male family members at home, it was thought that women would transfer the same submissive mentality to the workplace. Because women workers were less likely to assert their demands or organize against management, women workers were recruited in large numbers whenever factory owners were in need of mill hands.[129]

To promote women workers' status, the Production Line of Women Workers' Solidarity (*Nügong tuanjie shengchanxian*)—hereafter referred to as Women Workers' Solidarity—was established in 1991. As a moderate labor organization that sought to reform labor relations within the capitalist economy, its mission was to unite women laborers, improve their working conditions, and enhance their socioeconomic status. As a non-governmental organization consisting of labor activists and left-wing intellectuals, it offered job referrals and free advice to women workers. From the perspective of Women Workers' Solidarity, it is an outdated assumption for the industrialists to dispense with women's labor on the grounds that a woman's place is at home. In contemporary Taiwan, a double income is essential for a working-class household to make ends meet.[130]

In response to the demand of Women Workers' Solidarity and other non-governmental organizations,[131] in 1995 the Council of Labor Affairs[132] appropriated government money to create model childcare facilities at various industrial complexes. A portion of the budget was also allocated to subsidize private and public daycare centers. Half a million working mothers were estimated to be beneficiaries of the government's program. With the provision of these facilities, some working-class women were able to retain their jobs after having children.[133] The Kuomintang government's subsidy of daycare centers was reminiscent of the rural childcare facilities spearheaded by the Taiwan Provincial Women's Association during the 1950s.[134]

During the early 1990s, the Taiwanese government also developed a foreign labor policy to permit temporary guest workers from certain Southeast Asian countries to work in Taiwan's service, manufacturing, and construction sectors. According to Anru Lee's analysis of the relationship between patriarchy and industrial capitalism, male capitalists exploited female foreign workers' marginal status and transient labor in order to maintain low wages. Some small factory owners exploited the labor of their wives, sisters, and daughters to save the costs of hiring additional workers. With the above-mentioned strategies for saving labor costs, male industrial capitalists who opted to keep their factory production in Taiwan rather than outsourcing it abroad could still maximize their capital accumulation.[135]

To advocate reforms on immigration policies and improve the treatment of foreign workers, a coalition of non-governmental labor organizations, human rights associations, and the Awakening Foundation allied with foreign workers to stage a mass rally in December 2005. As a concession to the demands of the demonstrators, the Council of Labor Affairs announced that a guest worker in Taiwan is now permitted to directly negotiate a transfer from his or her former employer to a new employer without having to go through a private labor broker. Also, the government extended a guest worker's maximum duration of stay in Taiwan from six to nine years.[136]

In addition to convincing the government to liberalize its policies toward guest workers, labor activists and feminist advocates in Taiwan have urged the government to reform its naturalization policy. Since the late 1980s, new immigrants in Taiwan are by and large brides of Taiwanese businessmen who had outsourced their factories and business ventures to mainland China. Still other Taiwanese males had been introduced to their brides from Southeast Asia through matchmaking services and marriage brokers.

To a certain extent, Taiwan's naturalization law is modeled after legal precedents in Western countries. It required the applicant to pass health examinations, reside in Taiwan, relinquish his or her original nationality, pass a Chinese-language test, and meet certain financial qualifications, such as showing documented proof of a steady and sufficient monthly income, or meeting the standard of property ownership. Since most of the applicants are women from Southeast Asia, these financial requirements placed an unreasonable financial burden on them. Many had to borrow money to meet the requirement or remained ineligible for citizenship. To expedite the naturalization process for economically disadvantaged women, the coalition of non-governmental organizations and women's groups has proposed that the government eliminate this financial requirement.[137]

The Gender Equality in Employment Act, 2001

As early as 1989, Yu Mei-nü[138] and other lawyers affiliated with the Awakening Foundation completed a draft bill for the equal employment of men and women (*Nannü gongzuo pingdengfa caoan*). In 1990, it was presented to the Legislative Yuan for deliberation.[139] One goal of the draft legislation was to provide a legal blueprint for a welfare policy geared toward the advancement of working women's status. To this end, the legislation stipulated that the central government should provide financial subsidies to local governments to establish and maintain childcare facilities and job training programs for women. Further, the initial bill called for all levels of government to establish agencies to provide job referrals and job training to homemakers who wish to reenter the workforce. In order to ensure proper enforcement, commissions on gender equality at the workplace were to be established in the Executive Yuan and local governments to inspect and monitor cases of gender discrimination in the workplace. In the spirit of gender equality, the law was written to be applicable to gender discrimination against both male and female employees.[140]

In the section of the draft pertaining to the rights of equal employment, the text stated that employers should not discriminate against women in job advertisements, in the process of hiring, or in the employees' job placements and promotions. If a man and a woman have the same skill, responsibility, and seniority, they should receive the same pay for completing the same work. Moreover, the work unit should offer the same benefits, job training, and educational programs to its male and female employees. Finally, the draft legislation stated that there should be no gender disparity in the criteria for job dismissal and retirement. Female employees shall not be pressured to leave their jobs due to marriage, pregnancy, delivery, or motherhood.[141]

Sections of the bill concerning rules and regulations for filing complaints and issuing penalties stated that the employees or job seekers who found employers in violation of the law should present their case to the Commission on Gender Equality. The Commission was vested with the authority to conduct investigations into the employers' misconduct. If the employer was found guilty of misconduct, the employer would have been obliged to pay the employee or the job seeker for any damage incurred. In specific, legally defined instances of misconduct, the employer would also have been obliged to pay a fine.[142]

Due to the strong opposition of Taiwanese industrialists and businesses to the Equal Employment Bill, the Kuomintang-dominated Legislative Yuan postponed its passage . In the 1990s, the Awakening Foundation's draft bill for the equal employment of men and women underwent several revisions. By 1999, the Executive Yuan finalized an alternative draft, the Gender Equality in Employment Bill (*Liangxing gongzuo pingdengfa caoan*). In the Kuomintang government's bid to join the World Trade Organization, the bill was drafted in order to raise Taiwan's labor standard in the eyes of the international community.[143]

The final version of the bill that passed the Legislative Yuan in 2001 stipulates eight weeks of paid maternity leave, like the legal provisions in the ROC Factory Law of 1929.[144] Moreover, a pregnant woman who has a miscarriage is eligible for a maternity leave ranging from five days to four weeks, depending on the duration of pregnancy. Consistent with the spirit of the Awakening Foundation's draft bill, the Act of 2001 stipulates that employers would be fined for providing different benefits to men and women and for violating the principle of equal pay for equal work.[145] The law also stipulates that companies with thirty or more employees will be required to pay a fine for a failure to respond appropriately to complaints of sexual harassment or to set clear guidelines for the companies' policies. The law also requires that companies set clear guidelines for the prevention of sexual harassment, the filing of sexual harassment complaints, and the punishment of employees who violate the rules. In the law, sexual harassment is defined as follows: "Any case in which (when an employee is at work) any person (including a client) uses speech or behavior that amounts to a request for sexual favors, is of a sexual nature, or shows gender discrimination, and does so in such a way as to create an intimidating, or offensive work environment, thereby infringing upon or interfering with the dignity, personal freedom, or work performance of the individual."[146]

In addition to the law's acknowledgment of sexual harassment as an impediment to good job performance, the Gender Equality in Employment Act stipulated that male employees with newborn infants are given two days off. In order to be eligible for a two-year unpaid leave of absence for childcare, the employee must have worked for one year or more in a firm of at least thirty employees. The law also states that a parent is eligible to apply for a leave of absence from work for no more than two years to care for a child three years of age or younger. To lighten the employers' financial burden, the government promises to absorb the cost of a parent's insurance policy during an employee's leave.[147] Lastly, the Act obliges companies with more than 250 employees to establish childcare facilities with the aid of government subsidies.[148]

The passage of the Act is only the first step toward its actual implementation. Based on the provision in the Awakening Foundation's 1989 bill, the Gender Equality in Employment Act states that the Council of Labor Affairs is vested with the authority to establish a Commission on Gender Equality in Employment at both central and local governments. These commissions consist of five to eleven members who serve a two-year term. Each commission includes at least two representatives each from labor and non-governmental women's organizations. Under the leadership of Ch'en Chu, Chairwoman of the Council of Labor Affairs, the Council recommended that at least half of all members on the Commission be women. The Commission would oversee the work units' compliance with the law and investigate cases of gender discrimination in the workplace. On International Women's Day in 2002, the Gender Equality in Employment Act went into effect.[149] As of December 2007, all employees are eligible for a maximum of two years unpaid parental leave to take care of a child three years of age or younger, regardless of the number of employees in the workplace. A week of family leave is now available for employees in workplaces with over five employees. A father of a newborn infant can now have three days of paid leave instead of two.[150]

The Women's Rights Association, Women's Political Participation, and Contested National Identities

As we have seen, the trend toward greater legal protection for women and citizens' greater respect for the rule of law are indicative of Taiwan's emergence as a liberal democracy. In response to the citizens' demands, the Kuomintang government began to appropriate more resources for the study and teaching of Taiwanese languages and history. As a regime dominated by the mainlander minority, Kuomintang-sponsored historiography and pedagogy had emphasized the study and research of Chinese history and the use of Mandarin, the national language of China. To ensure the loyalty of the Taiwanese majority to the Chinese nation, the martial law regime banned the use of Taiwanese languages and dialects in the school system.[151]

According to Chang Yen-hsien, a scholar of Taiwanese history, the research and writing of Taiwanese history went through three phases in the postwar era. From 1945 through 1965, the compilation and editing of Taiwanese historical records were mostly done by intellectuals outside the academy. In order to pass Kuomintang censorship, Taiwanese scholars purposefully left out politically sensitive and taboo subjects such as the discussion of the February 28th massacre in 1947, the White Terror in the 1950s, and the Taiwanese people's aspiration for independence from China. Since universities were by and large mainlander-dominated institutions from 1945 through the late 1970s, scholars tended to interpret Taiwanese history from the perspective of mainland China. For instance, notable scholars such as Fang Hao and Kuo

T'ing-yi attributed Taiwan's modernization in the late nineteenth century to Chinese reformers' administrative and development policies. To them, mainland Chinese culture was the civilizing influence over the island at the periphery. They also regarded Chinese nationalism as the motivating force behind the Taiwanese people's resistance against Dutch colonization in the seventeenth century and Japanese occupation in the early twentieth century. By interpreting Taiwanese history as a local branch of Chinese history in accordance with the Kuomintang's claim that Taiwan is a part of China, the distinctive socio-historical experiences of the Taiwanese seldom appeared in state-censored research monographs and school textbooks.[152]

Consistent with the Kuomintang's interpretation of Taiwan's status vis-à-vis the mainland, historians from the West perceived Taiwan as a mirror image and a microcosm of mainland China. Since Communist China in the 1960s was inaccessible to most China scholars from the West, Taiwan became the only available site for Western scholars to conduct research about China. But as mainland China began to open itself up to the West beginning in 1978, many Western scholars of Chinese studies no longer needed to go to Taiwan to study China. Coupled with the demands of Taiwan's movement for greater democratization and the right to self-determination in the late 1970s, Taiwanese historians both inside and outside academe began to interpret Taiwan's historical development from the perspective of the Taiwanese people's experiences rather than from the Kuomintang's Sino-centric perspective.[153]

With the revocation of martial law in 1987, scholars began to discuss and analyze the historical significance of the previously forbidden political topics. In the post–martial law era, research and teaching of Taiwanese history and language has increased dramatically on college campuses.[154] According to Yun Fan,[155] the establishment of the Taipei Association for the Promotion of Women's Rights in 1994— referred to here as the Women's Rights Association (Nüquanhui)—was indicative of the trend toward Taiwanization. One of the missions of the Women's Rights Association was the preservation of oral histories and historical records of Taiwanese women's experiences.[156]

In opposition to the Kuomintang's vision of Taiwan's eventual unification with the mainland, most members of the Women's Rights Association were supporters of the pro-Taiwan Independence platform of the Democratic Progressive Party (DPP). In contrast to the Awakening feminists' nonpartisan strategy for legislative lobbying, some in the Women's Rights Association campaigned for the DPP during elections in the 1990s. In recognition of their efforts, the political activists were given a voice in the formulation of the DPP's policies toward women.[157]

As early as 1947, the ROC Constitution granted suffrage to Chinese women and stipulated that a certain number of seats in the legislative bodies should be reserved for women. The ROC electoral law guaranteed women candidates ten percent of the seats in the Legislative Yuan. In the late 1940s, the quota was intended to promote women's political representation in the Legislative Yuan. Yet, Taiwanese society in the early 1990s had progressed to the extent that more women were interested in running for political office than the quota stipulated. In order to overcome women's electoral bottleneck, the feminist community recommended that the ten-percent quota be raised to a higher percentage. Most non-governmental women's organizations endorsed this proposal and viewed it as a means to prevent gender discrimination within the political power structure. Feminists saw the measure as a temporary solution to gradually overcome gender inequality in political representation and hoped that the quota system would be abolished after women's political representation reached forty percent in the government.[158]

Concurring with the stance of the feminist majority, P'eng Wan-ju,[159] the Executive Director of the DPP's Women's Department, advocated the inclusion of an amendment to the party bylaws that would set aside at least a quarter of all DPP nominations for female candidates. In the DPP's Party Congress in November 1996, P'eng lobbied for passage of this amendment. A few days after she was seen entering a taxicab outside the hotel where the Party Congress was held, P'eng's body was found in an empty lot. She had been raped and brutally stabbed several times. A day after P'eng's disappearance, the Party Congress passed the amendment guaranteeing women candidates a quarter of all DPP electoral nominations.[160]

After P'eng was murdered, a coalition of non-governmental women's organizations staged a mass rally in all major cities throughout Taiwan to protest sexual assault and the government's ineptness in ensuring women's safety. Consequently, the Legislative Yuan passed the Sexual Assault Treatment and Prevention Act and Penal Code no. 37 on Traffic Regulation. Authored by lawyers in the Modern Women's Foundation, the Sexual Assault Treatment and Prevention Act stipulates that victims of sexual assault have the option of holding the trials behind closed doors. The act also obliges local governments to provide victims of sexual assault with professional psychological and legal counseling. Lastly, it stipulates that the central government must create a database with fingerprints and DNA of all known offenders of sexual assault. Penal Code no. 37 on Traffic Regulation stipulates that taxi drivers with previous records of murder, robbery, and/or sexual assault in police files shall be prohibited from obtaining license plates.[161]

Thus, the tragedy of P'eng's death in 1996 galvanized several policy and legislative reforms. As part of Taiwan's democratization program, the year

1996 also marked the first time that the voters in Taiwan could elect their own president. Four pairs of running mates ran a tight race. Among these, there was only one woman: vice presidential candidate Wang Ch'ing-fung. As a leading feminist activist, Wang dedicated her life to rescuing victims of juvenile prostitution and the sex trade. During meetings for devising the women voters' strategies, several feminist leaders suggested that the feminist community endorse Wang's candidacy to galvanize women voters' support for her.[162]

During one of the meetings, several proponents of Taiwan Independence expressed their reservations about supporting Wang's candidacy. While the feminists did not object to Wang herself, they did not support her presidential running mate, Ch'en Li-an. Running as a nonpartisan independent, Ch'en was nonetheless a mainlander who envisioned Taiwan's eventual unification with mainland China. An emotionally charged debate ensued. While some feminists insisted that women vote for the Ch'en-Wang pair to demonstrate women's solidarity, others insisted that crucial political issues, such as voters' national identity, should be taken into serious consideration before women cast their votes. During the 1996 election, the controversy over the different priorities remained unresolved.[163] With 76 percent of Taiwan's eligible voters casting their votes, the Ch'en-Wang pair carried only 10 percent of the popular vote, the lowest among the four pairs.[164]

In contrast to the lack of consensus among feminists in 1996, most feminists in the presidential election of 2000 supported the DPP's choice of Lu Hsiu-lien as the vice presidential running mate of Chen Shui-bian, the former mayor of Taipei. The feminist community's support for Lu could be attributed to her stature as the pioneer feminist of postwar Taiwan and the DPP's concurrence with feminists' demand to fill a quarter of all top cabinet posts with women. With the DPP's victory in the election of 2000, Lu became Taiwan's first woman vice president.[165]

In line with the DPP's campaign promise, President Chen filled several top cabinet posts with women from political and academic communities. Virtually all female appointees to the DPP government's cabinet posts were highly qualified individuals who had either previous political experiences or educational backgrounds to fit their job descriptions.[166] Subsequently, the Kuomintang also enacted a new policy that guaranteed women a least a quarter of the party's nominations during electoral campaigns for seats in the Legislative Yuan.[167]

After the early 1970s, the mainlander-dominated Kuomintang's recruitment of Taiwanese into the upper echelons of officialdom eased ethnic tensions and enhanced peaceful coexistence between the mainlanders and the

Taiwanese. Yet, as Taiwan democratized in the 1990s, tensions along the lines of ethnic and national identities reemerged from beneath the surface during every presidential election.[168] Inasmuch as Taiwan's national question remained unresolved, many voters felt the necessity to scrutinize the national identity of every presidential and vice presidential candidate. Just as a minority of mainlanders supported Taiwan Independence, some Taiwanese support the island's eventual unification with mainland China. Nonetheless, generally, most mainlanders in Taiwan would prefer the island's unification with a democratic China in the future. Conversely, most Taiwanese consider Taiwan a de facto independent state. Hence, it is conceivable that some pro-unification feminists chose not to vote for Lu Hsiu-lien due to her Taiwanese background and pro-independence stance. As a proponent of Taiwan Independence, Lu claims that Taiwan is already a sovereign state. Any change in the political status of Taiwan vis-à-vis the mainland should have the consent of the majority of Taiwan's residents.[169]

In 2001, the DPP administration invited Lee Yuan-chen and Yu Mei-nü from the Awakening Foundation and several women from other sectors of the civil society to join the Council for the Promotion of Women's Rights (*Funü quanyi cujin weiyuanhui*). As an advisory task force under the Executive Yuan, its members consist of representatives from non-governmental women's organizations, experts and scholars of women's issues, and officials from various ministries in the executive branch of the central government. As part-time volunteers who represent women's interests in civil society, these non-governmental representatives and scholars met with government officials every three or four months to assess women's needs, promote communication between civil society and the government, formulate pro-women policies, and monitor the state's implementation of these policies.[170]

In response to the Council's insufficient budget and its ineffectiveness in implementing gender-related policies, in 2003 the Awakening Foundation and 10 other women's NGOs demanded that the government establish the Commission on Gender Equality (*Liangxing pingdeng weiyuanhui*). Based on the concept of *gender mainstreaming* (*xingbie zhuliuhua*) advocated by the United Nations Commission on the Status of Women, the Awakening Foundation lobbied the Taiwanese government and all major political parties to hasten the creation of the commission. Unlike the advisory capacity of part-time volunteers in the Council for the Promotion of Women's Rights, the Commission on Gender Equality will be a cabinet within the Executive Yuan with a budget and a full-time paid staff with expertise on women's issues to formulate gender-related policies and monitor different branches of the government in their progress on implementing gender equity policies.

The policy of gender mainstreaming also mandated that at least a third of all elected and appointed officials of every governmental agency should be women. Annually, women's groups committed to the stated goals and principles of the UN Commission on the Status of Women would gather in New York to update each other about the progress made in each country and exchange ideas for further improvement. Although Taiwan has not been a member of the United Nations since 1971, the Awakening Foundation, as an NGO, has sent representatives to attend the UN Commission on the Status of Women in New York.[171]

Conclusion

In retrospect, there were ample instances of continuity between the strategies of feminist activists under the martial-law regime and in the post–martial law era. Similar to Lu Hsiu-lien's earlier vision of cooperative home economics, Lee Yuan-chen demanded that social studies textbooks emphasize the sharing of housework by male and female members of a family.[172] Like the social services provided by Lu Hsiu-lien's hotline in the 1970s,[173] the Taipei Women's Rescue Foundation and the Warm Life Association provided free legal and psychological counseling to women in the post–martial law period. In both the 1970s and 1980s, the autonomous women's movement was essentially an elite-sustained movement whose mission was to educate the public about the need for women's self-development and for greater gender equality. As a women's movement without government sponsorship, the feminists of postwar Taiwan sustained their publications and activities primarily with volunteer work and private donations.[174]

While continuities in movement strategy from the authoritarian period to the post–martial law era existed, new strategies and feminist discourses also emerged in the context of Taiwan's democratization. In 1987, the rally against juvenile prostitution and the sex trade marked the first public demonstration on behalf of women and girls in postwar Taiwan.[175] With more sociopolitical space in which to express their views, feminists in the post–martial law era were less compromising with Confucian-oriented gender roles than Lu Hsiu-lien had been during the 1970s. Awakening feminists were explicitly critical of gender bias and authoritarian tendencies in the Kuomintang's national education system.[176]

In the post–martial law era, legislative lobbying became an essential component of feminist strategy. This was in direct contrast to the absence of legislative lobbying in their strategies during the 1970s. Feminist lawyers also contributed to the authorship of draft amendments to family laws, the

Domestic Violence Prevention Bill, the Sexual Assault Treatment and Prevention Bill, and the Gender Equality in Employment Bill.[177] Feminist activists toured the island to familiarize the Taiwanese public with the bills, gathered signatures for petitions, and lobbied in the Legislative Yuan.[178] In the Gender Equality in Employment Act of 2001, the visions of the autonomous women's movements in the 1920s, 1970s, and 1980s for socialized childcare, maternity leaves, and equal opportunities in the workforce became legal provisions.

The easing of the Kuomintang's anti-communist campaign created a political environment that enabled the emergence of left-wing labor organizations such as Women Workers' Solidarity. Likewise, Marxist feminism became a category of analysis in Taiwan's feminist discourse. The feminists who used Marxist feminism to analyze the causes of oppression of women workers attributed it to the mutually reinforcing relationship between patriarchy and capitalism.[179]

By comparison, the concept of *woman-identified woman* in lesbian feminism critiqued the interlocking relationship between patriarchy and heterosexism.[180] In the post–martial law era, a young generation of feminists lifted their self-censorship and incorporated this concept and other themes associated with sexual liberation into their feminist discourse.[181] In contrast to the authoritarian regime's refusal to grant a copyright to Lu Hsiu-lien in 1976 for *New Feminism* on the grounds that the book promoted sexual promiscuity, the nascent democracy enabled Ho Ch'un-jui's perspective on women's sexual freedom to play a major part in Taiwan's feminist discourse in 1994 and thereafter.[182]

Conclusion

As we have seen, Taiwan's democratization in the post–martial law period facilitated the diversification of feminist discourses and non-governmental women's organizations. The revision of family laws and the enactment of the Gender Equality in Employment Law also significantly enhanced women's rights and status. To a large extent, these changes fulfilled the autonomous women's movements' goals for gender equality. Due to the long history of authoritarian political culture in twentieth-century Taiwan, it was not until the post–martial law era that the government began to meet the feminist activists' demands. The rise of Japanese militarism and ultra-nationalism in the early 1930s, the Kuomintang's suppression of Taiwanese intellectuals during the February 28th massacre in 1947, and the White Terror in the 1950s and 1960s all contributed to a highly repressive political climate in Taiwan that was not conducive to the reemergence of an autonomous women's movement.

With the decline of the autonomous movement in the early 1930s, government-affiliated women's organizations continued to flourish under the auspices of the Japanese colonial government until Japan's military defeat in 1945.[1] In postwar Taiwan, the Chinese Women's Anti-Aggression League affiliated with the Kuomintang had many goals similar to those of the Patriotic Women's Association under the patronage of the Japanese colonial government.[2] Both government-affiliated women's organizations offered seminars for the improvement of Taiwanese women's fluency in national languages. During the colonial era, the national language of Taiwan was Japanese. It was switched to Mandarin Chinese in 1945.[3]

Both government-affiliated organizations were the institutional instruments of their respective governments for mobilizing women in their war efforts.[4] Whereas the Patriotic Women's Association served Japanese nationalism and Japan's war effort in the colonial period, the Chinese Women's Anti-Aggression League mobilized women to serve the Kuomintang's anti-communist campaign and Chinese nationalism in 1950 and thereafter. Members of both women's organizations offered moral support to troops on military bases. They also raised funds for disabled soldiers and families of the war dead.[5]

In philanthropy, both the Patriotic Women's Association and the Chinese Women's Anti-Aggression League raised funds and provided relief services for victims of natural disasters. To foster traditional wifely virtues and motherhood, the government-affiliated women's organizations in both periods provided training programs in homemaking and childcare. To integrate married women's roles as both homemakers and productive workers, each organization offered seminars on handicraft skills and emphasized women's positions as earners of their families' supplementary incomes in cottage industries.[6]

In both the Japanese colonial era and the postwar Kuomintang period, the farmers' associations in rural Taiwan also offered similar training for rural women. As an institution that originated in the Japanese colonial era, the farmers' association was a government-affiliated organization in each village and county. While Taiwan was under Japanese colonial rule, in mainland China Madame Chiang organized upper- and middle-class women to educate rural women about domestic sciences and ways to improve their hygiene and literacy in the New Life movement.[7]

In 1955, the Kuomintang government in Taiwan assigned the responsibility of implementing this rural educational program to the farmers' associations in various localities. The Kuomintang not only ordered the farmers' associations to train home economics teachers for instructing rural women, they were also obliged to contribute money for the program's implementation. The vast majority of instructors were female high school graduates who underwent training in household management. Similar to the training programs of the New Life movement in the 1930s, the home economics instructors of the farmers' associations in postwar Taiwan taught rural women the skills that conformed to traditional women's domestic responsibilities. These included methods of keeping food and dwellings clean, making home improvements, taking care of personal hygiene, and managing household budgets.[8]

In many ways, the rural women's educational program in postwar Taiwan was a continuation of Madame Chiang's endeavor in the New Life movement. As a regime from mainland China, the Kuomintang government utilized rural institutions established during the Japanese colonial period to launch rural women's educational programs. While both the Japanese colonial government and the Kuomintang supported young single women's temporary roles as full-time workers in factories and service industries, both governments expected married women to return home and contribute to Taiwan's economic development in cottage industries. Through ideological indoctrination in educational programs, both regimes reinforced married women's roles as household managers, good mothers and wives, and family educators of children who would become productive citizens of their respective nations.[9]

The Kuomintang-affiliated Taiwan Provincial Women's Association also created seasonal childcare facilities to alleviate rural women's double burden in the postwar era. In the 1920s and early 1930s, the Taiwan Communist Party and the left-wing Taiwan Farmers' Union integrated the creation of rural childcare facilities into their women's policies. Despite the collapse of both autonomous organizations in the 1930s, some women's rights activists in the Taiwan Farmers' Union later joined the Taiwan Provincial Women's Association. Thus, the women activists of the autonomous social movement in the Japanese colonial era implemented their rural childcare program in the Kuomintang-affiliated Taiwan Provincial Women's Association during the postwar period.[10]

During the Japanese colonial era and postwar Taiwan, the ample human and financial resources of the government-affiliated organizations enabled them to establish local chapters in every city and town on the island.[11] In contrast, the autonomous women's movements in both periods faced a shortage of funds as well as infiltration by government informants. In the 1920s, the establishment of moderate non-governmental associations was possible with police permission. Once permission was granted, the associations were under the surveillance and speech censorship of the colonial police. The ascendancy of the radical left in the Taiwan Cultural Association and the Taiwan Farmers' Union in 1927 and the Tokyo government's campaign to arrest suspected communists beginning in 1929 precipitated the disintegration of both non-governmental associations and their respective women's movements.[12]

In postwar Taiwan, the martial law regime's imposition of the wartime Civic Bodies Organization Law made it virtually impossible for the autonomous women's movement to establish a non-governmental organization. To circumvent the Kuomintang's proscription of the freedom of association, the creation of publishing houses became a common organizational strategy for the movement.[13] With the revocation of the Civic Bodies Organization Law in 1986 and the lifting of martial law in 1987, the Awakening Publishing House was converted into a foundation—a non-governmental civic organization. In order to enable the transformation of the autonomous women's movement from an elite-sustained organization to a mass-based movement, the Awakening Associations in various cities were established beginning in 1994. Unlike the elite-sustained organizational model that centered foundation resources and decision making in Taipei, the Awakening Associations launched mass membership drives in their respective localities.[14]

Following the Chinese cultural-intellectual approach, women's rights activists in both the 1920s and the post–1972 era assumed that the transformation of people's cultural values and belief systems were prerequisites for other social changes. As such, activists made speeches in various cities to disseminate feminist ideas among the masses. They hoped that their writings and speeches would transform the male-centered beliefs of the Taiwanese populace. In both the 1920s and postwar Taiwan, liberal feminists contended that laws and policies were formulated from a strictly male perspective. In order to give women a voice in the political process, social and political activists in the 1920s advocated the establishment of the Taiwan Parliament, universal suffrage, and political participation of all men and women in colonial Taiwan.[15] In the postwar era, the ROC Constitution of 1947 granted women the right to vote. In postwar Taiwan, feminists urged women to vote and run for political office.

Starting in the 1970s, moderate liberal feminists sought to revise gender-biased family laws and penal codes within the ROC's existing legal framework. The passage of the abortion bill in 1984 marked the first time that feminist activists were able to gather signatures and petition in the Legislative Yuan.[16] As a result of this success, liberal feminists began drafting other legislation pertaining to women and utilized legislative lobbying and petition drives as strategies to accomplish their goals. With the revocation of martial law in 1987, the freedom to organize and stage public demonstrations also created new means for feminist activists to express their collective voice.[17]

In the 1970s and 1980s, Taiwan's autonomous women's movement was institutionally independent of the labor and democracy movements. Most feminists neither supported nor opposed the authoritarian regime. Under martial law, the feminists' political neutrality was a strategy for minimizing the government's interference with their activities and for ensuring the support of apolitical middle-class women in urban Taiwan.[18] Its institutional independence from other social and political movements in postwar Taiwan enabled it to prioritize issues pertaining to women over labor and other political issues.

Conversely, in colonial Taiwan the autonomous women's movement was an integral part of the island's anti-colonial and labor movements. Both the revolutionary left wing and the moderate reformist wing of Taiwan's labor and anti-colonial movements formulated policies for advancing women's status. Activists in the women's movement protested against Japanese capitalists' exploitation of Taiwanese peasants and workers and the second-class citizenship of the Taiwanese in the Japanese Empire.[19] In colonial Taiwan, the most notable examples of female leadership were Yeh T'ao of the Taiwan Farmers' Union and Hsieh Hsueh-hung of the Taiwan Communist Party.[20] In the 1920s, women activists in left-wing movements were inspired by the agendas of the Women's Department of the Russian Communist Party. Like their Soviet counterparts, women activists in the Taiwanese left-wing organizations advocated women workers' rights to obtain paid maternity leaves and freedom and equality to participate in waged labor and politics.[21] From the mid-1920s through the early 1930s, Taiwanese left-wing radicals actively supported strikers by offering advice on collective bargaining and on strategies for staging strikes.[22]

In contrast to the left-wing orientation of many women's liberation advocates in the 1920s, virtually all the left-wing activists during the postwar martial law period were imprisoned or silenced as a consequence of the Kuomintang's anti-communist campaign. Between 1950 and 1965, the primary functions of the Kuomintang-controlled labor unions included the implementation of the party-state's labor policies, the surveillance of workers' activities, and the prevention of Chinese Communist infiltration and ideological influence.[23] In this anti-communist political climate, virtually no autonomous left-wing organization independent of Kuomintang control emerged until the mid-1980s.[24] Because strikes were forbidden under martial law, feminist activists in the 1970s and early 1980s did not take a critical stand against the capitalist establishment to the same extent as their counterparts in the 1920s. In the 1970s, Lo Yeh-ch'in[25] was a writer on labor relations for the feminist Pioneer Press. Instead of urging women workers to take a confrontational stand against management, Lo merely advocated the cooperation of labor unions, the Kuomintang government, and capitalists to improve working conditions, social benefits, and wages for female workers.[26]

Beginning in the 1970s, Simone de Beauvoir's *The Second Sex* exerted significant influence on Taiwanese feminist discourse.[27] Yet, virtually no feminist in postwar Taiwan concurred with de Beauvoir's contention that a radical transformation from a capitalist socioeconomic structure to a socialist society was a necessary prerequisite for gender equality. Instead, both Hsiu-lien Annette Lu and Lee Yuan-chen opted for the creation of a welfare state through the enactment of legislation for paid maternity leaves and socialized childcare to facilitate working mothers' full participation in the capitalist economy.[28] Under the martial law regime, Lu never referred to the professionalization of childcare in the public domain as socialism. Mindful of the authoritarian regime's anti-leftist stance, she used the politically neutral phrase *cooperative home economics* to designate the idea.[29]

A year after the lifting of martial law, several Awakening feminists adopted Marxist feminism for their analysis of gender inequality in paid work and women's unpaid domestic labor. They also began to side with organized labor and to echo colonial Taiwanese activists' critique of industrial capitalism and patriarchy as the twin sources of women workers' oppression.[30] Starting in 1991, Women Workers' Solidarity sought to reform labor relations within the capitalist economy. It gave counsel to women strikers and offered strategies for collective bargaining.[31] This moderate reformist strategy resembled the Taiwan Populist Party's approach to reforming labor relations within the capitalist economy of colonial Taiwan.[32]

Just as Marxism reemerged as an explicit category of analysis in feminist discourse of the post–martial law era, Taiwan's national question once again became a contested issue. In 1994, the Taipei Women's Rights Association became the first feminist organization in postwar Taiwan to explicitly declare the mission of preserving Taiwanese women's historical experiences. In contrast to *Awakening*'s nonpartisan strategy for legislative lobbying, most members of the Women's Rights Association were supporters of the Democratic Progressive Party's pro-Taiwan independence platform. As such, they affirmed Taiwan's de facto independent status as a nation-state and opposed the Kuomintang's One China policy. This Taiwan-centered feminist perspective was in stark contrast to the silence of the autonomous women's movement on the question of Taiwanese national identity under the martial law regime.[33] In the context of the Kuomintang's anti-communist agenda in the 1970s, Hsiu-lien Annette Lu was the only feminist who openly advocated Taiwanese self-determination and peaceful coexistence between the two ethnic Chinese states.

Despite Lu's struggle against the Kuomintang's ideological hegemony, her narrative of Chinese women's history in *New Feminism* was strongly influenced by the Kuomintang's historical interpretation. Under the state censorship of the martial law regime, Lu's *New Feminism* did not take into account the Chinese Communists' contribution to the discourse on gender equality during the New Culture movement (1915–23) and the First United Front (1923–27) in mainland China or the Taiwanese women's movement under Japanese colonial rule. These omissions attested to the powerful impact of Kuomintang historiography in shaping Lu's historical narrative in the 1970s.

In the election of 1996, a controversy arose in the feminist community over whether women's solidarity should take precedence over women's national identities.[34] Nonetheless, there was a general consensus in Taiwan that the island's national question vis-à-vis mainland China should be resolved through peaceful means. Comparatively, colonial Taiwan's social and political activists were divided over whether to pursue independence through radical militant means or to seek the island's cultural and political autonomy through moderate reformist means within the legal framework of imperial Japan's Meiji Constitution.[35]

In colonial Taiwan and in the postwar period, liberal feminists such as Huang P'u-chun and Lee Yuan-chen considered gender-specific personalities and behavioral patterns to be consequences of social conditioning rather than as biologically predetermined qualities. They were committed to the notion that both men and women shared a common humanity and were thus more alike than different.[36] In both periods, liberal feminists defined feminism as a modern and rational ideology that sought to awaken women's gender consciousness and advocate women's freedom for pursuing self-development and economic independence. Both Huang and Lee contended that women's economic independence would enhance their autonomy and status in the family and would fulfill their social obligations to contribute to Taiwan's socioeconomic progress.

Young women have made great strides in the attainment of higher education and in workforce participation as a result of liberal feminists' advocacy and the new opportunities created during and after the 1970s. In 1971, women accounted for 36.9 percent of students who passed the college entrance examination, 31.5 percent of the Taiwanese workforce, 34.8 percent of professionals and technical specialists, and 8.9 percent of managers and administrators.[37] In 1970, the fertility rate was four children per woman. As Taiwan makes its transition to a post-industrial society in the twenty-first century, the fertility rate has dropped to 1.3 children per woman in 2002. In the same year, women comprised 49.1 percent of college students, 41.3 percent of the Taiwanese workforce, 43.6 percent of professionals and technical specialists, 14.6 percent of managers and administrators, and 22.2 percent of candidates who won electoral seats in Taiwan's Legislative Yuan.[38] As more women became well educated and self-reliant, a sizable minority of Taiwanese women and men chose to remain single. A new term, *single nobility (dansheng guizu)*, was coined to denote middle-class single people's high standard of living and freedom from familial responsibilities.

Whereas liberal feminism enhanced women's status in the public domain, the Confucian family-centered ideology in Taiwanese society created the context for relational feminists in the 1920s and the post–1972 period to conceptualize women's roles as managers of household affairs and educators of children in the family.[39] Relational feminism posited egalitarian relationships in the family and society without eliminating gender-role differentiation in the domestic realm.[40] In postwar Taiwan, Annette Lu's Confucian-oriented educational experience contributed to the relational strand evident in *New Feminism*. Imbued with the Confucian notion of the rectification of names, Lu urged mothers, wives, and daughters to fulfill the specific obligations attached to the gender roles they were socially expected to play. She posited that the function of parenting could only be properly fulfilled within the marital context.[41] In contrast, Lee Yuan-chen, in the post–martial law era, suggested that motherhood should be a legitimate option for single women.[42]

In the early 1980s, Lee Yuan-chen incorporated American theorist Jean Baker Miller's woman-centered perspective into her feminist thought. Lee suggested that everyone could benefit if men adopted non-violent and cooperative behavior more typical of women. Thus, the male-dominated culture's emphases on competition and power struggle in an authoritarian and hierarchical environment would be replaced by a more cooperative and egalitarian culture.[43] Lee's vision of influencing the dominant male-oriented culture with women's culture influenced Annette Lu, who, as the Vice President of Taiwan from 2000 through 2008, applied the ethos of women's culture to international relations. In the new global village, Lu posited that the ethos of non-violence, peaceful coexistence, and cooperation for mutual benefit between nations should replace the traditional ethos of power struggle and military dominance of one nation over another.[44]

As public opinion on various issues became more diverse and contentious after the lifting of martial law, feminist discourse in Taiwan also became more pluralistic. Activists in the Homemakers' Union for Environmental Protection spoke out against industrial pollution and advocated public policies to promote recycling and ecological balance.[45] As a partial solution to environmentalists' demands for air and water safe from the hazards of industrial pollution, Taiwanese labor-intensive industries began to outsource their factory production to mainland China and Southeast Asia in the late 1980s. Consequently, they reduced Taiwan's industrial pollution and also took advantage of cheaper labor in these less industrialized economies.[46]

According to Janet Salaff, the manufacturing sector in Taiwan has experienced a labor shortage since the mid-1970s. As more young single women obtained higher education, they preferred white-collar jobs in the professional and service sectors rather than blue-collar factory work. Ever since Taiwan's transformation into a newly industrialized society in the 1980s, more young Taiwanese women have been employed in white-collar occupations than in blue-collar jobs. Since the mid-1980s, married women of the middle-aged cohort have been recruited in large numbers to work in the manufacturing sector. Because most middle-aged female workers were not as well educated as the younger cohort, the former had few occupational options but to participate in blue-collar factory jobs.[47]

Since the Taiwanese government's legalization of foreign labor in the early 1990s, many middle-aged Taiwanese women workers have toiled in factories alongside guest workers from Southeast Asia. According to Anru Lee's analysis of the mutually reinforcing relationship between patriarchy and industrial capitalism, male capitalists exploited female foreign workers' marginal status and transient labor in order to maintain the low wages of Taiwan's female-dominated electronic and textile industries. With this strategy for saving on labor costs, male industrial capitalists who opted to keep their factory production in Taiwan rather than outsourcing it abroad could still maximize their capital accumulation.[48]

Whereas some foreign workers were employed in the manufacturing sector, others worked as housekeepers and caretakers of small children and the elderly in middle-class families. Due to the Confucian family-centered ideology, most Taiwanese families chose to take care of their ailing parents at home rather than sending them to nursing homes. Prior to the introduction of foreign labor, most families expected married women to bear the primary responsibility for housework, child rearing, and care for elderly parents-in-law. After the introduction of foreign labor from Southeast Asia, many middle-class families hired foreign maids to perform these tasks. This domestic help alleviated the burden on middle-class women and enabled them to focus on their careers or enjoy more leisure. Thus, within the broader context of the global capitalist system, we can see the interlocking relationships between inequalities along the lines of national origin, gender, and class in Taiwanese society.[49]

Whereas Marxist feminism analyzed the mutually reinforcing relationship between industrial capitalism and Confucian patriarchy in contemporary Taiwanese society, the concept of woman-identified woman and other ideas associated with lesbian feminism critiqued the connections between patriarchy and heterosexism. In the post–martial law era, these ideas have emerged from the margins of Taiwanese social discourse to become major strands of radical feminist discourse.[50] In contrast to relational feminism's conception of a heterosexual couple as the basic unit of society, lesbian feminism validated the primacy of emotional and erotic bonds between female partners.[51]

After 1994, the nascent democratic society enabled Josephine Ho's perspective on sexual liberation to permeate Taiwan's feminist discourse.[52] In *The Gallant Woman*, Ho advocated women's sexual self-determination and autonomy. In a sense, Ho's vision of a pluralistic society that respects women's diverse sexual preferences and practices was a logical extension of Lee Yuan-chen's liberal democratic vision of a socially tolerant society that respects an individual's rights and freedom to determine his or her life.[53]

During the latter half of the 1990s, there was an ideological rift between liberal feminists and their radical counterparts in *Awakening*.[54] The difference in the perspectives of liberal and radical feminists was evident in the controversy over licensed prostitution. While most radical feminists advocated prostitutes' right to work in their profession, most liberal and relational feminists considered prostitution male exploitation of women's bodies.[55] These differences notwithstanding, they were united in their commitment to women's participation in political leadership.

With the DPP's victory in the presidential election of 2000, the opposition party replaced the Kuomintang as the ruling party for the first time in fifty years. As the DPP's vice presidential candidate, Hsiu-lien Annette Lu, the postwar pioneer feminist and democracy leader, was elected Taiwan's first female vice president.[56] This breakthrough set a precedent for future administrations.

Notes

Introduction

1. Taiwan is approximately one hundred miles off the coast of mainland China.

2. Lee Yuan-chen, "Feminist Movement," 109–15.

3. The Kuomintang regime of the Republic of China (ROC) on Taiwan established the Taiwan Council for Documents and Records (*Taiwansheng wenxian weiyuanhui*) in 1949 to compile historical documents on the first Sino-Japanese War (1894–95), the cession of Taiwan to Japan, the Japanese occupation of Taiwan (1895–1945), the military defeat and surrender of Japan to the Kuomintang government in 1945, and the retrocession of Taiwan to the ROC government in 1945. The Council also compiled and translated Japanese-language court proceedings of Taiwanese martyrs who resisted Japanese colonial rule and commissioned new publications, including chronicles of major events and historical sketches of armed resistance of the Taiwanese under Japanese occupation. From the perspective of Chinese nationalism, the Council's historical sketches depicted Taiwanese anti-colonial resistance (1895–1945) as the same nationalistic struggle as the anti-Japanese resistance during the second Sino-Japanese war on mainland China (1937–45). Although sections of *Taiwan's General Historical Records* (*Taiwansheng tongzhi*), compiled and edited by the Council, acknowledged the contributions of the Japanese colonial government in building infrastructure and promoting vocational skills and functional literacy in Japanese among the Taiwanese, the historical narrative was critical of the colonial government's attempts to destroy Chinese culture and exploit the natural and human resources of colonial Taiwan to serve Japanese imperialism. The Kuomintang's historical narrative did not acknowledge the Taiwanese people's ambivalence about their Chinese identity vis-à-vis mainland China in the twentieth century. The Council compiled and translated the Japanese colonial government's policy documents and colonial laws to serve as references for the Kuomintang's governance of post-1945 Taiwan. Lastly, the Council compiled local gazettes and genealogies of notable families in order to record histories of various localities in Taiwan, and collected and edited biographies of notable Taiwanese

in the twentieth century. See Wang, Shih-ch'ing, *Taiwan yanjiu*, 1–185; Li, Ju-he, *Taiwan wenjiao*, 52–54, 160–71; and Ch'en, Tse, ed., *Taiwan qianqi*, 1–3.

4. See Yang, Ts'ui, *Riju shidai*.

5. Yu, Chien-ming, "Taiwan diqu de fuyun," 548–49.

6. I use the term "hard authoritarianism" to designate the highly repressive political culture in certain periods of Taiwanese history in which the government suppressed virtually all autonomous voices critical of the government. In contrast, the term "soft authoritarianism" characterizes the periods of Taiwanese history in which the government loosened its control to permit social and political dissent within the limited purview set by the authoritarian government. The terms "soft authoritarianism" and "hard authoritarianism" are used by C. L. Chiou to characterize the two types of authoritarianism in different periods of postwar Taiwan. In this book, I use the two terms to differentiate the two types of authoritarianism in both the Japanese colonial period and the postwar era. See Chiou, " National Affairs Conference," 18–21.

7. Yu, Chien-ming, "Taiwan diqu de fuyun," 549; and Yang, Ts'ui, *Riju shidai*, 602.

8. From 1895 to 1919, military governors-general ruled Taiwan. Chen, Edward I-te, "Formosan Political Movements," 481.

9. Yang, Ts'ui, *Riju shidai*, 138, 217.

10. Yu, Chien-ming, "Taiwan diqu de fuyun," 548–49.

11. Yang, Ts'ui, *Riju shidai*, 602.

12. For examples of the programs and activities of the government-affiliated women's organizations in colonial Taiwan, see Yu, Chien-ming, "Taiwan diqu de fuyun," 423–33.

13. Ibid., 435–67.

14. See Diamond, Norma, "Women under Kuomintang," 3–45.

15. Roy, *Taiwan*, 153–54.

16. Ku, Yen-lin, "Selling Feminist Agenda," 427n.

17. Hinsch, "Metaphysics and Reality," 591–98.

18. Mann, "Women in East Asia," 63–65.

19. Ibid., 67–72.

20. Ibid.

21. Classical Confucianism originated in the later Zhou dynasty (770–221 B.C.E.).

22. Hinsch, "Metaphysics and Reality," 591–98.

23. Mann, "Women in East Asia," 71–72.

24. Ibid., 56–57, 73–76.

25. Ibid., 83–85.

26. Tsurumi, *Japanese Colonial Education*, 18–28, 123–24; and Yang, Ts'ui, *Riju shidai*, 137–55, 594.

27. For Chinese terms of various strands of feminism, see Fang, "Nüxing zhuyi," 6–7.

28. Ku, Yen-lin, "Feminist Movement," 13–14, 14n.

29. Lu, Hsiu-lien, *Xinnüxing zhuyi*, 149.

30. Offen, "Defining Feminism," 143.

31. Cheng, Shu-ju Ada, "Contemporary Autonomous Women's Movement," 13–14.

32. Offen, "Defining Feminism," 146.

33. Ibid., 136–39,153; and Lu, Hwei-syin, "Transcribing Feminism," 239–40.

34. Lu, Hwei-syin, "Transcribing Feminism," 239–41.

35. Offen, "Defining Feminism," 140–51.

36. Lee, Bernice, "Women and Law," 36–37.

37. Lu, Hwei-syin, "Transcribing Feminism," 224–25.

38. Ibid., 233–37.

39. Lee, Yuan-chen, interview, 1 July 1998.

40. The industrialized and democratic societies of northeast Asia include Japan, South Korea, and Taiwan.

41. See Smith, *Global Feminisms*, 7.

42. This Chinese term was coined by Yu Chien-ming. See Yu, "Taiwan diqu de fuyun," 548.

43. There were two major types of interest groups in Taiwan during the 1960s and 1970s. The first type consisted of trade associations, such as farmers' associations, labor unions, professional associations, and commercial and industrial associations that had accumulated substantial financial and human resources and were thus brought under the Kuomintang party-state's direct control. The party cells imposed financial supervision and leadership selection on these organizations. Due to these government-affiliated organizations' political orientation, they served as transmission belts to carry out the party-state's policies and mobilize their members for supporting the Kuomintang candidates during election campaigns. In contrast to this first type of interest group, a second type of interest group in Taiwanese civil society was by and large organized along the lines of culture, academics, social services, athletics, and religious affiliation. Unlike the mass membership and ample resources of the first type of interest group, the second type of interest groups were limited in financial and human resources and were nonpolitical in their relationship with the Kuomintang. Beginning in the 1970s, the Kuomintang tended to give the second type of interest group a higher degree of institutional and financial autonomy than the first type. See Tien, *Great Transition*, 45–63. Based on Tien Hung-mao's definition of the two categories of interest groups in postwar Taiwan, this study contends that the government-affiliated women's organizations belonged to the first type, whereas the autonomous women's movement in the 1970s and thereafter belonged to the second type of interest group organized to represent women's interests rather than to carry out the government's directives.

44. Yu Chien-ming, "Taiwan diqu de fuyun," 403–6.

45. Yang, Ts'ui, *Riju shidai*, 602–3.

46. Yu, Chien-ming, "Taiwan diqu de fuyun," 548–49; and Cheng, Shu-ju Ada, "Autonomous Women's Movement," 1–2, 15–17.

47. Yang, Ts'ui, *Riju shidai*, 137–55.

48. Lu, Hsin-yi, "Imagining New Women," 79–81.

49. Yang, Ts'ui, *Riju shidai*, 599; and Yu, Chien-ming, "Taiwan diqu de fuyun," 549.

50. Yu, Chien-ming, "Taiwan diqu de fuyun," 549.

51. See Ku, Yen-lin, "Feminist Movement."

52. Ku, Yen-lin, "Selling Feminist Agenda," 423–27.

53. See the introductory chapter of Rupp and Taylor, *Survival in Doldrums;* and Fan, "From Politics without Parties," 16–17, 23.

54. Most women activists obtained their professional and academic training in colonial Taiwan, China, or Japan. Tsurumi, *Japanese Colonial Education*, 148, 209–11.

55. Ku, Yen-lin, "Feminist Movement," 15.

56. Freeman, Jo, *Women's Liberation,* 44.

57. Fan, "From Politics without Parties," 33. For similar content of Fan's paper, see Fan, "Activists in a Changing Political Environment," 122–66.

58. Wang, Tsai-wei, "Feminism and Formation," 84–86, 135.

59. Lu, Hsin-yi, "Imagining New Women," 81–83.

60. Yang, Ts'ui, *Riju shidai,* 58–60.

61. See Chiang, May-ling Soong, *Jiang furen yanlunji.*

62. Chu, Ming, *Tamen de xuehan,* 20.

63. See Tang, Wen-hui Anna, "Explaining Social Policy."

64. Chien, Ying-ying, "From Utopian," 36.

65. Cheng, "Autonomous Women's Movement," 93–94.

66. Lee, Yuan-chen, interview, 1 July 1998.

67. Lu, Hwei-syin, "Transcribing Feminism," 239–41.

68. Fan, "From Politics without Parties," 36.

Chapter 1: Feminist Discourses and Women's Movements under Japanese Colonial Rule, 1895–1945

1. Yang, Ts'ui, *Riju shidai,* 132–68.

2. Ibid., 138, 217, 599.

3. Yu, Chien-ming, "Taiwan diqu de fuyun," 548–49.

4. Ibid.; Yang, Ts'ui, *Riju shidai,* 602.

5. "Malayo-Polynesian" and "Austronesian" are terms that Western anthropologists have used to denote the indigenous population in Taiwan. *Yuanzhumin* is the term that Taiwan's indigenous peoples have used for self-identification since Taiwan's democratization in the 1980s. Literally, it means "original inhabitants" in Mandarin Chinese. Currently, Taiwan's Malayo-Polynesian indigenes comprised 1.5 percent of the island's population. The vast majority of Taiwan's population is ethnically Han Chinese. Taiwan's total population was 3.7 million in 1927. By 1943, its population had risen to six million. Taiwan's current population is about 23 million.

6. Diamond, Jared, *Guns, Germs, and Steel,* 339–45.

7. Andrade, "Pirates, Pelts, and Promises," 296n, 299.

8. Roy, *Taiwan,* xi; and Rigger, *From Opposition to Power,* 3–4.

9. Andrade, "Pirates, Pelts, and Promises," 296–301.

10. During Japanese colonial rule over Taiwan, it was also quite common for Japanese males to marry indigenous women for cementing political alliances between the Japanese colonial authorities and various indigenous communities. The Japanese colonial state paid several indigenous wives of Japanese males to serve as interpreters and cultural intermediaries between their communities and the Japanese colonial authorities. Barclay, "Cultural Brokerage," 323–52.

11. Roy, *Taiwan,* 4–6, 23–27; and Rigger, *From Opposition to Power,* 3–4.

12. Diamond, Norma, "Middle Class Family," 854–55.

13. Yu, Chien-ming, "Taiwan diqu de fuyun," 403–5.

14. See Katz, "Governmentality and its Consequences," 387–403.

15. Roy, *Taiwan,* 36.

16. The reign of Emperor Taisho lasted from 1912 to 1926.

17. Ts'ai, P'ei-huo, *Taiwan minzu*, 77.

18. Chen, Edward I-te, "Formosan Political Movements," 486–87; and Ching, *Becoming "Japanese,"* 57.

19. Tsurumi, *Japanese Colonial Education*, 186.

20. The bill for universal male suffrage only applied to adult males in Japan's home islands. Male adults in the Japanese colonies of Taiwan and Korea were excluded. Japanese colonization of Korea lasted from 1910 to 1945. Chen, Edward I-te, "Formosan Political Movements," 486.

21. "Taiwan de funü yundong," 2; and "Funü yundongzhe," 2.

22. "Riben funü," 2.

23. "Moni xuanju," 8.

24. Ts'ai, P'ei-huo, *Taiwan minzu*, 321–23.

25. Ibid., 552.

26. Chen, Edward I-te, "Formosan Political Movements," 490.

27. Yang, Ts'ui, *Riju shidai*, 506.

28. Ibid., 21.

29. Chen, Edward I-te, "Formosan Political Movements," 491.

30. Ibid., 478, 491.

31. Chiang, Wei-shui, "Taiwan minzhongdang," 8; and "Minzhongdang," 4. For the policies and bylaws of the left-wing political parties in imperial Japan, see "Riben ge wuchan zhengdang de zhenrong," *Taiwan minbao* no. 199, 8; no. 200, 8; and no. 201, 8.

32. "Minzhongdang," 4.

33. Male and female intellectuals in colonial Taiwan contributed to feminist discourse in the 1920s. According to Yang Ts'ui, the four main topics in colonial Taiwan's feminist discourse were women's autonomy in marriages, economic independence, and gender and ethnic equality in educational opportunities and political participation. Yang, Ts'ui, *Riju shidai*, 174.

34. Yang, Ts'ui, *Riju shidai*, 152–53. The May Fourth movement was an anti-imperialistic intellectual movement aimed at strengthening China via the wholesale adoption of Western culture and radical rejection of traditional Chinese culture. In its early stage, proponents of liberal democracy dominated the movement. In its latter stage, Russian populism, anarchism, and Marxism-Leninism became influential. After the establishment of the Chinese Communist Party in 1921, Marxism-Leninism became the dominant strand of thought among the May Fourth intellectuals. See Schwarcz, *Chinese Enlightenment*.

35. Yang, Ts'ui, *Riju shidai*, 152.

36. Lee, Bernice J. "Women and Law in Republican China," 36–39.

37. See Chang, Yueh-ch'eng, "Funü yundong de renshi," 9.

38. Yang, Ts'ui, *Riju shidai*, 597.

39. Su, Yi-chen, "Xinshidai de funü," 13–16.

40. Yang, Wei-ming, "Lun hunyin," 32–37; and Jizhe, "Sixiangjie," 34–35.

41. Chang, Li-yun, "Qinai de jiemeimen," 12–13.

42. Ts'ai, Tun-yao, "Women Taiwan," 8.

43. "Minzhongdang," 4.

44. During the Japanese colonial era, foster daughters (*yangnü*) were legally differen-

tiated from *tongyangxi*. A foster daughter was a legal minor whose natal parents gave her away to her foster parents without the explicit purpose of marrying her to her foster parents' son when she came of age. Conversely, a *tongyangxi* was a legal minor whose natal parents gave her away to the parents of her betrothed. After the arrival of the Chinese Nationalist government in 1945, its civil codes eliminated the Japanese colonial distinction between foster daughters and *tongyangxi*, lumped these two categories together into one legal category, and regarded all of them as foster daughters. Kuo, Wen-hua, "Taiwan jiating jihua," 97.

45. Yang, Ts'ui, *Riju shidai*, 49–57.

46. Takenaka, *Shokuminchi Taiwan*, vol. 3, 138–40, 287–88.

47. Yang, Ts'ui, *Riju shidai*, 182; Tsurumi, *Japanese Colonial Education*, 221; and Diamond, Norma, "Middle Class Family," 854.

48. K'o, "Taiwan qingnian," 7.

49. Lu, Hsin-yi, "Imagining 'New Women,'" 88–91.

50. Jayawardena, *Feminism and Nationalism*, 244–46.

51. Yang, Wei-ming, "Lun hunyin," 34–37.

52. Yu, Chuan, "Jiu sixiang," 10.

53. Ts'ai, Hsiao-ch'ien, "Cong lianai dao jiehun," *Taiwan minbao* no. 90, 15–16; and no. 91, 13–14.

54. Tzu, "Xiqu chengli," 8.

55. Huang, P'u-chun, "Nannü chabie," 35–6.

56. Wu, "Nüzi xinhanxue," 9–10; and Ch'en Ying, "Nüzi jiaoyu," 19–20.

57. Huang, P'u-chun, "Nannü chabie," 34–36.

58. Ibid.

59. "Furen jiefang," 1.

60. "Funü shengji," 4.

61. Offen, "Defining Feminism," 119–57.

62. Chang, Yüeh-ch'eng, "Funü yundong de renshi," 10.

63. Chiang, Wei-shui, "Taiwan minzhongdang," 8. There were 3.7 million Taiwanese and 180,000 Japanese in colonial Taiwan in the 1920s. Tsurumi, *Japanese Colonial Education*, 183.

64. "Taiwan jiaoyu," 2.

65. Chiang, Wei-shui, "Taiwan minzhongdang," 8.

66. Tsurumi, *Japanese Colonial Education*, 105.

67. "Shuzi shang," 2.

68. Tsurumi, *Japanese Colonial Education*, 117–31.

69. Ibid., 182.

70. Chen, Edward I-te, "Formosan Political Movements," 482–84.

71. Tsurumi, *Japanese Colonial Education*, 18, 148.

72. Ibid., 18–28.

73. Roy, *Taiwan*, 42.

74. Japanese was officially designated as colonial Taiwan's national language from 1896 to 1945. Chou, Wan-yao, "Kominka Movement," 49.

75. Tsurumi, *Japanese Colonial Education*, 71.

76. Ibid., 72–73.

77. Han, "Fuxuan fuyu," 10.

78. The universities and colleges in Japan's home islands did not give preference to Japanese applicants to the same extent as the Taihoku Imperial University. Tsurumi, *Japanese Colonial Education*, 123–24.

79. See Chang, Tzu-hui, *Taiwan shiren zhi*; and *Zouguo liangge shidai*.

80. Yang, Ts'ui, *Riju shidai*, 499–504.

81. Ibid., 504.

82. Ibid., 594.

83. For more examples of female-oriented occupations, see Takenaka, *Shokuminchi Taiwan*, vol. 4, 82–83.

84. Yamakawa Hitoshi was a Japanese Marxist intellectual. See Yang, Ts'ui, *Riju shidai*, 261–64, 288–89.

85. Yang, Ts'ui, *Riju shidai*, 259–70.

86. Chen, Edward I-te, "Formosan Political Movements," 478–91.

87. Ching, *Becoming "Japanese,"* 57–58, 85–86.

88. Chen, Edward I-te, "Formosan Political Movements," 484–91.

89. The Third International instructed the Japanese Communist Party to provide guidance for the creation of the Taiwan Communist Party in 1928. Organizationally, the Taiwan Communist Party was a branch party of the Japanese Communist Party, but it also had close ties with the Chinese Communist Party. Because the Japanese colonial government regarded the Taiwan Communist Party as an illegal organization, Hsieh Hsueh-hung, a founder of the party, implemented communist policies regarding women by infiltrating legal left-wing organizations such as the Taiwan Farmers' Union and the Taiwan Cultural Association. Ch'en, Fang-ming, *Hsieh Hsueh-hung*, 83–86, 237; and Chen, Edward I-te, "Formosan Political Movements," 478.

90. Yang, Ts'ui, *Riju shidai*, 353, 366–67.

91. Ibid., 506, 598–99; and Chen, Edward I-te, "Formosan Political Movements," 491.

92. Tsurumi, *Japanese Colonial Education*, 223; and Yang, Ts'ui, *Riju shidai*, 174.

93. Ch'en, Fang-ming, *Hsieh Hsueh-hung*, 53–56.

94. Ibid., 55–70.

95. Yang, Ts'ui, *Riju shidai*, 366–77.

96. This oversimplification of the woman question in left-wing discourses of colonial Taiwan was similar to the nationalistic discourses of other colonized peoples in the 1920s. Hongnong gao, "Funü jiefang yundong," 8; and Yang, Ts'ui, *Riju shidai*, 596.

97. Like Hsieh, the Russian Communist Party also opposed the separation of its women's movement from the proletarian movement. See Lapidus, *Women in Soviet Society*, 71.

98. Ch'en, Fang-ming, *Hsieh Hsueh-hung*, 110–11.

99. Ibid.

100. "Zhuluo funü kenqinhui," 8.

101. Yang, Ts'ui, *Riju shidai*, 141, 528.

102. "Furen zhishi jieji," 3.

103. Yang, Ts'ui, *Riju shidai*, 564.

104. "Taiwan shehui yundong," 8; and "Guoqu yinianjian," 7.

105. "Zhuluo funü xiejinhui," 13; and "Guoqu yinianjian," 7.

106. P'an, "Taiwan funü," 8.

107. See Lin, Yu-sheng, *Crisis of Chinese Consciousness.*

108. Yang, Ts'ui, *Riju shidai,* 506–7.

109. Chen, Edward I-te, "Formosan Political Movements," 486–87.

110. Fujieda, "Japan's First Phase of Feminism," 334.

111. "Funü shengji," 3.

112. In 1931, Hsieh and 107 other communists were arrested in Taiwan. In 1940, she was released from prison for medical treatment. Ch'en, Fang-ming, *Hsieh Hsueh-hung,* 111, 239–45; and Chen, Edward I-te, "Formosan Political Movements," 477, 491.

113. "Kangofu yosei," 1–3; and Takenaka, *Shokuminchi Taiwan,* vol. 1, 79–80, 135–37.

114. "Kangofu yosei," 3–4; and Takenaka, *Shokuminchi Taiwan,* vol. 4, 45–49, 135.

115. Garon, *Molding Japanese Minds,* 122; and Sievers, *Flowers in Salt,* 217n.

116. Yang, Ts'ui, *Riju shidai,* 58; and Takenaka, *Shokuminchi Taiwan,* vol. 1, 132–35.

117. Tavares, "Japanese Colonial State," 363.

118. Ibid., 361–81

119. Takenaka, *Shokuminchi Taiwan,* vol. 1, 139–46.

120. In 1929, Japanese residents in Taiwan comprised one-fifth of the membership in the Taiwan chapters of the Patriotic Women's Association. Yang, Ts'ui, *Riju shidai,* 59; and Takenaka, *Shokuminchi Taiwan,* vol. 1, 132–35; and vol. 4, 136–38.

121. Yang, Ts'ui, *Riju shidai,* 58–60.

122. Chou, Wan-yao, "Kominka Movement," 41.

123. Roy, *Taiwan,* 39.

124. Ibid., 13, 41–43.

125. The legend of Goddess Matsu was based on the life of a fisherman's daughter named Lin Mo-niang. Born on Meichou Island near China's Fujian Province in 960 C.E., Lin was known for using her paranormal power to save fishermen and seafarers from drowning. When Chinese immigrants from coastal Fujian Province settled in Taiwan, they brought the Taoist deity with them. Roy, *Taiwan,* 13, 53.

126. Chou, Wan-yao, "Kominka Movement," 41–49.

127. Yang, Ts'ui, *Riju shidai,* 59.

128. Ibid., 62, 595; and Takenaka, *Shokuminchi Taiwan,* vol. 4, 135–38.

129. Takenaka, *Shokuminchi Taiwan,* vol. 1, 131–37.

130. Ibid., 136–37, 212–15.

131. Garon, *Molding Japanese Minds,* 141.

132. Takenaka, *Shokuminchi Taiwan,* vol. 4, 40–43, 97–100.

133. Ibid.,198–99; and Garon, *Molding Japanese Minds,* 143.

134. Garon, *Molding Japanese Minds,* 181–86; and Takenaka, *Shokuminchi Taiwan,* vol. 4, 198, 231.

135. Tsurumi, *Japanese Colonial Education,* 221–23.

136. Sievers, *Flowers in Salt,* 190; and Takenaka, *Shokuminchi Taiwan,* vol. 4, 231–32.

137. Takenaka, *Shokuminchi Taiwan,* vol. 3, 232–33; and vol. 4, 175.

138. Chou, Wan-yao, "Kominka Movement," 66; and Lu, Hsin-yi, "Imagining 'New Women,'" 80.

139. Takenaka, *Shokuminchi Taiwan,* vol. 4, 173–74, 239–40, 262–70, 291, 342.

140. Offen, "Defining Feminism," 119–57.

141. Yang, Ts'ui, *Riju shidai,* 59–60, 205, 217, 257.

142. Chou, Wan-yao, "Kominka Movement," 68.

Chapter 2: *The Kuomintang Policies on Women and Government-Affiliated Women's Organizations*

1. Lin, Yu-sheng, *Crisis of Chinese Consciousness,* 6.
2. See Lu, Meiyi, "Awakening of Chinese Women," 65–67; and Yang, Ts'ui, *Riju shidai,* 174.
3. Yang, Ts'ui, *Riju shidai,* 169–252.
4. Lu, Meiyi, "Awakening of Chinese Women," 65–67.
5. Ibid., 62–66.
6. Eastman, *Abortive Revolution,* 3.
7. Croll, *Feminism and Socialism,* 121–23.
8. See Lapidus, *Women in Soviet Society,* 63–73.
9. Croll, *Feminism and Socialism,* 123–24.
10. Ibid., 124–43.
11. Honig, *Sisters and Strangers,* 209.
12. Thornton, *Disciplining the State,* 92.
13. Croll, *Feminism and Socialism,* 136, 148–51.
14. Thornton, *Disciplining the State,* 92, 101–5.
15. Croll, *Feminism and Socialism,* 148–51.
16. Chiang, Nora Lan-hung and Yen-lin Ku, *Past and Current Status,* 26n, 27.
17. Jayawardena, *Feminism and Nationalism,* 189–90.
18. Diamond, Norma, "Women under Kuomintang," 8.
19. Eastman, *Seeds of Destruction,* 216–18.
20. Eastman, *Abortive Revolution,* 6–8, 285.
21. Thornton, *Disciplining the State,* 73–86, 97–115.
22. Eastman, *Abortive Revolution,* 5–9, 285–86.
23. Eastman, *Seeds of Destruction,* 2.
24. Hinder, "China's New Factory Law," 152–54.
25. Civil codes and factory laws were promulgated in order to convince the Western Powers that China had become a modern nation-state that deserved to be treated as an equal partner. These laws were drafted based on Western standards. Hinder, "China's New Factory Law," 152–54; and Croll, *Feminism and Socialism,* 155–56.
26. Lee, Bernice J., "Women and Law," 28.
27. Lu, Hsiu-lien, *Xinnüxing zhuyi,* 61. Based on the penal codes of the Ming (1368–1644) and Qing (1644–1911) dynasties, the only instance in which a married man could be branded as an adulterer was when he had a sexual relationship with a married woman. On the other hand, a married woman who had a sexual relationship with any man other than her husband was punished as an adulteress. Lee, Bernice J., "Women and Law," 20–21.
28. A wife's property generally consisted of her dowry and her independent assets prior to her marriage. Based on the stipulation of the civil code, a wife's property is under her ownership. But in actuality, her husband's right to control her property served to invalidate her de facto ownership of her property. Chiang Nora Lan-hung and Yen-lin Ku, *Status of Women,* 14–19; and Lu, Hsiu-lien, *Xinnüxing zhuyi,* 63–66.
29. Ibid.
30. Ibid.

31. Chiang, Nora Lan-hung and Yen-lin Ku, *Status of Women*, vii.

32. In the 1930s, the rural peasantry represented 85 percent of the Chinese population. During the same decade, 98.7 percent of rural Chinese women were illiterate. Lee, Bernice J., "Women and Law," 39; and Croll, *Feminism and Socialism*, 167–73.

33. Croll, *Feminism and Socialism*, 156.

34. Eastman, *Abortive Revolution*, 36–49, 61, 74–81.

35. Ibid., 64–73.

36. Culp, "Rethinking Governmentality," 532–46.

37. De Bary, Chan, and Tan, *Sources of Chinese Tradition*, 138–44.

38. Culp, "Rethinking Governmentality," 531–32, 543.

39. Ibid., 540–42.

40. De Bary, Chan, and Tan, *Sources of Chinese Tradition*, 139–43.

41. In primary education, only 2 percent of students were girls in 1907. By 1936, girls represented 19.3 percent of the student body. In secondary education, only 9.8 percent of students were girls in 1911. By 1930, girls represented 17.6 percent of the student population. In higher education, only 2.5 percent were women in 1922. By 1936, it increased to 15.2 percent. Lu, Hsiu-lien, *Xinnüxing zhuyi*, 55.

42. Croll, *Feminism and Socialism*, 158–66.

43. Chiang, May-ling Soong, *China Shall Rise*, 53–61.

44. Croll, *Feminism and Socialism*, 159–68.

45. Chao, "With Madame on My Mind," 117–18.

46. Eastman, *Abortive Revolution*, 70.

47. Croll, *Feminism and Socialism*, 160–70.

48. Ibid., 164.

49. Chiang, May-ling Soong, *War Messages*, 323–32.

50. Ibid., 328.

51. Croll, *Feminism and Socialism*, 170.

52. Ibid., 159–62.

53. Diamond, Norma, "Women under Kuomintang," 6–8.

54. Ibid., 11–13.

55. Croll, *Feminism and Socialism*, 157.

56. Ono, *Chinese Women*, 117.

57. Croll, *Feminism and Socialism*, 178–82.

58. Chiang, May-ling Soong, *We Chinese Women*, 2–4; and Takenaka, *Shokuminchi Taiwan*, vol. 4.

59. Chiang, May-ling Soong, *Jiang furen yanlunji*, 710–45.

60. Croll, *Feminism and Socialism*, 180–83.

61. Ch'en, Fang-ming, *Hsieh Hsueh-hung*, 282.

62. Ibid., 280–88.

63. Ibid., 294.

64. Ibid., 287.

65. Rigger, *Politics in Taiwan*, 67.

66. Yu, Chien-ming, "Taiwan diqu de fuyun," 454–56.

67. Ch'en, Fang-ming, *Hsieh Hsueh-hung*, 278.

68. This estimate was based on "The Report on the Study of the February 28th Incident" issued by the Executive Yuan of the ROC government.

69. Due to Hsieh Hsueh-hung's leadership role in an armed resistance against the Kuomintang troops during the February 28th incident, she fled to Hong Kong during the latter stage of the uprising to escape persecution. Ch'en, Fang-ming, *Hsieh Hsueh-hung,* 309–49.

70. In postwar Taiwan, mainlanders are commonly known as *waishengren* (people from outside of the province). Demographically, the mainlanders represent 14 percent of Taiwan's current population, whereas the Taiwanese comprise 86 percent. Among Taiwan's total population, 70 percent are Hoklo Taiwanese who trace their ancestral origin to Fujian Province, 14.5 percent are Hakka Taiwanese who trace their origin to Guangdong Province, and 1.5 percent are the indigenous Malayo-Polynesian peoples.

71. Since the Kuomintang government fled to Taiwan in 1949, the national (central) government and the Taiwan provincial government have had overlapping jurisdiction over the same territory of Taiwan. Since 1949, The Republic of China (ROC) on Taiwan has functioned as a de facto independent state with its own territory, population, jurisdiction, economy, and military that are mutually exclusive and independent of Communist China. Yet, the Kuomintang's adherence to the One China policy and its lack of official diplomatic recognition by the international community all contributed to the ambiguous national status of the ROC on Taiwan vis-à-vis the People's Republic of China (PRC) on the mainland. To reflect the majority opinion of Taiwan's citizenry, President Lee Teng-hui of Taiwan shifted away from the One China policy in 1999 by stating that the relationship between the ROC on Taiwan and the PRC on the mainland is a special state-to-state relationship between two ethnic Chinese states. He compared Taiwan's relationship to the PRC with the relationship between North and South Korea and East and West Germany before unification. Though his redefinition and clarification of Taiwan's national identity have promoted Taiwan's de facto independent statehood, it has also prompted the PRC to step up its campaign to prevent other nations from recognizing Taiwan's sovereignty in the international community. Due to these political factors, the question of whether Taiwan is a part of China or an independent sovereign state remains a controversial issue in the international community. See Wachman, "Taiwan," 183–203.

72. Wachman, "Competing Identities," 62. In the 1940s, most Taiwanese spoke the Hoklo (Minnan) dialect of coastal Fujian province across the Taiwan Strait. Since it was a unique dialect spoken by the inhabitants of a few cities and villages in coastal southeastern China, most mainlanders found the Hoklo dialect unintelligible upon their arrival in Taiwan. Whereas the Taiwanese spoke Japanese, Hoklo, Hakka, or Malayo-Polynesian languages in 1945, mainlanders spoke Mandarin and their respective dialects from mainland China. As the national language of China, Mandarin was a northern Chinese dialect unintelligible to most Taiwanese in 1945.

73. On December 10, 1979, editors of *Formosa,* the magazine of Taiwan's democracy movement, organized a demonstration in the city of Kaohsiung to commemorate International Human Rights Day. During the mass rally, scuffles broke out between public security forces and demonstrators. Subsequently, the Kuomintang arrested the editors of *Formosa* who had organized the rally. Meanwhile, the magazine's director, Hsu Hsin-liang, was touring the United States and was granted permission to stay in the U.S. for political asylum. In 1980, Hsu mentioned the term *wailai zhengquan* for the first time in the foreword of the complete volume of the magazine's back issues. The term was used to protest the indictments and courts-martial of *Formosa* staffers. As Taiwan was transformed

into a democracy in the 1990s, Lee Teng-hui, then the president of Taiwan, popularized the term *wailai zhengquan* to refer to the Kuomintang regime.

74. Wachman, "Competing Identities," 17–62; and Vecchione, *Tug of War.*

75. Since the 1970s, the cultures of the mainlanders and the Taiwanese have gradually integrated in Taiwan. As Taiwan democratized in the 1990s, the notion that Taiwan should be an independent state has become one of the mainstream ideas in Taiwan's political discourse. Meanwhile, the PRC government on the mainland has indicated that it would use military force against Taiwan if the island were to declare independence. The PRC's bellicose stance against the nascent Taiwanese democracy has also intensified the distrust of the Taiwanese populace with regard to mainland China's authoritarian political culture. Since most people in Taiwan and mainland China are ethnically Chinese, the duality of both sameness and difference in Taiwan's relationship with China persists. Wachman, "Competing Identities," 17–62; and Vecchione, *Tug of War.*

76. Rigger, *Politics in Taiwan,* 63–64.

77. Ibid., 70–71; and Roy, *Taiwan,* 83–90.

78. Roy, *Taiwan,* 90.

79. Rigger, *Politics in Taiwan,* 25, 58.

80. Ngo, "Civil Society," 8.

81. Tang, "Explaining Social Policy," 16, 38, 59–61.

82. Gallin, "Women, Family," 76.

83. Tang, "Explaining Social Policy," 43, 88–89.

84. Diamond, Norma, "Middle Class Family," 856.

85. In 1971, 38 percent of Taiwan's factory workers and 90 percent of all workers in Taiwan's electronics industry were female. Diamond, Norma, "Middle Class Family," 854; and Diamond, Norma, "Women under Kuomintang," 6.

86. Tang, "Explaining Social Policy," 43, 88–89.

87. Lu, Hsiu-lien, *Xinnüxing zhuyi,* 77.

88. Diamond, Norma, "Middle Class Family," 856.

89. In 1998, the revised Labor Standard Law prohibits employers' dismissal of women employees in service and banking industries on the basis of marital status or pregnancy. Prior to the revision of the labor law, it was a common practice in these industries to lay off female employees once they were married or became pregnant. Lee, Yuan-chen, "Taiwan fuyun," 6.

90. Lu, Hsiu-lien, *Xinnüxing zhuyi,* 73–79.

91. Ibid., 13, 76–77; and Chiang, Nora Lan-hung, and Yen-lin Ku, *Status of Women,* 10–11.

92. Cheng, Lucie, and P.C. Hsiung, "Women, Export-Oriented Growth," 325.

93. Ibid., 343–49.

94. Yu, Chien-ming, "Taiwan diqu de fuyun," 494–95.

95. Ku, Yen-lin, "Feminist Movement," 13. In the 1950s and 1960s, Cheng-yi Chang and Hsin-hua Lee both received their education in Taiwan's public schools. Upon their entry into high school, excerpts from the Five Confucian Classics and Four Books were recited in the national-literature courses. Traditional gender roles were instilled in the consciousness of adolescents. Since the national education system forbade children to speak Taiwanese dialects in schools, Lee's and Chang's Taiwanese identity was preserved

via the use of Hoklo Taiwanese at home and the oral traditions of their parents' colonial experiences under Japanese rule. With the National Institute of Compilation and Translation's publication of the junior-high textbook, *Renshi Taiwan* (Getting to Know Taiwan), in 1997, Taiwanese experiences under Japanese colonial rule were comprehensively taught in the national education system for the first time in postwar Taiwan.

96. Ku, Yen-lin, "Feminist Movement," 13.

97. Lee, Yuan-chen, "Quanwei jiaoyu," 4.

98. Cheng, Shu-ju Ada, "Contemporary Autonomous Women's Movement," 29.

99. Kuo, Wen-hua, "Taiwan jiating jihua," 66–76.

100. Offen, "Defining Feminism," 119–57.

101. Ku, Yen-lin, "Feminist Movement," 14.

102. Yu, Chien-ming, "Taiwan diqu de fuyun," 493–94.

103. Chiang, May-ling Soong, *Jiang furen yanlunji*, 803.

104. Kuo, Wen-hua, "Taiwan jiating jihua," 69.

105. Ibid., 76–79.

106. In 1957, there were 4.7 children per married couple in Taiwan.

107. Chiang, Nora Lan-hung, and Yen-lin Ku, *Status of Women*, 27–28.

108. Cheng, Shu-ju Ada, "Contemporary Autonomous Women's Movement," 62; Zhonghua funü fangong lianhehui, *Fulian sanshinian*, 188; and Yu, Chien-ming, "Taiwan diqu de fuyun," 548.

109. Beahan, "Feminism and Nationalism," 401–13.

110. Croll, *Feminism and Socialism*, 45–55, 68–70.

111. Cheng, Shu-ju Ada, "Contemporary Autonomous Women's Movement," 56–60; and Yu, Chien-ming, "Taiwan diqu de fuyun," 548.

112. Kuo, Wen-hua, "Taiwan jiating jihua," 69–74.

113. Chiang, Nora Lan-hung, and Yen-lin Ku, *Status of Women*, 32; and Chiang, May-ling Soong, *Jiang furen yanlunji*, 803.

114. Chiang, May-ling Soong, *Jiang furen yanlunji*, 840.

115. Chiang, Nora Lan-hung, and Yen-lin Ku, *Status of Women*, 32–33; and Diamond, Norma, "Women under Kuomintang," 16–18.

116. Diamond, Norma, "Women under Kuomintang," 16–17.

117. Chu, Ming, *Tamen de xuehan*, 20. From the 1950s through the 1970s, Chu Ming was an activist who advocated the concepts of home economics, family planning, and village nursery schools among rural women.

118. Ibid., 21–24.

119. During both the Japanese colonial era and postwar Taiwan, the farmer's association served as a cooperative credit union in each rural community. It would purchase improved new seeds and fertilizers at wholesale prices and redistribute them to its members. The farmers' associations supported the colonial government's program for the expansion of rural electrification. After the arrival of the Kuomintang in 1945, the new regime also used the farmers' associations as institutional means for rural reconstruction in the 1950s, including the dissemination of new agricultural technology and distribution of new seeds and fertilizers. In 1955, the Kuomintang government assigned the responsibility of implementing its home economics educational program to the farmers' associations in various rural communities and ordered the associations to train home economics teachers for

instructing rural women. Consistent with the New Life advocates' belief in women's gender roles as household managers and educators, all home economics instructors for the rural women's educational program were female high school graduates who underwent three weeks of training in home economics and human relations. The home economics teachers taught rural women the methods of household budgeting and the manufacturing of handicrafts to start family sideline businesses. Chu, Ming, *Tamen de xuehan*, 25–27.

120. Ibid., 21–23.

121. Ibid., 22–23.

122. Chiang, Nora Lan-hung, and Yen-lin Ku, *Status of Women*, 32–33; and Diamond, Norma, "Women under Kuomintang," 16–18.

123. Eastman, *Abortive Revolution*, 220–22; and Eastman, *Seeds of Destruction*, 219–25.

124. Chiang, Nora Lan-hung, and Yen-lin Ku, *Status of Women*, 32.

125. *Ershinian lai de Taiwan funü*, 49; Chiang, May-ling Soong, *Jiang furen yanlunji*, 752–55; and Diamond, Norma, "Women under Kuomintang," 15.

126. Chiang, May-ling Soong, *Jiang furen yanlunji*, 792, 908–13.

127. Diamond, Norma, "Women under Kuomintang," 15.

128. With the support of the Chinese Women's Anti-Aggression League, more than 12,000 houses for military personnel were built. Kuo, Wen-hua, "Taiwan jiating jihua," 72–74.

129. Ershinian lai de Taiwan funü, 43.

130. Kuo, Wen-hua, "Taiwan jiating jihua," 78. The Chinese Women's Anti-Aggression League considered all female civil officials to be its members. It required these officials to take several hours off per month to sew a pair of pants for military personnel. As the section chief of the Commission of Laws and Regulations in the Executive Yuan during the mid-1970s, Hsiu-lien Annette Lu was required to report to the sewing factory on a monthly basis. As postwar Taiwan's pioneer feminist, she was troubled by this obligation and felt that women could contribute to the nation in more productive ways than the sewing of military uniforms. Lu, Hsiu-lien Annette, "Women's Liberation," 296, 303n.

131. Yu, Chien-ming, "Taiwan diqu de fuyun," 470–72, 486–90.

132. Chiang, Nora Lan-hung, and Yen-lin Ku, *Status of Women*, 27–28; and Kuo, Wen-hua, "Taiwan jiating jihua," 75.

133. Yu, Chien-ming, "Taiwan diqu de fuyun," 482.

134. Rigger, *From Opposition to Power*, 16.

135. Roy, *Taiwan*, 85–86.

136. Yu, Chien-ming, "Taiwan diqu de fuyun," 482–89.

137. Chiang, Nora Lan-hung, and Yen-lin Ku, *Status of Women*, 27–28.

138. Yu, Chien-ming, "Taiwan diqu de fuyun," 483.

139. Kuo, Wen-hua, "Taiwan jiating jihua," 87.

140. Yet, the marriage and family laws promulgated during the Nanjing decade were male-centered. In this sense, they contradicted the gender equality clause in the 1947 ROC Constitution. This contradiction was not resolved until the Legislative Yuan's passage of the revised family laws in 1996. Lee, Yuan-chen, "Taiwan fuyun," 4; and Lu, Hsiu-lien, *Xinnüxing zhuyi*, 60–67.

141. Chiang, May-ling Soong, *Jiang furen yanlunji*, 766–67; and Kuo, Wen-hua, "Taiwan jiating jihua," 86–87.

142. Kuo, Wen-hua, "Taiwan jiating jihua," 84.

143. Ibid., 81–85.

144. Roy, *Taiwan*, 99.

145. Chu, Ming, *Tamen de xuehan*, 71–72.

146. Consistent with the trend of industrialization, the proportion of women in the workforce engaged in the agricultural sector dropped from 64 percent in 1975 to 16 percent in 1983, while the percentage in manufacturing and commerce increased from 16.5 percent in 1975 to 58.5 percent in 1983. Chiang, Nora Lan-hung, and Yen-lin Ku, *Status of Women*, 6–7.

147. Kung, *Factory Women*, xiii–xiv.

148. Roy, *Taiwan*, 153–54.

149. Rigger, *Politics in Taiwan*, 10–11; and Rigger, *From Opposition to Power*, 18–19.

150. Ngo, "Civil Society," 9–10.

151. Rigger, *From Opposition to Power*, 17.

152. Roy, *Taiwan*, 158–59, 170; and Rigger, *Politics in Taiwan*, 119.

153. Rigger, *From Opposition to Power*, 19.

154. Roy, *Taiwan*, 153–54.

155. Ngo, "Civil Society," 9–10.

156. Ku, Yen-lin, "Feminist Movement," 15–16.

157. The Kuomintang regime's propaganda machine consisted of Taiwan's mass media and educational system. These two Kuomintang-controlled institutions were the party-state's instruments of indoctrinating the populace with Kuomintang policies and ideologies. Before martial law was lifted in 1987, the party-state and its military owned the vast majority of Taiwan's printed and electronic media.

158. Ku, Yen-lin, "Feminist Movement," 15.

Chapter 3: Hsiu-lien Annette Lu: The Pioneering Stage of the Postwar Autonomous Women's Movement and the Democratic Opposition, 1972–79

1. In 1977, angry voters in the city of Chungli burned down the local police station to protest the fraudulent electoral process for the county magistrate of Taoyuan. In response to the incident, Chiang Ching-kuo terminated his policy of liberalizing Taiwan's politics. It was not until the 1980s that the Kuomintang reintroduced the policy of political liberalization. Chiou, "National Affairs Conference," 19.

2. Lu, Hsiu-lien, *Taiwan liangxinhua*, 188–206.

3. Lu, Hsiu-lien, *Xinnüxing zhuyi*, 219; Lu, Hsiu-lien Annette, "Women's Liberation," 290–301; and Ku, Yen-lin, "Feminist Movement," 15.

4. The first edition of *New Feminism* was published in 1974. According to Lu, the 1977 and 1986 editions were identical in content. Herein I refer to the 1986 edition as it is more comprehensive in its coverage of Lu's ideas. See Lu, Hsiu-lien, *Xinnüxing zhuyi*, v.

5. Chien, "From Utopian," 36.

6. Lu, Hsiu-lien, *Xinnüxing zhuyi*, 215; and Shih, Shu-ch'ing, *Cong nüren*, 139–40.

7. Lee, Yuan-chen, telephone interview, 1 July 1998.

8. Lu also cited Yang Mei-hui's Chinese annotated summary of Margaret Mead's *Sex and Temperament in Three Primitive Societies* as a text that she consulted to formulate *New Feminism*. See Lu, Hsiu-lien, *Xinnüxing zhuyi*, 277. The Chinese summary of Mead's work was compiled in Yang, Mei-hui, *Funü wenti xinlun yucong*.

9. Li, Wen, *Zongheng wushinian*, 5.

10. Lu, Hsiu-lien, *Shuyishu tuohuang*, 4–10.

11. Government Information Office, *Hsiu-lien Annette Lu*. Because Lu was interested in a comparative study of American and modern Chinese laws, in 1969 she decided to get another law degree in the U.S.

12. Lu, Hsiu-lien, *Shuyishu tuohuang*, 4–10.

13. Rubinstein, "Lu Hsiu-lien," 256.

14. Rubinstein, "Lu Hsiu-lien," 257–58. When Lu pioneered the women's movement, the pen pal lent her his moral support as a friend. Lu, Hsiu-lien, *Shuyishu tuohuang*, 11–12.

15. Rubinstein, "Lu Hsiu-lien," 258.

16. Lu, Hsiu-lien, *Shuyishu tuohuang*, 4–13; and Lu, *Xinnüxing zhuyi*, 197, 289.

17. Lu, Hsiu-lien, *Xinnüxing zhuyi*, 222.

18. Ibid., 237.

19. Rubinstein, "Lu Hsiu-lien," 262; and Ku, Yen-lin, "Feminist Movement," 16, 16n.

20. Lu, Hsiu-lien, *Xinnüxing hequhecong*, 90–91.

21. Similar to the Chinese intellectuals' conceptualization of women's contribution to the economy as a means to enhance the wealth and power of the Chinese nation in the twentieth century, Lu envisioned women's contribution to Taiwan's economy as a means to enhance the island's wealth and power. Ku, Yen-lin, "Changing Status," 179; and Lu, Hsiu-lien, *Xinnüxing hequhecong*, 1–23.

22. Government Information Office, *Hsiu-lien Annette Lu*; and Lu, Hsiu-lien, *Xinnüxing hequhecong*, 1–23.

23. Lu, Hsiu-lien, *Xinnüxing hequhecong*, 73; and Lu, Hsiu-lien, *Liangxing wenti*, 47.

24. Lu, Hsiu-lien, *Xinnüxing hequhecong*, 81.

25. In the Ming (1368–1644) and Qing (1644–1911) dynasties, a husband could kill his adulterous wife with impunity. Lee, Bernice J., "Women and Law," 20–21; Lu, Hsiu-lien, *Xinnüxing zhuyi*, 38; and Lu, Hsiu-lien, *Xinnüxing hequhecong*, 79–83.

26. The district court of Hsinchu gave Chung Chao-man a prison sentence of seven and a half years for the murder of his wife. Lu, Hsiu-lien, *Xinnüxing hequhecong*, 73.

27. Lu, Hsiu-lien Annette, "Women's Liberation," 293.

28. Lu, Hsiu-lien, *Xinnüxing zhuyi*, 223; Lu, Hsiu-lien Annette, "Women's Liberation," 293; and Ku, Yen-lin, "Feminist Movement," 15n.

29. Lu, Hsiu-lien, *Shuyishu tuohuang*, 72–117.

30. Lu, Hsiu-lien Annette, "Women's Liberation," 294–95; and Lu, Hsiu-lien, *Shuyishu tuohuang*, 56–61.

31. Lu, Hsiu-lien Annette, "Women's Liberation," 295.

32. Under Lu's leadership, the women's rights advocates included 31 signatories of an application for the creation of the Contemporary Women's Association in Taipei in 1972. In 1976, Lu recruited 68 new volunteers to work for her rape crisis hotline in Kaohsiung.

Adding these numbers together, one determines that approximately 100 volunteers had worked for the autonomous women's movement in the 1970s. Lu, Hsiu-lien, *Xinnüxing zhuyi*, 233; and Lu, Hsiu-lien, *Shuyishu tuohuang*, 24–25. For a description of the elite-sustained character of the American Women's Liberation movement during the Second Red Scare, see the introductory chapter of Rupp and Taylor, *Survival in Doldrums*.

33. Tang, "Explaining Social Policy," 16, 38, 59–61.

34. For a summary of American liberal feminists' lobbying strategies, see chapters eight and nine of Rupp and Taylor, *Survival in Doldrums*.

35. Lu, Hsiu-lien, *Xinnüxing zhuyi*, 233.

36. Chiang, Nora Lan-hung, and Yen-lin Ku, *Status of Women*, 32–33; Diamond, Norma, "Women under Kuomintang," 16–18; and Lu, *Xinnüxing zhuyi*, 231–32.

37. Chiang, Nora Lan-hung, and Yen-lin Ku, *Status of Women*, 32–33; and Diamond, Norma, "Women under Kuomintang," 16–18.

38. Chiang, Nora Lan-hung, and Yen-lin Ku, *Status of Women*, 32; Lu, Hsiu-lien, *Xinnüxing zhuyi*, 243; and Lu, Hsiu-lien, *Taiwan liangxinhua*, 188–206.

39. Lu, Hsiu-lien, *Xinnüxing zhuyi*, 231–32; and Lu, Hsiu-lien, *Xinnüxing hequhecong*, 94–95.

40. Lu Hsiu-lien, *Xinnüxing zhuyi*, 235–37.

41. Lu, Hsiu-lien, *Taiwan liangxinhua*, 188–206.

42. Ku, Yen-lin, "Feminist Movement," 16; Lu, Hsiu-lien Annette, "Women's Liberation," 295; and Lu, Hsiu-lien, *Taiwan liangxinhua*, 188–206.

43. Ch'en, Hsiu-chih, "Lu Hsiu-lien," 8.

44. Lu, Hsiu-lien, *Xinnüxing zhuyi*, 142, 221–27.

45. For more analysis of the cultural-intellectual approach, see Lin, Yu-sheng, *Crisis of Chinese Consciousness*.

46. Lu, Hsiu-lien, *Xinnüxing hequhecong*, 202–3.

47. According to the ROC civil code of 1929 and 1930, a husband had the right to manage and dispose of his wife's property and income after marriage. In most cases, the wife could not dispose of her own property without her husband's consent. Essentially, a woman lost her financial independence upon marrying her husband. During the roundtable discussion, the proposed individual property that separates the property of husband and wife would allow a married woman freedom to dispose of and manage her own money and property. Her husband would have no right to manage or dispose of her individual property without her consent. As for the relaxation of divorce restrictions, the civil code stipulated that instances of abuse that cause marital cohabitation to be unbearable should be a legitimate ground for divorce. Yet, due to the social conservatism of Taiwanese society, the law was interpreted strictly rather than liberally. If a husband refused to divorce his wife, one instance of physical abuse substantiated by a medical record generally would not be enough to convince a judge to grant the abused wife the divorce. In order to ensure an abused wife's well-being, the participants of the roundtable discussion recommended that one instance of physical abuse substantiated by credible medical proof should suffice for a judge to grant the divorce. Rather than granting child custody to the father as stipulated in the family law, the roundtable discussants recommended negotiation between the divorced couple to reach an agreement. If a mutual agreement could not be reached, then the court should either grant joint custody to both parents or grant custody to the

parent who could serve the best interest of the child. Lu, Hsiu-lien, *Xinnüxing hequhe-cong*, 208–50.

48. Ibid., 130–31.

49. Ibid., 138–43.

50. Ku, Yen-lin, "Feminist Movement," 15.

51. As feminist scholars and activists, both Ku and Lee published several articles on the history of the Chinese women's movement and postwar Taiwan's autonomous women's movement.

52. Ku, Yen-lin, "Feminist Movement," 15n.

53. Ibid., 17; Lu, Hsiu-lien, *Shuyishu tuohuang*, 18–19; and Lu, Hsiu-lien, *Xinnüxing zhuyi*, 239–41.

54. While Lu toured the United States, she visited a rape crisis center in St. Louis, Missouri. After collecting data and literature about sexual assault from the center, she did some research on the statistics of criminal cases upon her return to Taiwan. Based on the ROC statistics compiled in 1973, 74 percent of the rape cases were committed by male perpetrators who knew the female victims. Lu, Hsiu-lien, *Xinnüxing hequhecong*, 122–27; and Lu, Hsiu-lien, *Bangta zhengqu*, 152–53.

55. Ibid.

56. Lu, Hsiu-lien, *Shuyishu tuohuang*, 22–23.

57. Women comprised ninety percent of the volunteers at the hotline. The volunteers ranged from retired women doctors and midwives to young professional women, college students, and housewives. Lu, Hsiu-lien, *Shuyishu tuohuang*, 22–23; Lu, Hsiu-lien, *Xinnüxing zhuyi*, 242–45; and Lu, Hsiu-lien Annette, "Women's Liberation," 294.

58. Lu, Hsiu-lien, *Shuyishu tuohuang*, 24–25.

59. Ibid., and Ku, "Feminist Movement," 17.

60. Ku, Yen-lin, "Feminist Movement," 17; and Lu, Hsiu-lien, *Taiwan liangxinhua*, 188–206.

61. Rubinstein, "Lu Hsiu-lien," 267–68.

62. Ku, Yen-lin, "Feminist Movement," 16; and Lu, Hsiu-lien Annette, "Women's Liberation," 298.

63. There were approximately an equal number of women writers, translators, and volunteers from mainlander and Taiwanese backgrounds at the Pioneer Press. The founders of the press were Lu Hsiu-lien, Shih Shu-ch'ing, Wang Chung-p'ing, and Ts'ao Yu-fang. After Shih obtained her master's degree in the Department of Theater at the City University of New York, she returned to Taiwan to become a fiction writer. Wang obtained her bachelor's degree in the Department of Economics at Tung-hai University and also became a professional writer. Lastly, Ts'ao was a graduate of the World College of Journalism and Communications in Taipei. She became the editor-in-chief of the press as well as a fiction writer and essayist. See Lu, Hsiu-lien, *Shuyishu tuohuang*, 21–22; Shih, Shu-ch'ing, *Cong nüren*, 3–4; and Ts'ao, Yu-fang, *Tamen weisheme*, 5–6.

64. Lee, Yuan-chen, telephone interview, 1 July 1998.

65. Ku, Yen-lin, "Feminist Movement," 17.

66. Lo Lo-chia was a graduate of the English Department at Taiwan's National Normal University.

67. Lu, Hsiu-lien, *Xinnüxing zhuyi*, 244; Lu, Hsiu-lien Annette, "Women's Liberation," 294; and Ku, Yen-lin, "Feminist Movement," 17.

68. Rubinstein, "Lu Hsiu-lien," 268.

69. Ku, Yen-lin, "Feminist Movement," 17, 17n.

70. Government Information Office, *Hsiu-lien Annette Lu;* and Lu, Hsiu-lien Annette, "Women's Liberation," 296.

71. Lu, Hsiu-lien, *Xinnüxing zhuyi*, 139–42.

72. Ibid., 155.

73. Lu, Hsiu-lien Annette, "Women's Liberation," 297. Born in England, Mary Wollstonecraft (1759–97) has long been regarded as the mother of Anglo-American liberal feminism. In the spirit of English liberalism and French Enlightenment, Wollstonecraft called for women's educational opportunities, economic independence, and political rights. On the other hand, she also validated women's role as educators of children in the family. See the Pioneer Press' Chinese translation of Mary Wollstonecraft's *A Vindication of the Rights of Woman* (1792) in Shih, Shu-ch'ing, *Cong nüren*, 43–65.

74. Lu, Hsiu-lien, *Xinnüxing zhuyi*, 124–25, 146–55.

75. Ibid., 192.

76. Lu, Hsiu-lien Annette, "Women's Liberation," 297; and Beauvoir, *Second Sex*, 714–32.

77. Lu, Hsiu-lien, *Xinnüxing zhuyi*, 120–26.

78. Ibid., 121.

79. Ibid.

80. Ibid., 152–55.

81. Ibid.

82. Hinsch, "Metaphysics and Reality," 591–98.

83. Lu, Hsiu-lien, *Xinnüxing zhuyi*, 167.

84. Beauvoir, *Second Sex*, 605.

85. Lu, Hsiu-lien, *Xinnüxing zhuyi*, 149–52.

86. Ibid.

87. In the Confucian vision of hierarchical order and social harmony, *the rectification of names* was the notion that people's attitudes and behavior should properly conform with their specific titles, positions, and roles in the family and society. For instance, a ruler should act like a ruler in fact as well as in name, so that there is an agreement between one's title and one's actual behavior. Every name and position in social and familial relationships carried with it certain duties and responsibilities. Confucius said, "Let the ruler be a ruler, the subject a subject, the father a father, the son a son." Confucius, *Analects,* 114; De Bary, Chan, and Tan, *Sources of Chinese Tradition*, 18; and Fung, *Short History,* 41–42.

88. Lu, Hsiu-lien, *Xinnüxing zhuyi*, 149–52.

89. *The Book of Rites* (*Li Ji*), one of the five Confucian classics, stated that a young girl should follow and obey her father. After she is married, she should follow and obey her husband. After the death of her husband, she should follow and obey her son. Lu, Hsiu-lien, *Xinnüxing zhuyi*, 36–38, 89, 115.

90. Ibid., 60, 143–44; and Friedan, *Feminine Mystique*, 370.

91. Lu, Hsiu-lien, *Xinnüxing zhuyi*, 133–56, 193, 213.

92. Ibid., 150–55.

93. Ibid., 145–55; and Mead, *Sex and Temperament*, 321–22.

94. Friedan, *Feminine Mystique*, 336–75.

95. Lu, Hsiu-lien, *Xinnüxing zhuyi*, 145–57, 198–205; and Chien, "From Utopian," 36.

96. Lu, Hsiu-lien, *Xinnüxing zhuyi*, 204–9; and Beauvoir, *Second Sex*, 724.

97. See Confucius, *Analects*, 135.

98. Lu, Hsiu-lien, *Xinnüxing zhuyi*, 204–9.

99. Ibid., 105–9. A husband could be convicted of adultery, however, if his wife sued him with substantiated evidence.

100. Ibid., 110, 162, 174–75.

101. Ibid., 162, 210.

102. Ibid. During Taiwan's transition from an agrarian society to a newly industrializing society in the 1970s, the traditional practice of matchmaking was still prevalent. In these instances, love between a couple could develop either before or after marriage. Among the young modern couples, men and women dated on college campuses and in other social situations. In these instances, love came before marriage.

103. Ibid., 174–75.

104. Ibid., 174–75, 287.

105. Rubinstein, "Lu Hsiu-lien," 258.

106. Lu, Hsiu-lien, *Xinnüxing zhuyi*, 161–64; and Friedan, *Feminine Mystique*, 315–21.

107. Ibid., 160–63; and Beauvoir, *Second Sex*, 642–59.

108. Lu, Hsiu-lien, Xinnüxing zhuyi, 162–63.

109. Ibid., 163–170, 212; and Friedan, *Feminine Mystique*, 338–78.

110. Lu proposed that a home economics course be offered to students of both sexes in the secondary schools as part of the curriculum of compulsory universal education. Lu, Hsiu-lien, *Xinnüxing zhuyi*, 151–52, 168–69.

111. Ibid.,151–63; Chiang, Nora Lan-hung, and Yen-lin Ku, *Status of Women*, 28–32; and Hinsch, "Metaphysics and Reality," 592.

112. Lu, Hsiu-lien, *Xinnüxing zhuyi*, 150–63.

113. Lu, Hsiu-lien Annette, "Women's Liberation," 298.

114. Lu, Hsiu-lien, *Xinnüxing zhuyi*, xvi, 155, 280.

115. Lu's vision of a new woman capable of working outside the home and managing the household came from her mother's life experiences. As a child, Lu's mother was adopted by another family and never attended school. When Lu's mother came of age, she managed to learn enough practical skills to help her husband run the family business. She traveled throughout Taiwan to set up business connections and sell products. With their mother as a role model, Lu and her two sisters also participated in the running of the family business. Burdened with housework, Lu's mother nevertheless said with great pride that "there is not a single woman in our family who does not do a man's work. When we are at home, we do women's work. When we leave home, we do men's work." Government Information Office, *Hsiu-lien Annette Lu*; and Li, Wen, *Zongheng wushinian*, 5–6.

116. Lu, Hsiu-lien, *Xinnüxing zhuyi*, 150–55; and Ku, Yen-lin, "Feminist Movement," 16.

117. Lu, Hsiu-lien, *Xinnüxing zhuyi*, 155, 199.

118. Beauvoir, *Second Sex,* 679–715.

119. Lu, Hsiu-lien, *Xinnüxing zhuyi,* 216–17.

120. Similar to Gilman's vision, Lu advocated that housekeeping professionals should be trained in large numbers to provide services at a reasonable cost for working couples. These services should include shopping, cleaning, cooking, and laundry. Lu, Hsiu-lien, *Xinnüxing zhuyi,* 215; and Shih, Shu-ch'ing, *Cong nüren,* 139–40.

121. Ibid. Both Lu and Gilman felt that private companies that met certain standards and charged affordable fees could run daycare centers and hire professionals to provide these services to working couples.

122. Lu, Hsiu-lien, *Xinnüxing zhuyi,* 169, 216.

123. Lu, Hsiu-lien, *Liangxing wenti,* 96–9.

124. Ibid.

125. Ibid., 99–101.

126. Ibid.

127. Government Information Office, *Hsiu-lien Annette Lu.*

128. Lu, Hsiu-lien, *Liangxing wenti,* 100–107.

129. Ibid., 105.

130. Ibid., 102–7; and Lu, Hsiu-lien, *Xinnüxing zhuyi,* 183.

131. Lu, Hsiu-lien, *Xinnüxing zhuyi,* 4–6. John Stuart Mill was the leading voice of women's suffrage in the British Parliament in 1865 and thereafter. His feminist treatise, *The Subjection of Women,* was written with strong ideological influence from his wife, Harriet Taylor.

132. Ibid., 4–11.

133. Ibid., 12.

134. Eisenstein, *Contemporary Feminist Thought,* xii.

135. Lu, Hsiu-lien, *Xinnüxing zhuyi,* 16–17, 183.

136. Ibid., 46–53.

137. Ibid., 50–55.

138. Lu, Hsiu-lien, *Taiwan de guoqu,* 58–59.

139. Ibid.

140. Ibid., 59–61, 96–108. Metaphorically, Lu referred to Taiwan as a girl given away by her biological parent (China) to her foster parent (Japan) in the Treaty of Shimonoseki in 1895.

141. Ibid., 62–63.

142. As Taiwan's vice president (2000–2008), Lu's stance on Taiwan's national identity vis-à-vis the PRC has remained consistent since 1978. See Lu, Hsiu-lien, *Taiwan de guoqu,* 241; Lu, Hsiu-lien, "Tan fatong," 20–21; and Lu, Hsiu-lien, *Taiwan liangxinhua,* 229–42.

143. Rigger, *From Opposition,* 20–21.

144. Ibid., 20–21.

145. Roy, *Taiwan,* 167; and Kagan, *Chen Shui-bian,* 64.

146. Roy, *Taiwan,* 168.

147. Ku, Yen-lin, "Feminist Movement," 17. With the assistance of Amnesty International in West Germany, Lu was released for treatment of her thyroid cancer in 1985. Li, Wen, *Zongheng wushinian,* 314.

148. Rigger, *From Opposition,* 21–22.

149. Ku, Yen-lin, "Feminist Movement," 17; and Lu, Hsiu-lien Annette, "Women's Liberation," 301–2, 304n; and Fan, "From Politics without Parties," 13–16.

150. Cheng, Shu-ju Ada, "Contemporary Autonomous Women's Movement," 82.

151. Diamond, Norma, "Women under Kuomintang," 8.

152. Lu, Hsiu-lien, *Xinnüxing zhuyi,* 36–38, 89, 151–56.

153. Ibid., xvi, 150–55, 215–17; Lu, Hsiu-lien Annette, "Women's Liberation," 298; and Cheng, Shu-ju Ada, "Contemporary Autonomous Women's Movement," 82.

154. Yang, Ts'ui, *Riju shidai,* 174, 603; and Lu, Hsiu-lien, *Xinnüxing zhuyi,* 162–74.

155. Huang, P'u-chun, "Nannü chabie," 36; and Lu, Hsiu-lien, *Xinnüxing zhuyi,* 160–63.

156. Chang, Yueh-ch'eng, "Funü yundong," 10; Lu, Hsiu-lien, *Xinnüxing zhuyi,* 60, 143–44; and Yang, Ts'ui, *Riju shidai,* 89–90.

157. Huang, P'u-chun, "Nannü chabie," 35; and Lu, Hsiu-lien, *Taiwan liangxinhua* 91–95.

158. Lu, Hsiu-lien, *Xinnüxing zhuyi,* 280; and Lu, Hsiu-lien Annette, "Women's Liberation," 303n.

159. Cheng, Shu-ju Ada, "Contemporary Autonomous Women's Movement," 94–95; and Chiang, Nora Lan-hung, "Women in Taiwan," 239–40.

Chapter 4: Lee Yuan-chen and Awakening, 1982–89

1. Ku, Yen-lin, "Feminist Movement," 17.

2. Jean Baker Miller was an American psychoanalyst who conceived of women's psychological experiences as the source of their collective empowerment and the creation of a woman-centered culture. Eisenstein, *Contemporary Feminist Thought,* 63–68. The Chinese translation of Miller's *Toward a New Psychology of Women* was published in *Awakening* in several installments, from 10 November 1982 to 10 February 1984.

3. Lee, telephone interview, 1 July 1998.

4. Kunming is the capital of Yunnan province in southwestern China.

5. Ku, Yen-lin, "Feminist Movement," 17–18.

6. Ibid.; and Lee, telephone interview, 1 July 1998.

7. In the 1970s, writers of the Native Soil Literary movement depicted the daily lives and problems of ordinary people to expose the socioeconomic injustice in Taiwanese society. The writers attempted to distinguish the folk culture of ordinary Taiwanese people from the Kuomintang government's emphasis on the historical narratives of military heroes and political leaders in mainland China.

8. Lee, Yuan-chen, *Funü kaibuzou,* 160–63; and Ku, Yen-lin, "Feminist Movement," 18.

9. Ibid.; and Cheng, Shu-ju Ada, "Contemporary Autonomous Women's Movement," 96–97.

10. Lee, Yuan-chen, *Funü kaibuzou,* 163–64; and Lee, written correspondence to the author, 18 February 2001.

11. Lee, Yuan-chen, "Funü yundong," 5–6; Lee, Yuan-chen, *Funü kaibuzou,* 70–71, 87–88; and Lu, Hsiu-lien, *Xinnüxing zhuyi,* 145–55.

12. Cheng, Shu-ju Ada, "Contemporary Autonomous Women's Movement," 93–94.

13. Lee, Yuan-chen, telephone interview, 1 July 1998.

14. *Awakening* Editorial Board, "Fakanci," 4; Ku, Yen-lin, "Feminist Movement," 15; and Lu, Hsiu-lien, *Xinnüxing zhuyi*, 160–63.

15. Fan, "From Politics without Parties," 27.

16. Po, "Tekanci," 4–5; Ku, Yen-lin, "Changing Status," 182; and Ku, Yen-lin, "Feminist Movement," 18.

17. Lee, Yuan-chen, "Funüzhou huodong," 7–9; and Lee, Yuan-chen, "Funü yundong," 5.

18. Liu, Hsiu-fang, "Xinliangxing guanxi," 5–8; and Ku, Yen-lin, "Feminist Movement," 18.

19. Lee, Yuan-chen, *Funü kaibuzou*, 151.

20. Lee, Yuan-chen, "Liangxing kongjian," 5; and Lee, Yuan-chen, "Liangxing dou xuyao," 1.

21. Lee, Yuan-chen, "Liangxing shehui," 51; Lee, Yuan-chen, *Funü kaibuzou*, 86–88; and Miller, *New Psychology*, 29–39.

22. Lee, Yuan-chen, "Liangxing kongjian," 5; Lee, Yuan-chen, "Liangxing shehui," 50–51; and Lee, Yuan-chen, *Funü kaibuzou*, 89–90, 152–53.

23. Lee, Yuan-chen, "Cong muxing," 11–12; Lee, Yuan-chen, "Zuo yige," 5; Lee, Yuan-chen, "Sheilai guanxin," 7; and Lee, Yuan-chen, *Funü kaibuzou*, 133–36, 152–53.

24. Lee, Yuan-chen, "Funüzhou huodong," 7; and Lee, Yuan-chen, "Rang women," 6–7.

25. Wang, Tsai-wei, "Feminism and Formation," 167–71.

26. Ibid.

27. Lee, Yuan-chen, "Cong muxing," 11; and Eisenstein, *Contemporary Feminist Thought*, 63–68.

28. Lee, Yuan-chen, "Cong muxing," 12; Lee, Yuan-chen, *Funü kaibuzou*, 102; and Miller, *New Psychology*, 128.

29. Lee, Yuan-chen, *Funü kaibuzou*, 102.

30. Lee, Yuan-chen, "Liangxing shehui," 50–51; Lee, Yuan-chen, *Funü kaibuzou*, 85–86; Miller, *New Psychology*, 21–26; and Eisenstein, *Contemporary Feminist Thought*, 64–68.

31. Lee, Yuan-chen, *Funü kaibuzou*, 89. For information about ways in which elections served as a catalyst for Taiwan's democratization, see Rigger, *Politics in Taiwan*, 11, 26–29.

32. Lee, Yuan-chen, "Funü xinzhi jijinhui," 7; Eisenstein, *Contemporary Feminist Thought*, 64–68; and Miller, *New Psychology*, 25–27, 116.

33. Lee, Yuan-chen, *Funü kaibuzou*, 85–86; and Miller, *New Psychology*, 25, 116.

34. Lee, Yuan-chen, "Funü xinzhi jijinhui," 7.

35. Lee, Yuan-chen, *Funü kaibuzou*, 89; Lee, Yuan-chen, "Liangxing kongjian," 5; Li, "Nannü ruhe," 41–42; Lu, *Xinnüxing zhuyi*, 150–51; and Mead, *Sex and Temperament*, 319–22.

36. Lee, Yuan-chen, *Funü kaibuzou*, 156.

37. Lee, Yuan-chen, "Liangxing dou xuyao," 1.

38. Lee, Yuan-chen, "Nannü ruhe," 42; and Lee, Yuan-chen, *Funü kaibuzou*, 71, 133.

39. Lu, Hsiu-lien, *Xinnüxing zhuyi*, 163; and Lee, Yuan-chen, *Funü kaibuzou*, 120.

40. Lee, Yuan-chen, "Sheilai guanxin," 7–8; Lee, Yuan-chen, "Zuo yige," 5; and Beauvoir, *Second Sex*, 522.

41. The legislation was a eugenic law, since one of its main goals was to reduce the births of infants with birth defects. Ku, Yen-lin, "Feminist Movement," 19.

42. Negative effect on family life generally meant that a family already had too many children to afford an additional child. Lu, Hsiu-lien, *Liangxing wenti*, 104.

43. Yeh, Ch'ih-ling, "Weisheme yao," 5–6.

44. Ku, Yen-lin, "Feminist Movement," 19.

45. Lu, Hsiu-lien, *Liangxing wenti*, 100–7; and Lu, Hsiu-lien, *Xinnüxing zhuyi*, 183.

46. Ku, Yen-lin, "Feminist Movement," 19. In 1986, Lee criticized the government for its failure to provide enough obstetricians to meet the high demand for abortion. Lee, Yuan-chen, "Funü yundong," 6.

47. Lee, Yuan-chen, telephone interview, 1 July 1998.

48. Lee, Yuan-chen, *Funü kaibuzou*, 70–71, 87–88, 120; Lee, Yuan-chen, "Funü yundong," 5–6; and Lu, Hsiu-lien, *Xinnüxing zhuyi*, 145–63.

49. Lee, Yuan-chen, "Cong muxing," 11; and Eisenstein, *Contemporary Feminist Thought*, 63–68.

50. Lee, Yuan-chen, "Cong muxing," 12; Lee, Yuan-chen, *Funü kaibuzou*, 102; and Lu, Hsiu-lien, *Xinnüxing zhuyi*, 215.

51. Lu, Hsiu-lien, *Liangxing wenti*, 100–7; Lu, Hsiu-lien, *Xinnüxing zhuyi*, 183; and Ku, Yen-lin, "Feminist Movement," 19.

Chapter 5: The Autonomous Women's Movement and Feminist Discourse in the Post–Martial Law Era

1. Lee, Yuan-chen, "Funüzhou huodong," 7.

2. Hsu Shen-shu had strong ties with *Awakening*. In 1987, she organized housewives in Taipei to establish the Homemakers' Union for Environmental Protection. Yeh, Sheng-hung, "Xinhuanjin zhufu," 13.

3. Cheng, Shu-ju Ada, "Contemporary Autonomous Women's Movement," 114.

4. Yeh, Sheng-hung, "Xinhuanjin zhufu," 12–13; and Ch'en, Hsiu-hui, "Zhufu lianmeng," 15.

5. Cheng, Shu-ju Ada, "Contemporary Autonomous Women's Movement," 115; and Ch'en, Hsiu-hui, "Zhufu lianmeng," 15.

6. Awakening Foundation, "Minjian funü," 2.

7. Ibid.; and Awakening Foundation, "1988 fanhe xuanyan," 6.

8. Ch'en, Hsiu-hui, "Zhufu lianmeng," 15; and Lee, Yuan-chen, "Funü yundong," 5; and Minjian tuanti, "Xiuzheng minqin shupian," 29.

9. Proliferation of the sex trade and juvenile prostitution in the 1960s and 1970s may be attributed to Taiwan's integration into the global capitalist economy and to the Vietnam War. During the war, Taiwan, along with Hong Kong, South Korea, Thailand, and the Philippines, became popular destinations for American troops' rest and relaxation. As a consequence, prostitution became part of Taiwan's tourism industry. Japanese businessmen and Taiwanese males also frequented Taiwanese brothels. A disproportionate number of prostitutes were from the economically disadvantaged Malayo-Polynesian minority. Thus, racism, classism, sexism, and neo-colonialism in the global capitalist system were all

factors that contributed to the unequal and exploitative relationships between prostitutes and their clientele. Lee, Yuan-chen, "Taiwan fuyun," 2.

10. McCaghy and Hou, "Taiwan," 284–87; and Cheng, Shu-ju Ada, "Contemporary Autonomous Women's Movement," 120.

11. Ku, Yen-lin, "Feminist Movement," 19–20. As a feminist associate of Hsiu-lien Annette Lu in the 1970s, Yen-lin Ku is a professor of English and gender studies at National Chiao-tung University in Hsinchu, Taiwan.

12. Awakening Foundation, "Minjian funü," 4–5.

13. Lee, Yuan-chen, telephone interview, 1 July 1998.

14. Sui, "Taiwan fuyun," 21.

15. McCaghy and Hou, "Taiwan," 291–95.

16. Ibid.

17. Established in 1988, the Garden of Hope Foundation (*Taibeishi lixing shehui fuli shiyei jijinhui*) provides job training and shelter for teenage prostitutes who seek a new way of life. See Wang, Tsai-wei, "Feminism and Formation," 483.

18. McCaghy and Hou, "Taiwan," 292–94; Cheng, Shu-ju Ada, "Contemporary Autonomous Women's Movement," 120–21; and Awakening Foundation, "Minjian funü," 4–5.

19. Lee, Yuan-chen, "Taiwan fuyun," 2.

20. Cheng, Shu-ju Ada, "Contemporary Autonomous Women's Movement," 108.

21. Fan, "From Politics without Parties," 13, 16, 21n, 22–28.

22. Ibid., 22–23, 33.

23. "Taibeishi funü xinzhi," 21–22.

24. Huang, Chang-ling, personal interview, 20 July 2006. Born in Taipei in 1963, Huang Chang-ling obtained her Ph.D. in 1999 from the University of Chicago. Huang is Associate Professor of Political Science at National Taiwan University and President of the Awakening Foundation.

25. Sun, Ruei-suei, telephone interview, 14 July 2003. Born in 1967, Sun Ruei-suei was a coordinator of Taiwan's Intercollegiate Women Students' Conference (*Jiemei ying*) in 1990 and a co-founder of the Center for Gender and Space at the Graduate Institute of Building and Planning at National Taiwan University. Her award-winning master's thesis dealt with the politics of housing pertaining to single women's identity and space. After receiving her Ph.D. from UCLA, Sun has been a faculty member at the National Taiwan University for the Arts (*Guoli Taiwan yishu daxue*) and a board member of the Awakening Foundation.

26. Fan, "From Politics without Parties," 23, 27–28.

27. Lee, Yuan-chen, "Nide yipiao," 1; Lee, Yuan-chen, "Funü xinzhi," 7; and Fan, "From Politics without Parties," 13–16, 26–28.

28. "Taibeishi funü xinzhi," 21–22.

29. According to *Awakening*, women's historical contributions to Taiwanese society were underrepresented in the textbooks. See Awakening Foundation, "Dui jiaoyu gaige," 2.

30. Ch'ao, "Xiaomennei," 1–4.

31. Lee, Yuan-chen, "Quanwei jiaoyu," 4–7.

32. Ibid.; and Lee, Yuan-chen, "Taiwan fuyun," 9.

33. Lee, Yuan-chen, "Taiwan fuyun," 8–9.

34. Gender Equity Education Act, 1–6.

35. Tseng, Chao-nuan, *Funü xinzhi*, 64.

36. Chiang, Nora Lan-hung, "Personal Essay," 182–84.

37. In 1994, the newsletter's title was changed to *Funü yu xingbie yanjiu tongxun*. In 2003, it was renamed *Forum in Women's and Gender Studies* (*Fuyan zongheng*).

38. In 2002, it was renamed *Journal of Women's and Gender Studies* (Nüxue xuezhi).

39. Hsieh, Hsiao-chin, "Women's Studies," 136–37. Hsieh Hsiao-chin was the coordinator of the Research Program on Gender and Society at National Tsinghua University from 1991 through 1993.

40. Ku, Yen-lin, "Cong yizhi," 246–59.

41. Ku, Yen-lin, "Yangtou ruhe bian gourou," 4–6.

42. Chiang, Nora Lan-hung, "Personal Essay," 180–87.

43. Hsieh, Hsiao-chin, "Women's Studies," 138–39.

44. Ibid.

45. Ibid., 136–39.

46. Ku, Yen-lin, "Cong yizhi," 260–62.

47. Wang, Tsai-wei, "Feminism and Formation," 488; and Fan, "From Politics without Parties," 28–39.

48. Ku, Yen-lin, "Cong yizhi," 261–62.

49. See Hsieh, Han, and Yen, "Appendix."

50. Awakening Foundation, "Fuyun zongzi," 17; and Awakening Foundation, "Minjian funü," 3.

51. Sui, "Taiwan fuyun, 20–23; and Awakening Foundation, "Minjian funü," 3.

52. Lu, Hwei-syin, "Transcribing Feminism," 229–41.

53. Chang, Man-chun, "Wanqing xiehui," 15; and "Minfa qinshupian xiufa," 12.

54. Chiou, "National Affairs Conference," 27; and Fan, "From Politics without Parties," 25–26.

55. "Xiuzheng minfa qinshupian," 1–2.

56. Minjian tuanti, "Xiuzheng minqin shupian," 29; and Li, Ch'ing-ju, "Zouchu hunyin," 11.

57. Sui, "Minfa qinshupian," 25–28.

58. "Minfa qinshupian xiufa," 12; and Lee, Yuan-chen, "Taiwan fuyun," 3–4.

59. Lee, Yuan-chen, "Taiwan fuyun," 3–4; and "Chilai de shanyi," 1.

60. In the mid-1990s, the three political parties were the Kuomintang, the Democratic Progressive Party (DPP), and the New Party. While the DPP included many political dissidents from the Democracy movement, most New Party members were former Kuomintang members who broke away from the party.

61. Lee, Yuan-chen, "Taiwan fuyun," 3–4.

62. Tseng, Chao-nuan, *Funü xinzhi*, 26–28.

63. Established in 1987, the mission of the Modern Women's Foundation is to provide legal services and emotional support for female victims of domestic violence, rape, and other forms of physical and sexual assault. Its attorneys drafted legislative bills for the prevention of sexual assault and domestic violence. Lee, Yuan-chen, "Taiwan fuyun," 4; and Wang, Tsai-wei, "Feminism and Formation," 484.

64. "Liberating Women."

65. Tseng, Chao-nuan, *Funü xinzhi,* 29, 55, 63–64.

66. Sui, "Taiwan fuyun," 22–23; and T'ao, "Yige nüren zhuzhi," 9–10.

67. Sun, telephone interview, 14 July 2003.

68. Sui, "Taiwan fuyun," 22–23; T'ao, "Yige nüren zhuzhi," 9–10; and Shuai Jen, "Dui tade ganjue," 12–14.

69. Sun, telephone interview, 14 July 2003.

70. In 1970, New York-based Radicalesbians' "Woman-Identified Woman" was presented as a position paper at the Second Congress to Unite Women. See the Chinese translation of the text in Radicalesbians, "Nüren rentong nüren," 2–4.

71. Ibid.; and Sui, "Taiwan fuyun," 22–23.

72. Radicalesbians, "Nüren rentong nüren," 2–4; Hu, "Yinü chugui," 13–16; and Rich, "Compulsory Heterosexuality," 631–60.

73. Hu, "Yinü chugui," 13–16.

74. "Waijiaodu huodongbiao," 11.

75. Lorde, "Qingse zhi yong," 5–6. Also see Lorde, "Qingyu de liyong," 24–28.

76. Lorde, "Qingse zhi yong," 5–6; Tseng, Chao-yuan, "Women zhexie," 12–13; and Sun, "Congxin sikao qingyu," 16–18.

77. Lorde, "Cong chenmo," 10–11; Tseng, Chao-yuan, "Women zhexie," 12; and Yeh, Hsiu-wen, "Fansheng Shouzha," 15–16.

78. Sun, telephone interview, 14 July 2003, Wichita.

79. "Waijiaodu huodongbiao," 11; Sui, "Taiwan fuyun," 22; Lorde, "Nianling, zhongzhu," 8; and Tseng, Chao-yuan, "Women zhexie," 14.

80. Tseng, Chao-yuan, "Women zhexie," 15; Lorde, "Shengqi zhi yong," 11–12; and Lorde, "Cong chenmo," 11.

81. Tseng, Chao-yuan, "Women zhexie," 13–14; Lorde, "Shengqi zhi yong," 11–12; and Shuai Jen, "Dui tade," 12–14.

82. Tseng, Chao-yuan, "Women zhexie," 14–15.

83. *Nüpengyou,* "Xishou zhi qian," 16–18.

84. Rich, "Compulsory Heterosexuality," 631–60; Women zhijian, "Nütongxinglian," 24–25; and "Waijiaodu huodongbiao," 11

85. Women zhijian "Nütongxinglian," 24–25.

86. *Nüpengyou,* "Xishou zhi qian," 16–18; and Lee, Yuan-chen, "Taiwan fuyun," 6–7.

87. In Taiwan and Hong Kong, the movement to promote the rights of gays and lesbians has been known as *tongzhi yundong* (comrades' movement) since the 1990s.

88. Lee, Yuan-chen, "Taiwan fuyun," 6–7.

89. Hu, "Yinü chugui," 13–16; and "Nütongzhi fuyun," 1.

90. *Nüpengyou,* "Xishou zhi qian," 16–18.

91. Ku, Ming-chun, "Nüxing zhuyi," 19–20.

92. *Nüpengyou,* "Xishou zhi qian," 16–18; Xinzhi gongzuoshi, "Chaijie hunyin," 10–13; and Lee, Yuan-chen, "Taiwan fuyun," 10.

93. Lee, Yuan-chen, "Taiwan fuyun," 10.

94. Ch'iu, "Cong falu," 25–26.

95. Ibid.; and Huang, Chao-yuan, "Cong gongfa," 27–28.

96. "Women yao shuochu," 23.

97. Lee, Yuan-chen, "Taiwan fuyun," 4; and Huang, Chao-yuan, "Cong gongfa," 28.

98. Ho Ch'un-jui is a professor of English and heads the Research Center for Sexuality and Gender Studies at the National Chung-yang University in Chungli, Taiwan.

99. See Ho, "Haoshuang nüren," *Awakening*, 10. The Chinese transliteration of the poem reads: Wo-yao xing-gao-chao, Bu-yao xing-sao-rao. Ni-zai xing-sao-rao, Wo-jiu dong jian-dao.

100. Ibid.; Chang, Hsiao-hung, "Shi qingyu jiefang," 13; and Fan, "From Politics without Parties," 36–37.

101. Fan, "From Politics without Parties," 36.

102. Ho, "Haoshuang nüren," *Awakening*, 10–11.

103. Ibid.

104. Ho, "Xingsaorao," 20–22; and Ho, "Haoshuang nüren," *Awakening*, 11–12.

105. Ho, "Xingsaorao," 20.

106. Ho, "Haoshuang nüren," *Awakening*, 10–12.

107. Lee, Yuan-chen, *Funü kaibuzou*, 156.

108. Fan, "From Politics without Parties," 38.

109. "Nüren lianxian," 20; and Fu-jen Lai-tsu, "Qingyu chuzheng," 18.

110. A speech by Chang Chuan-fen, 12 October 1995, at The Ohio State University, Columbus. Chang Chuan-fen graduated from the sociology department at National Taiwan University (NTU). She was a member of the Awakening Foundation, X-Centric, and the NTU Women's Studies Club. Professionally, she worked as a journalist and an editor on women's issues at *China Times* (*Zhongguo shibao*), a major newspaper in Taiwan. The information on the Taiwanese society's responses to Ho Ch'un-jui's stance on women's sexual liberation is based on notes I took while attending Chang Chuan-fen's talk during her lecture tour in the United States.

111. Ho, "Haoshuang nüren," *Awakening*, 10–12; and lecture by Chang Chuan-fen.

112. Lecture by Chang Chuan-fen.

113. Ho, "Xingsaorao," 22; and lecture by Chang Chuan-fen.

114. Wang, Min-ch'uan, "Duiyu feichang," 4–6.

115. Lee, Yuan-chen, "Taiwan fuyun," 7–8.

116. The Awakening Foundation supported the licensed prostitutes' plea for a two-year grace period for humanitarian reasons. But the foundation did not support the legalization of prostitution on a permanent basis. Sun, telephone interview, 14 July 2003.

117. Lee, Yuan-chen, "Taiwan fuyun," 8.

118. For analysis of biographical and generational profiles of abolitionists and sexual liberationists, see Fan, "Activists in Changing Political Environment," 158–60.

119. Lee, Yuan-chen, "Taiwan fuyun," 8.

120. Fan, "From Politics without Parties," 42–43.

121. Lee, Yuan-chen, "Taiwan fuyun," 8.

122. McCaghy and Hou, "Taiwan," 296.

123. Mo, "Women's Groups," 3.

124. Ibid.

125. Born in 1949, Ts'ao Ai-lan received her master's degree in special education from the University of Utah. She returned to Taiwan to advocate for disabled and women workers. She was a founder of *Awakening* in 1982.

126. Ts'ao, Ai-lan, *Xinshidai Taiwan*, 178–81; and Ch'en, Su-hsiang, "Nügong jiemei," 11.

127. Ch'en, Su-hsiang, "Laojifa," 23–24.

128. Ts'ao, Ai-lan, *Xinshidai Taiwan*, 178–81.

129. Ibid.; and Ch'en, Su-hsiang, and Cheng, Ts'un-chi, "Nügong yundong," 20–21.

130. Ch'en, Su-hsiang, and Cheng, Ts'un-chi, "Nügong yundong," 20–22.

131. Another notable non-governmental organization that offers similar services to women workers is the Grassroots Women Workers' Center (*Jiceng funü laogong zhongxin*). Established in 1988, it was sponsored by the Taiwan Presbyterian Church. Wang, Tsai-wei, "Feminism and Formation," 487.

132. The Council of Labor Affairs is a cabinet in the Executive Yuan of the Taiwanese government. It is equivalent to the Ministry of Labor in other countries.

133. Lin, Yu-pao, and Ni Chia-chen, "Laoweihui," 29.

134. Chu, Ming, *Tamen de xuehan*, 20.

135. Lee, Anru, *Harmony and Prosperity*, xiv–xv, 8, 111–62.

136. "CLA to Offer Foreign Workers," and Wang, "Fan nugong dayouxing," 37–38.

137. "Activists Slam Naturalization Policy."

138. Born in 1955, Yu Mei-nü (Dagmar Mei-nü Yu) passed the bar examination in Taiwan in 1981 and graduated from the master's program of the School of Law at National Taiwan University in 1985. She was then admitted into the doctoral program of jurisprudence at Johann Wolfgang Goethe University in Germany. From 1982 through 1991, she was a legal consultant/columnist for *Awakening*. Yu has chaired the committees that drafted the Equal Employment Bill and the amendments to the family laws. Since 1992, she has served as Director of the International Federation of Women Lawyers in Taiwan. In 2001, Yu became a Commissioner on the Council for the Promotion of Women's Rights in the Taiwanese government and the President/Spokesperson of the National Union of Taiwan Women's Associations. Yu, Mei-nü, personal interview, 28 July 2006.

139. Lee, Yuan-chen, "Taiwan fuyun," 6.

140. Ibid.; and Yu, Mei-nü, "Nannü gongzuo," 13–16.

141. Yu, Mei-nü, "Nannü gongzuo," 13–16.

142. Ibid.

143. Lee, Yuan-chen, "Taiwan fuyun," 6.

144. "New Law," and Hinder, "China's New Factory Law," 152–54.

145. "New Law."

146. Ibid.

147. Ibid.

148. "Law Passed."

149. "Workplace Gender Equality."

150. Department of Labor Standards, "Revised articles," 1.

151. Cheng, Robert, "Language Unification," 357–69.

152. Farris, "Social Discourse," 325; Chang, Yen-hsien, "Taiwanshi yanjiu," 76–86; Chang, Yen-hsien, "Chongjian Taiwanren," 4–5; and Chang, Yen-hsien, "Taiwanren yishi," 72.

153. Chang, "Taiwanshi yanjiu," 82–86.

154. Cheng, Robert, "Language Unification," 362; and Chang, Yen-hsien, "Chongjian Taiwanren," 4.

155. Yun Fan was a leader of the student movement for Taiwan's democratization. In 2000, she received her Ph.D. from Yale University. Currently, she is a faculty member in the sociology department of National Taiwan University and a board member of the Awakening Foundation.

156. Fan, "From Politics without Parties," 28–31. A good example of preserving the oral history of Taiwanese women's experiences was Shen Hsiu-hua's book on the life experiences of widows who lost their husbands in the February 28th incident of 1947. Her book in 1997 was the first comprehensive study on the widows. Shen's research methodology consisted of interviewing February 28th widows of diverse class backgrounds. As a compilation of biographical accounts that honored the widows' emotional trauma, it also demonstrated the ways in which many widows raised their children amidst economic hardships. See Shen, Hsiu-hua, *Chamuoren de 228.*

157. Fan, "From Politics without Parties," 30–35.

158. Lee, Yuan-chen, "Taiwan fuyun," 5.

159. Born in 1949, P'eng Wan-ju received her B.A. from the department of Chinese Literature at National Normal University in 1971. In 1988, she was Secretary General of the Awakening Foundation. From 1990 through 1992, P'eng was a member of the board of directors of the Homemakers' Union and Foundation for Environmental Protection, the Taiwan Women's Rescue Foundation, and the Warm Life Association. During the last few years of her life, P'eng contributed to the formulation of the DPP's policies on government-subsidized childcare facilities, legislative reforms for gender equality in the workplace, the amendments to gender-biased family laws, and on penalties for perpetrators of sexual and domestic violence. See P'eng, *P'eng Wan-ju jinian,* vol. 1; and Lee, Yuan-chen, "Taiwan fuyun," 5n.

160. See "Remembering P'eng Wan-ju," 12.

161. Lee, Yuan-chen, "Taiwan fuyun," 4; and "Liberating Women."

162. Fan, "From Politics without Parties," 45–46.

163. Ibid.

164. Lim, "Taiwan's Presidential Election," 5.

165. Lee, Yuan-chen, "Taiwan fuyun," 5.

166. See Ch'en, Hsiu-chih, *"Lu Hsiu-lien."* In 2000, about 20 percent of all Taiwan's elected representatives in the Legislative Yuan were women. Lu, Hsiu-lien, *Taiwan liangxinhua,* 84–86.

167. See Table 4 in Huang, Chang-ling, "Strength in Numbers," 295.

168. Chiou, "National Affairs Conference," 19; and Fan, "From Politics without Parties," 45–47.

169. Lu, Hsiu-lien, *Taiwan liangxinhua,* 229–42.

170. Huang, Chang-ling, personal interview, 20 July 2006.

171. Tseng, Chao-nuan, *Funü xinzhi,* 11–17, 53, 66; Fanchiang, "NGOs," and Huang, personal interview, 20 July 2006.

172. Lee, Yuan-chen, "Quanwei jiaoyu," 4–7.

173. Ku, Yen-lin, "Feminist Movement," 17.

174. Lee, Yuan-chen, "Taiwan fuyun," 2; and Fan, "From politics without parties," 16, 22–23, 27–28.

175. Ibid; and Lee, Yuan-chen, telephone interview, 1 July 1998.

176. See April issue of *Awakening,* 1988.

177. Fan, "From Politics without Parties," 14–15.

178. "Minfa qinshupian xiufa," 12; and Lee, Yuan-chen, "Taiwan fuyun," 3–4.

179. Ts'ao, Ai-lan, *Xinshidai Taiwan,* 178–81; and Ch'en, Su-hsiang, "Nügong jiemei," 11.

180. Radicalesbians, "Nüren rentong nüren," 4; Hu, "Yinü chugui," 13–16; and Rich, "Compulsory Heterosexuality," 631–60.

181. *Nüpengyou,* "Xishou zhi qian," 16–18; and Lee, Yuan-chen, "Taiwan fuyun," 6–7.

182. Ku, Yen-lin, "Feminist Movement," 16; and Fan, "From Politics without Parties," 36.

Conclusion

1. Yang, Ts'ui, *Riju shidai,* 58.

2. Yu, Chien-ming, "Taiwan diqu de fuyun," 548.

3. Yang, Ts'ui, *Riju shidai,* 59; and Kuo, Wen-hua, "Taiwan jiating jihua," 86–87.

4. Yu, Chien-ming, "Taiwan diqu de fuyun," 548.

5. Chiang, Nora Lan-hung, and Yen-lin Ku, *Status of Women,* 32; Chiang, May-ling Soong, *Jiang furen yanlunji,* 803; and Yang, Ts'ui, *Riju shidai,* 58–62.

6. Chiang, Nora Lan-hung, and Yen-lin Ku, *Status of Women,* 28–32; and Yang, Ts'ui, *Riju shidai,* 58–62.

7. Croll, *Feminism and Socialism,* 160–70; and Chu, Ming, *Tamen de xuehan,* 25–27.

8. Chu, Ming, *Tamen de xuehan,* 25–27.

9. Yang, Ts'ui, *Riju shidai,* 62, 261–64, 595; Diamond, Norma, "Women under Kuomintang," 14; and Diamond, Norma, "Middle Class Family Model," 856.

10. Yang, Ts'ui, *Riju shidai,* 353, 367; Huang, Hua, "Nüzhonghaojie," 37–38; and Chu, Ming, *Tamen de xuehan,* 20–24.

11. Yang, Ts'ui, *Riju shidai,* 58–65; and Chiang, Nora Lan-hung, and Yen-lin Ku, *Status of Women,* 27–32.

12. Chen, Edward I-te, "Formosan Political Movements," 491; and Yang, Ts'ui, *Riju shidai,* 599.

13. Fan, "From Politics without Parties," 19; and Ngo, "Civil Society," 10.

14. Fan, "From Politics without Parties," 19, 33; and "Taibeishi funü xinzhi," 21–22.

15. Huang, P'u-chun, "Nannü chabie," 35–36; Ts'ai, Tun-yao, "Women Taiwan," 8; and Chang, Yueh-ch'eng, "Funü yundong de renshi," 10.

16. Ku, Yen-lin, "Changing Status of Women," 183; and Ku, Yen-lin, "Feminist Movement," 19.

17. Fan, "From Politics without Parties," 14–15, 36–37.

18. Ibid., 13–19, 26. As feminist activists in the 1970s, Lu Hsiu-lien and Lee Yuan-chen's participation in the democracy movement were exceptions rather than the rule. In the early 1970s, the democracy movement emerged at around the same time as the autonomous women's movement. In contrast, the labor movement (independent of the Kuomintang's control and patronage) did not emerge until the early 1980s. Shen, Tzong-Ruey, "Modes of State Control," 126; Ku, Yen-lin, "Changing Status of Women," 179; and Lu, Hsiu-lien Annette, "Women's Liberation," 302–4n.

19. Yang, Ts'ui, *Riju shidai,* 21, 64–65, 138, 217, 599.
20. See Huang, Hua, "Nüzhonghaojie," 37–38; and Ch'en, Fang-ming, *Hsieh Hsueh-hung pingzhuan.*
21. Yang, Ts'ui, *Riju shidai,* 353, 367, 596.
22. Chen, Edward I-te, "Formosan Political Movements," 478–91.
23. Shen, Tzong-Ruey, "Modes of State Control," 111–30.
24. On 1 May 1984, the Taiwan Supporting Organization for Labor Laws was established independent of the Kuomintang's control. It was committed to the amendment of labor laws via legislative reform. Shen, Tzong-Ruey, "Modes of State Control," 126.
25. Born in 1947, Lo Yeh-ch'in obtained her master's degree in labor relations and became a consultant for Taiwanese industries and the Pioneer Press. Shih, Shu-ch'ing, *Cong nüren,* 4.
26. Chu, Ming, *Tamen de xuehan,* 95–105, 121. Since the authoritarian regime prioritized economic development and orderly industrial production over workers' welfare, the Kuomintang-sponsored labor unions were not effective channels for workers to air their grievances. Moreover, many leaders of the labor unions were employers and capitalists with Kuomintang party membership. This fact rendered the labor unions ineffective as organizations for the protection of workers' rights. Shen, Tzong-Ruey, "Modes of State Control," 116–30.
27. Lee, telephone interview, 1 July 1998.
28. Lu, Hsiu-lien, *Xinnüxing zhuyi,* 215–17; Lee, Yuan-chen, "Cong muxing," 12; and Lee, Yuan-chen, *Funü kaibuzou,* 102–4.
29. Lu, Hsiu-lien, *Xinnüxing zhuyi,* 215.
30. T'ang, "Taiwan nügong," 1–2; and Yang, Ts'ui, *Riju shidai,* 594.
31. Ch'en Su-hsiang, and Cheng Ts'un-chi, "Nügong yundong," 20–22.
32. "Taiwan minzhongdang chuxian," 4–5; and Ch'en Su-hsiang, and Cheng Ts'un-chi, "Nügong yundong," 20–22.
33. Fan, "From Politics without Parties," 30–32.
34. Ibid., 45–46.
35. Lan, "Under the Shadow," 44–52; and Tsurumi, *Japanese Colonial Education,* 199–209.
36. Lee, Yuan-chen, "Cong muxing," 11; and Huang, P'u-chun, "Nannü chabie," 34–36.
37. Chou, Bi-ehr, "Changing Patterns," 344; and Lu, Hsiu-lien, *Xinnüxing zhuyi,* 84.
38. *Shuzi gaosu ni,* 8–17.
39. Wu, "Nüzi xinhanxue," 9–10; Ch'en, Ying, "Nüzi jiaoyu," 19; and Cheng, Shu-ju Ada, "Contemporary Autonomous Women's Movement," 114.
40. Offen, "Defining Feminism," 145–46.
41. Lu, Hsiu-lien, *Xinnüxing zhuyi,* 150–63.
42. Lee, Yuan-chen, *Funü kaibuzou,* 120.
43. Lee, Yuan-chen, "Funü xinzhi jijinhui," 7; and Lee, Yuan-chen, *Funü kaibuzou,* 85–86. Also see Eisenstein, *Contemporary Feminist Thought,* 64–68; and Miller, *New Psychology,* 25–27, 116.
44. Lu, Hsiu-lien, *Taiwan liangxinhua,* 198–203.
45. Yeh, Sheng-hung, "Xinhuanjin," 12–13.

46. Kung, *Factory Women*, xv.

47. Ibid., xiii–xv.

48. Lee, Anru, *Harmony and Prosperity*, xiv–xv, 8, 111–62.

49. Awakening Foundation, "Nünü xiangting," 39. For analysis of inequalities along the lines of gender, national origin, and class in Taiwanese society, see Lee, Anru, *Harmony and Prosperity*, 131–65.

50. Ts'ao, Ai-lan, "Taiwan fuyun xinshiyei," 6–9; and Radicalesbians, "Nüren rentong nüren," 4.

51. *Nüpengyou*, "Xishou zhi qian," 16–18; Lee, Yuan-chen, "Taiwan fuyun," 6–7; and Offen, "Defining Feminism," 135–36.

52. Fan, "From Politics without Parties," 36.

53. Ho, "Haoshuang nüren," Awakening Foundation, 10–12; and Lee, Yuan-chen, *Funü kaibuzou*, 156.

54. Ho, "Xingsaorao," 22.

55. Lee, Yuan-chen, "Taiwan fuyun," 8.

56. Lu, Hsiu-lien, *Taiwan liangxinhua*, 64–68.

Bibliography

"Activists Slam Naturalization Policy." *Taiwan Headlines,* 26 July 2007.

Aikoku Fujinkai, Taiwan Honbu. *Aikoku fujinkai Taiwan honbu enkakushi* (The institutional historical record of Patriotic Women's Association's Taiwan headquarters). Taihoku: Aikoku fujinkai Taiwan honbu, 1941.

Andrade, Tonio. "Pirates, Pelts, and Promises: The Sino-Dutch Colony of Seventeenth-Century Taiwan and the Aboriginal Village of Favorolang." *Journal of Asian Studies* 64, no. 2 (May 2005): 295–322.

Awakening Foundation. "Dui jiaoyu gaige zhi yijian" (Some opinions concerning the educational reform). *Awakening,* 10 March 1988, 3.

———. Funü xinzhi shuangshi nianhua (The double-ten anniversary of Awakening). Taipei: Awakening Foundation, 2002.

———. "Fuyun zongzi piandisa" (Seeds of the women's movement are widely disseminated). *Awakening,* 1 April 1990, 17–18.

———. "Gongchang shiyei, fuyun pangguan?" (Licensed prostitutes are unemployed, women's movement observes from the sideline?). *Stir Quarterly* no. 5 (March 1998): 4–54.

———. "Minjian funü tuanti niandu xinzhanwang" (Women's civic organization's new prospects for the new year). *Awakening,* 10 January 1988, 1–5.

———. "Nünü xiangting, fandui nugong lianhe shengming gao" (Joint announcement by women uplifting each other to oppose slave labor). Taipei Awakening Association (January/February 2006): 39.

———. "1988 fanhe xuanyan" (The 1988 declaration for opposition to the building of nuclear power plants). *Awakening,* 10 April 1988, 6.

———. "1988 muqinjie xuanyan" (The 1988 declaration for Mother's Day). *Awakening,* 10 May 1988, 5.

———. "2005 funü xinzhi jijinhui niandu dashi: huiwu baogao" (Awakening Foundation's major events in 2005: The foundation's business report). *Taipei Awakening Foundation* (January/February 2006): 42–48.

Awakening Editorial Board. "Fakanci" (The opening statement for launching the first issue of *Awakening*). *Awakening*, 1 February 1982, 4.

———. "Yousheng baojianfa caoan zuotanhui" (The symposium on the draft of the Eugenic Protection Law). *Awakening*, 10 July 1982, 7–13.

Barclay, Paul. D. "Cultural Brokerage and Interethnic Marriage in Colonial Taiwan: Japanese Subalterns and Their Aborigine Wives, 1895–1930." *Journal of Asian Studies* 64, no. 2 (May 2005): 323–60.

Barlow, Tani E. *The Question of Women in Chinese Feminism*. Durham, N.C.: Duke University Press, 2004.

Beahan, Charlotte L. "Feminism and Nationalism in the Chinese Women's Press, 1902–1911." *Modern China* 1, no. 4 (October 1975): 379–416.

Beauvoir, Simone de. *The Second Sex*. Translated and edited by H. M. Parshley. New York: Alfred A. Knopf, 1971.

Bernhardt, Kathryn. *Women and Property in China, 960–1949*. Stanford, Calif.: Stanford University Press, 1999.

Bo, Ch'ing-jung. "*Funü xinzhi* de huigu yu qianzhan" (The retrospect and prospect of *Awakening*). *Awakening*, 1 December 1989, 1–2.

Bodenhorn, Terry, ed. *Defining Modernity: Guomindang Rhetorics of a New China, 1920–1970*. Michigan Monographs in Chinese Studies. Ann Arbor: University of Michigan Press, 2002.

Brinton, Mary C. *Women's Working Lives in East Asia*. Stanford, Calif.: Stanford University Press, 2002.

Brown, Melissa J. *Is Taiwan Chinese? The Impact of Culture, Power, and Migration on Changing Identities*. Berkeley: University of California Press, 2004.

Chang, Cheng-yi, and Hsin-hua Lee. Interview with author, 14 July 2001. Columbus, Ohio.

Chang, Hsiao-hung. "Shi qingyu jiefang haishi xingjiefang?" (Is it the liberation of erotic passion or sexual liberation?). *Awakening*, 5 October 1994, 13–14.

Chang, Hsiao-yen. "Cong Taiwan shehui de xiankuang yu zhanwang kan funü yundong: Hsiao Hsin-huang zhujiang" (Looking at the women's movement from the perspective of Taiwanese society's current situation and prospect: a speech by Hsiao Hsin-huang). *Awakening*, 10 February 1988, 18–21; and 10 April 1988, 21.

———. "Taiwan funü yundong yu nüxing yishi de fazhan: Ku Yen-lin zhujiang" (The Taiwanese women's movement and the development of women's consciousness, a speech by Ku Yen-lin). *Awakening*, 10 July 1987, 1–5.

Chang, Hui-Ching, and Rich Holt. "Symbols in Conflict: Taiwan (Taiwan) and Zhongguo (China) in Taiwan's Identity Politics." *Nationalism and Ethnic Politics* 13, no. 1 (2007): 129–65.

Chang, Li-yun. "Qinai de jiemeimen ya! Fenqi! Nuli!" (Dear sisters! Arise with courage! Put forth our efforts). *Taiwan minbao* no. 18 (21 June 1925): 12–13.

Chang, Man-chun. "Wanqing Xiehui: wo shi yige danqin muqin" (The Warm Life Association: I am a single mother). *Awakening*, 1 May 1989, 15.

Chang, Tzu-hui, ed. *Taiwan shiren zhi* (A record of who's who in contemporary Taiwan). Taibei: Guoguang chubanshe, 1946.

Chang Yen-hsien. "Chongjian Taiwanren fankang jingshengshi" (Reconstructing Taiwanese people's history of resistance). *Taiwan shiliao yanjiu* no. 2 (August 1993): 3–7.

———. "Taiwanren yishi huiyilu de chuxian" (The emergence of memoirs on Taiwanese consciousness). *Taiwan shiliao yanjiu* no. 11 (May 1998): 65–72.

———. "Taiwanshi yanjiu de xinjingsheng" (The new spirit of Taiwanese historical studies). *Taiwan shiliao yanjiu* no. 1 (February 1993): 76–86.

Chang, Yueh-ch'eng. "Funü yundong de renshi"(Understanding the women's movement). *Taiwan minbao* no. 145 (20 February 1928): 10.

Chao, Anne Shen. "With Madame on My Mind: A Mosaic of Impressions of the Madame." In *Madame Chiang Kaishek and her China*, ed. Samuel C. Chu, 112–20. Norwalk, Conn.: EastBridge, 2005.

Ch'ao, Teng-mei. "Xiaomennei de nanzun nübei: liangxing pingdeng jiaoyu zuotanhui" (Respecting males and debasing females in schools: a panel discussion on promoting gender equality in education). *Awakening*, 10 April, 1988, 1–4.

Chen, Dung-Sheng. "Taiwan's Social Changes in the Patterns of Social Solidarity in the Twentieth Century." *China Quarterly* no. 165 (March 2001): 61–82.

Chen, Edward I-te. "Formosan Political Movements under Japanese Colonial Rule, 1914–1937." *Journal of Asian Studies* 31, no. 3 (May 1972): 477–97.

Chen, Fen-ling. *Working Women and State Policies in Taiwan: A Study in Political Economy.* New York: Palgrave, 2000.

Ch'en, Fang-ming. *Hsieh Hsueh-hung pingzhuan* (A critical biography of Hsieh Hsueh-hung). Irvine, Calif.: Taiwan chubanshe, 1992.

Ch'en, Hsiu-chih. "Lu Hsiu-lien." In *Buiyiyang de nüren: xinzhengfu shiwei nüxing shouzhang de gushi* (Women unlike all others: the story of ten women chief administrators in the new government), ed. Li Ch'iung-si, 2–17. Taibei: Xianjue chubanshe, 2000.

Ch'en, Hsiu-hui. "Zhufu lianmeng jijinhui chengli ganyan" (Reflections on the establishment of the Homemakers' Union and Foundation for Environmental Protection). *Awakening*, 1 May 1989, 15.

Ch'en, K'un-shu. "Genben de hunyin gexinlun" (A discussion on the fundamentals of marriage reform). *Tai Oan Chheng Lian* no. 6 (15 December 1921): 22–31.

Ch'en, Su-hsiang. "Laojifa yu ni" (The labor standard law and you). *Awakening*, 1 September 1991, 23–24.

———. "Nügong jiemei de beige" (The melancholy song of women workers). *Awakening*, 1 December 1991, 10–11.

Ch'en, Su-hsiang, and Cheng Ts'un-chi. "Nügong yundong de chubu tantao" (A preliminary investigation of the women workers' movement). *Awakening*, 1 June 1991, 20–21.

Ch'en, Tse, ed. *Taiwan qianqi wuzhuang kangri yundong youguan dangan* (Relevant government files on Taiwan's early movement of armed resistance against Japan). Taichung: Taiwansheng wenxian weiyuanhui, 1977.

Ch'en, Ying. "Nüzi jiaoyu zhi biyao" (The necessity of women's education). *Tai Oan Chheng Lian* no. 2 (15 August 1920): 19.

Cheng, Lucie, and P. C. Hsiung. "Women, Export-Oriented Growth, and the State: The Case of Taiwan." In *The Role of the State in Taiwan's Development*, eds. J. D. Aberbach, David Dollar, and K. L. Sokoloff, 321–53. Armonk, N.Y.: M. E. Sharpe, 1994.

Cheng, Robert. "Language Unification in Taiwan." In *The Other Taiwan: 1945 to the Present*, ed. Murray A. Rubinstein, 357–69. Armonk, N.Y.: M.E. Sharpe, 1994.

Cheng, Shu-ju Ada. "The Contemporary Autonomous Women's Movement in Taiwan." Master's thesis, University of Oregon, 1994.

Chiang, Hui-na. "Zhufu canzheng" (Homemakers' political participation). *Awakening*, 1 November 1991, 11–13.

Chiang, May-ling Soong. *China Shall Rise Again*. New York: Harper and Brothers, 1941.

———. *Jiang furen yanlunji* (The collection of Madame Chiang's speeches). Edited by Wang Ya-ch'uan. Taibei: Zhonghua funü fangong lianhehui, 1977.

———. *Selected Speeches, 1943–1982*. Taipei: Chinese Women's Anti-Aggression League, 1984.

———. *War Messages and Other Selections*. Hankow: China Information Committee, 1938.

———. *We Chinese Women: Speeches and Writings during the First United Nations Year, February 12,1942–November 16, 1942*. New York: John Day, 1943.

Chiang, Nora Lan-hung. "A Personal Essay." In *Changing Lives: Life Stories of Asian Pioneers in Women's Studies*, ed. The Committee on Women's Studies in Asia, 172–88. New York: The Feminist Press at the City University of New York, 1994.

———. "Women in Taiwan: Linking Economic Prosperity and Women's Progress." In *Women in Asia: Tradition, Modernity, and Globalisation*, ed. Louise Edwards and Mina Roces, 229–46. Ann Arbor: The University of Michigan Press, 2000.

Chiang, Nora Lan-hung, and Yen-lin Ku. *Past and Current Status of Women in Taiwan*. Taipei: Women's Research Program, Population Studies Center, National Taiwan University, 1985.

Chiang, Nora Lan-hung, and Yu-yuan Pien. *The Role of Women in the National Development Process in Taiwan*. Taipei: Population Studies Center, National Taiwan University, 1985.

Chiang, Wei-shui. "Taiwan minzhongdang de zhidao yuanli yu gongzuo" (The guiding principles and work of the Taiwan Populist Party). *Taiwan minbao* no. 226 (16 September 1928): 8.

Chien, Ying-ying. "From Utopian to Dystopian World: Two Faces of Feminism in Contemporary Taiwanese Women's Fiction." *World Literature Today* 68, no. 1 (Winter 1994): 35–42.

"Chilai de shanyi" (The belated goodwill). *Awakening*, 5 October 1994, 1.

Ching, Leo T. S. *Becoming "Japanese": Colonial Taiwan and the Politics of Identity Formation*. Berkeley: University of California Press, 2001.

Chiou, C. L. "The 1990 National Affairs Conference and the Future of Democracy in Taiwan." *Bulletin of Concerned Asian Scholars* 25, no. 1 (January–March 1993): 17–33.

Ch'iu, Huang-ch'uan. "Cong falu guandian kan xingsaorao shensuquan yu feibangzui zhi guanlian" (Looking at the relationship between one's right to present a sexual harassment case at the court of law and the crime of slandering from a legal perspective). *Awakening*, 5 December 1995, 25–26.

Chou, Bi-ehr. "Changing Patterns of Women's Employment in Taiwan, 1966–1986." In *The Other Taiwan: 1945 to the Present*, ed. Murray A. Rubinstein, 330–54. Armonk, N.Y.: M. E. Sharpe, 1994.

Chou, Wan-yao. "The Kominka Movement in Taiwan and Korea: Comparisons and Interpretations." In *The Japanese Wartime Empire, 1931–1945*, ed. Peter Duus, Ramon H. Myers, and Mark R. Peattie, 40–68. Princeton, N.J.: Princeton University Press, 1996.

Chu, Ming, Lo Yeh-ch'in, Liu An-an, and Huang Han-lung, eds. *Tamen de xuehan, tamen de yanlei* (Their blood and sweat, their tears). Taibei: Tuohuangzhe chubanshe, 1976.

Chu, Yun-han, and Jih-wen Lin. "Political Development in Twentieth-Century Taiwan." *China Quarterly* no. 165 (March 2001): 102–29.

"CLA to Offer Foreign Workers One-Stop Service Center." *Taiwan Headlines*, 27 July 2007.

Clark, Cal, and Rose J. Lee. *Democracy and the Status of Women in East Asia.* Boulder: Lynne Rienner, 2000.

Confucius. *The Analects.* Translated with an Introduction by D.C. Lau. New York: Penguin Books, 1979.

Corcuff, Stephane, ed. *Memories of the Future: National Identity Issues and the Search for a New Taiwan.* Armonk, N. Y.: M.E. Sharpe, 2002.

Croll, Elisabeth. *Feminism and Socialism in China.* Boston: Routledge and Kagan Paul, 1978.

Culp, Robert. "Rethinking Governmentality: Training, Cultivation, and Cultural Citizenship in Nationalist China," *Journal of Asian Studies* 65, no. 3 (August 2006): 529–54.

Dai Nihon kokubo fujinkai junenshi (Ten-year history of the Greater Japan National Defense Women's Association). Tokyo: Dai Nihon kokubo fujinkai junenshi hensan jimusho, 1943.

Damm, Jens. "Same Sex Desire and Society in Taiwan, 1970–1987." *China Quarterly* no. 181(21 March 2005): 67–81.

De Bary, William Theodore, Wing-tsit Chan, and Chester Tan, eds. *Sources of Chinese Tradition.* Vols. 1–2. New York: Columbia University Press, 1960.

Department of Labor Standards, Council of Labor Affairs, Executive Yuan, Taiwan. "Revised Articles of Gender Equality in Employment Laws are Passed by Legislative Yuan." Taipei, 19 December 2007.

Diamond, Jared. *Guns, Germs, and Steel: The Fates of Human Societies.* New York: W. W. Norton, 1999.

Diamond, Norma. "The Middle Class Family Model in Taiwan: Woman's Place is in the Home." *Asian Survey* 13, no. 9 (September 1973): 853–72.

———. "The Status of Women in Taiwan." In *Women in China: Studies in Social Change and Feminism,* ed. Marilyn Young, 211–42. Ann Arbor: Center for Chinese Studies, University of Michigan, 1973.

———. "Women under Kuomintang Rule: Variations on the Feminine Mystique." *Modern China* 1, no. 1 (January 1975): 3–45.

"DPP Wins in Taoyuan County: Annette Lu's Bi-Election Victory Follows Murder of KMT Chief." *Taiwan International Review* no. 2 (March-April 1997): 2–3.

Eastman, Lloyd E. *The Abortive Revolution: China under Nationalist Rule, 1927–1937.* Cambridge, Mass.: Harvard University Press, 1974.

———. *Seeds of Destruction: Nationalist China in War and Revolution, 1937–1949.* Stanford, Calif.: Stanford University Press, 1984.

Edmonds, Richard L., and Steven M. Goldstein, eds. *Taiwan in the Twentieth Century: A Retrospective View.* Cambridge: Cambridge University Press, 2001.

Eisenstein, Hester. *Contemporary Feminist Thought.* Boston: G.K. Hall, 1983.

Ershinian lai de Taiwan funü bianji weiyuanhui, ed. *Ershinian lai de Taiwan funü* (Taiwanese women in the past twenty years). Taibei: Taiwansheng funü xiezuo xiehui, 1965.

Eskildsen, Robert. "Taiwan: A Periphery in Search of a Narrative." *Journal of Asian Studies* 64, no. 2 (May 2005): 281–94.

Fan, Yun. "Activists in a Changing Political Environment: a Micro-foundational Study of Social Movements in Taiwan's Democratic Transition, 1980s-1990s." Ph.D. diss., Yale University, 2000.

———. "From Politics without Parties to Politics with Parties: the Women's Movement in Taiwan's Political Transformation, 1980s—." In *Taiwan 2000—Envisioning a Pluralistic Future: Proceedings of the Sixth Annual Conference of the North American Taiwan Studies Association at Harvard University, Cambridge, Massachusetts, June 16-19, 2000.*

Fanchiang, Cecilia. "NGOs Push for Stronger Gender Equality Agency." Taipei: Government Information Office, Republic of China, Taiwan, 5 September 2003.

Fang, Shuang. "Nüxing zhuyi de sange zhuyao paibie" (The three main strands of feminism), *Awakening*, 1 December 1988, 6-7.

Farris, Catherine. "The Social Discourse on Women's Roles in Taiwan: A Textual Analysis." In *The Other Taiwan*, ed. Murray A. Rubinstein, 305-29. Armonk, N.Y.: M. E. Sharpe, 1994.

———. "Women's Liberation under 'East Asian Modernity' in China and Taiwan." In *Women in the New Taiwan: Gender Roles and Gender Consciousness in a Changing Society*, ed. Catherine Farris, Anru Lee, and Murray Rubinstein, 325-76. Armonk, N.Y.: M. E. Sharpe, 2004.

Freeman, Derek. *Margaret Mead and Samoa.* Cambridge, Mass.: Harvard University Press, 1983.

Freeman, Jo. *The Politics of Women's Liberation: A Case Study of an Emerging Social Movement and Its Relation to the Policy Process.* New York: David McKay, 1975.

Friedan, Betty. *The Feminine Mystique.* New York: Bantam Doubleday Dell Publishing, 1983.

Friedman, Edward. *China's Rise, Taiwan's Dilemmas and International Peace.* London: Routledge, 2005.

Fu-jen Lai-tzu. "Qingyu chuzheng" (Fighting the battle of sexuality). *Awakening*, 5 July 1995, 17-18.

Fujieda, Mioko. "Japan's First Phase of Feminism." In *Japanese Women: New Feminist Perspectives on the Past, Present, and Future*, ed. Kumiko Fujimura-Fanselow and Atsuko Kameda, 323-42. New York: The Feminist Press at the City University of New York, 1995.

Fung, Yu-lan. *A Short History of Chinese Philosophy.* Edited by Derk Bodde. New York: MacMillan, 1960.

"Funü gonglihui zhi huodong" (The activities of women's association for mutual encouragement and collective action). *Taiwan minbao* no. 71 (20 September 1925): 5.

"Funü shengji wenti" (Problems of women's livelihood). *Taiwan minbao* no. 129 (31 October 1926): 4.

"Funü yundongzhe naliqu?" (Where are the feminists?). *Taiwan minbao* no. 204 (15 April 1928): 2.

"Furen jiefang de dangmian wenti" (The immediate problems facing women's liberation). *Taiwan minbao* no. 76 (25 October 1925): 1.

"Furen zhishi jieji tuanjie! Taichung furen qinmuhui chengli" (The women intelligentsia unite! The Taichung women's friendship society is established). *Taiwan xinminbao* no. 333 (4 October 1930): 3.

Gallin, Rita S. "The Entry of Chinese Women into the Rural Labor Force: A Case Study from Taiwan." *Signs: Journal of Women in Culture and Society* 9, no. 3 (1984): 382–98.

———. "Women and the Export Industry in Taiwan." In *Women Workers and Global Restructuring*, ed. Kathryn Ward, 179–92. Ithaca, N.Y.: Cornell University Press, 1990.

———. "Women, Family, and the Political Economy of Taiwan." *Journal of Peasant Studies* 12, no. 1 (October 1984): 76–92.

Garon, Sheldon. *Molding Japanese Minds: The State in Everyday Life.* Princeton, N.J.: Princeton University Press, 1997.

Gates, Hill. *Chinese Working-Class Lives: Getting by in Taiwan.* Ithaca, N.Y.: Cornell University Press, 1987.

Gender Equity Education Act. (http://law.moj.gov.tw/Eng/Fnews/Fnewscontent), (downloaded on September 15, 2006), 1–6.

Gilmartin, Christina K., Gail Hershatter, Lisa Rofel, and Tyrene White. *Engendering China: Women, Culture, and the State.* Cambridge, Mass.: Harvard University Press, 1994.

Glosser, Susan L. *Chinese Visions of Family and State, 1915–1953.* Berkeley: University of California Press, 2003.

Government Information Office. *Hsiu-Lien Annette Lu: Tenth-Term Vice President of the Republic of China.* Taipei, 2000.

———. "ROC Vice President Lu Hsiu-lien Receives World Peace Prize." Taipei, 2001.

Greene, J. Megan. *The Origins of the Developmental State in Taiwan: Science Policy and the Quest for Modernization.* Cambridge, Mass.: Harvard University Press, 2008.

"Guoqu yinianjian de Taiwan sixiangjie" (Taiwan's intellectual circle in the past year). *Taiwan minbao* no.138 (2 January 1927): 7.

Han, Shih-lin. "Fuxuan fuyu he funü jiefang" (Women's liberation). *Taiwan minbao* no. 217 (15 July 1928): 10.

Hershatter, Gail. "State of the Field: Women in China's Long Twentieth Century." *Journal of Asian Studies*, vol. 63 no. 4 (November 2004): 991–1064.

Hinder, Eleanor M. "China's New Factory Laws as Affecting Women and Children." *The Chinese Recorder* (March 1931): 149–55.

Hinsch, Bret. "Metaphysics and Reality of the Feminine in Early Neo-Confucian Thought." *Women's Studies International Forum* 11, no. 6 (1988): 591–98.

Ho, Ch'un-jui. "Haoshuang nüren: nüxing zhuyi yu xingjiefang" (Gallant woman: feminism and sexual liberation). *Awakening*, 5 October 1994, 10–13.

———. *Haoshuang nüren: nüxing zhuyi yu xingjiefang* (Gallant woman: feminism and sexual liberation). Taibei: Huangguan wenxue chuban, 1994.

———. "Xingsaorao yu xingqishi" (Sexual harassment and gender discrimination). *Awakening*, 5 November 1995, 20–22.

Hongnong gao. "Funü jiefang yundong yu minzu jiefang yundong" (Women's liberation movement and national liberation movement). *Taiwan minbao* no. 220 (5 August 1928): 8.

Honig, Emily. *Sisters and Strangers: Women in the Shanghai Cotton Mills, 1919–1949.* Stanford, Calif.: Stanford University Press, 1986.

Hsieh, Hsiao-chin. "Women's Studies in Taiwan, 1985–1992." *Women's Studies Quarterly* no. 3 and 4 (1994): 132–45.

Hsieh, Hsiao-chin, Ling Han, and Sung-wen Yen. "Appendix: Women's and Gender Research Institutes/Organizations in Taiwan." In *Gender, Culture, and Society: Women's Studies in Taiwan,* ed. Wei-hung Lin and Hsiao-chin Hsieh. Seoul: Ewha Woman's University Press, 2005.

Hsieh, John Fuh-sheng, and Emerson M. S. Niou. "Measuring Taiwanese Public Opinion on Taiwanese Independence." *China Quarterly* no. 181 (March 2005): 158–68.

Hsiung, Ping-chun. "Between Bosses and Workers: The Dilemma of a Keen Observer and a Vocal Feminist." In *Women in the New Taiwan,* ed. Catherine Farris, Anru Lee, and Murray Rubinstein, 295–309. Armonk, N.Y.: M. E. Sharpe, 2004.

——. *Living Rooms as Factories: Class, Gender, and the Satellite Factory System in Taiwan.* Philadelphia: Temple University Press, 1996.

Hsu, Hsin-liang. "Rang women fenshen touru Taiwan geming de hongliu" (Let us commit our lives to the wave of Taiwanese revolution). In *Formosa: The Magazine of Taiwan's Democratic Movement.* Taibei: Meilidao zazhishe, 1980.

Hu, Shu-wen. "Yinü chugui" (Heterosexual women come out of the closet). *Awakening,* 5 July 1995, 13–16.

Huang, Chang-ling, Personal interview with author, 20 July 2006. The Awakening Foundation headquarters, Taipei, Taiwan.

——. "Strength in Numbers: Increasing Women's Political Participation in Taiwan" In *Gender, Culture, and Society: Women's Studies in Taiwan,* ed. Wei-hung Lin and Hsiao-chin Hsieh, 273–300. Seoul: Ewha Woman's University Press, 2005.

Huang, Chao-yuan. "Cong gongfa guandian kan xingsaorao shensuquan yu feibangzui zhi guanlian" (Looking at the relationship between one's right to present the sexual harassment case at the court of law and the crime of slandering from the perspective of public law). *Awakening,* 5 December 1995, 27–28.

Huang, Ch'ung-hua. "Duo bu duo, laoniang you quan jueding" (Women have the right to decide whether to have an abortion). *Awakening,* 1 June 1989, 8–9.

Huang, Hua. "Nüzhonghaojie Yeh T'ao nüshi" (A woman of great capability: Yeh T'ao). *Awakening,* 10 December 1983, 37–38.

Huang, Ling-na. "Guomindang ruhe huiying lingyiban renkou de shengyin" (How does the Kuomintang respond to the voices of the other half of population). *Awakening,* 10 August 1988, 5–9.

Huang, P'u-chun. "Nannü chabie chefei" (Abolition of gender disparities).*Tai Oan Chheng Lian* no. 1 (15 January 1921): 34–36.

Jayawardena, Kumari. *Feminism and Nationalism in the Third World.* London: Zed Books, 1986.

Jizhe. "Sixiangjie: hunyin zhi jinhua" (The world of thoughts: the evolution of marriage). *Tai Oan Chheng Lian* no.2 (15 August 1921): 34–35.

Judge, Joan. "Citizens or Mothers of China? Gender and the Meaning of Modern Chinese Citizenship." In *Changing Meanings of Citizenship in Modern China,* ed. Merle Goldman and Elizabeth J. Perry, 23–43. Cambridge, Mass.: Harvard University Press, 2002.

Kagan, Richard C. *Chen Shui-bian: Building a Community and a Nation.* Taipei: Asia-Pacific Academic Exchange Foundation, 2000.

——. "Feminist Art in Taiwan: Textures of Reality and Dreams." In *Women in the New Taiwan,* ed. Catherine Farris, Anru Lee, and Murray Rubinstein, 310–324. Armonk, N.Y.: M. E. Sharpe, 2004.

"Kangofu yosei" (Nurses' training). (www.avis.ne.jp/~shimoina/Yougo/youg009.htm), (downloaded on July 29, 2004), 1–14.

Katz, Paul. R. "Governmentality and Its Consequences in Colonial Taiwan: A Case Study of the Ta-pa-ni Incident of 1915." *Journal of Asian Studies* 64, no. 2 (May 2005): 387–424.

Kerr, George H. *Formosa Betrayed.* New York: Houghton Mifflin, 1965.

K'o, Liang. "Taiwan qingnian nannü jian kumen de yuanyin" (The causes of sadness between young men and women in Taiwan). *Taiwan minbao* no. 189 (1 January 1928): 7.

Kollontai, Alexandra. *Selected Writings of Alexandra Kollontai.* Translated by Alix Holt. Westport, Conn.: Lawrence Hill, 1978.

Ku, Ming-chun. "Nüxing zhuyi zhenying zhong de tongxinglian kongjuzheng" (Homophobia in the women's movement). *Awakening,* 5 October 1995, 18–21.

Ku, Yen-lin. "The Changing Status of Women in Taiwan." *Women's Studies International Forum* 11, no. 3 (1988): 176–86.

———. "Cong yizhi dao shenggen: funü yanjiu zai Taiwan (1985–1995)" (From transplant to taking roots: women's studies in Taiwan, 1985–1995). *Research on Women in Modern Chinese History* no. 4 (August 1996): 241–68.

———. "The Feminist Movement in Taiwan, 1972–87." *Bulletin of Concerned Asian Scholars* 21, no. 1 (1989): 12–22.

———. "Nannü zhi bie: youguan nannü xingbie de gezhong yanjiu" (The distinctions between men and women: concerning various studies on gender distinctions). *Awakening,* 1 February 1982, 5–8.

———. "Selling a Feminist Agenda on a Conservative Market: The *Awakening* Experience in Taiwan." In *Radically Speaking: Feminism Reclaimed,* ed. Diane Bell and Renate Klein, 423–28. North Melbourne, Victoria: Spinifex Press, 1996.

———. "Yangtou ruhe bian gourou: funü yanjiu zai Taiwan de zuori, jinri" (How did the goat's head become dog's flesh: women's studies in Taiwan's yesterday and today), *Awakening,* 1 August 1991, 4–6.

Kung, Lydia. *Factory Women in Taiwan,* with an introduction by Janet W. Salaff. New York: Columbia University Press, 1994.

Kuo, Mei-chin. "Mofan muqin zhenshi xiandai muqin de mofan?" (Are the model mothers really the true role models of modern mothers). *Awakening,* 10 July 1982, 39–40.

Kuo, Wen-hua. "1950 zhi 1970 niandai Taiwan jiating jihua: yiliao zhengce yu nüxingshi de tantao" (Taiwan's family planning: a study of medical policies and women's history, 1950–1970). Master's thesis, Taiwan National Tsinghua University, 1997.

Lan, Shi-chi Mike. "Under the Shadow of Benevolent Hegemony: The Taiwanese Discourse of Making Same/Keeping Difference of the 1920s." In *Taiwan 2000—Envisioning a Pluralistic Future: Proceedings of the Sixth Annual Conference of the North American Taiwan Studies Association at Harvard University, Cambridge, Massachusetts, June 16–19, 2000.*

Lao, Tzu. *Tao Te Ching.* Translated by D. C. Lau. London: Penguin Books, 1963.

Lapidus, Gail W. *Women in Soviet Society.* Berkeley: University of California Press, 1978.

"Law Passed for Working Women." *Taipei Times,* 7 December 2001.

Lee, Anru. *In the Name of Harmony and Prosperity: Labor and Gender Politics in Taiwan's Economic Restructuring.* Albany: State University of New York Press, 2004.

Lee, Bernice J. "Women and Law in Republican China." *Journal of the Oriental Society of Australia* 12 (1977): 16–41.

Lee, Yuan-chen. "Cong muxing tandao fuxing" (From a discussion of motherliness to fatherliness). *Awakening*, 10 August 1983, 10–12.

——. "8338 Funüzhou huodong zhongjieshao" (8 March 1983: A general introduction to the activities of women's week). *Awakening*, 10 March 1983, 6–9.

——. *Funü kaibuzou* (Women's forward march). Taibei: Shenghuo wenhua, 1988.

——. "Funü xinzhi jijinhui de changduancheng mubiao" (Awakening Foundation's long and short-term goals). *Awakening*, 10 January 1988, 7.

——. "Funü yundong de huigu yu zhanwang" (The prospect and retrospect of the women's movement). *Awakening*, 10 October 1986, 4–6.

——. "Fuyun de lixiang" (The ideals of women's movement). *Awakening*, 1 December 1989.

——. "How the Feminist Movement Won Media Space in Taiwan." In *Spaces of Their Own: Women's Public Sphere in Transnational China*, ed. Mayfair Mei-hui Yang, 95–115. Minneapolis: University of Minnesota Press, 1999.

——. "Liangxing dou xuyao funü xinzhi" (Both genders need Awakening). *Awakening*, 10 April 1986.

——. "Liangxing kongjian de duoyuan mianmao" (The multi-faceted spaces between genders). *Awakening*, 1 July 1989, 5.

——. "Liangxing shehui de xinlixiang" (New ideals of a gender-egalitarian society). *Awakening*, 10 December 1983, 48–52.

——. "Nide yipiao you liliang" (Your vote has power). *Awakening*, 1 November 1989, 1.

——. *Nüren de mingtian* (Women's tomorrow). Taibei: Jianxing wenhua, 1991.

——. "Quanwei jiaoyu de bihai zhi yi: xingbie qishi de guomin jiaoyu" (One of the problems of authoritarian education: gender discrimination in public education). *Awakening*, 10 March 1988, 4–7.

——. "Quefa liangxing jiaoyu de guomin jiaoyu" (The national education system lacks a gender-balanced curriculum). *Awakening*, 10 September 1983, 24–26.

——. "Rang women dajia yiqilai" (Let us all come together). *Awakening*, 10 April 1983, 6–7.

——. "Renquan de zuihou baolei: qing pingdeng zunzhong nütongxinglianzhe" (The last fortress of human rights: please respect lesbian's rights in the spirit of equality). *Awakening*, 1 May 1992, 2.

——. "Sheilai guanxin muqin de renquan" (Who would show concern for mothers' human rights). *Awakening*, 10 May 1983, 6–8.

——. "Taiwan fuyun ji qi zhengzhi yihan" (The Taiwanese women's movement and its political significance), 15 October 2000. (Photocopy). A paper supplied by Lee Yuan-chen to the author. Department of Chinese Language and Literature, Tamkang University, Taipei, Taiwan.

——. Telephone interview with author, 1 July 1998 and 25 August 2002. The Ohio State University, Columbus.

——, to the author, 18 February 2001 and 22 August 2002. Transcripts in the hand of the author. Written Correspondence from Tamkang University, Taipei, Taiwan to Columbus, Ohio.

———. "Zuo yige xinshidai de muqin" (Be a mother of the new era). *Awakening*, 1 May 1982, 4–5.

Lenin, V. I. *The Emancipation of Women*. New York: International Publishers, 1966.

"Liberating Women," *Taipei Journal*, 5 June 2001.

Li, Ch'ing-ju. "Zouchu hunyin misi" (Walking out of the illusion of marriage). *Awakening*, 5 March 1995, 11.

Li, Ch'ung-yueh. "Nannü ruhe huxiang xuexi: Lee Yuan-chen yu Po Yang duitan" (How should men and women learn from each other: a dialogue between Lee Yuan-chen and Po Yang). *Awakening*, 10 September 1983, 40–43.

Li, Ju-he. *Taiwan wenjiao shilue* (A historical sketch of Taiwan's culture and education). Taichung: Taiwansheng wenxian weiyuanhui, 1972.

Li, Laura Tyson. *Madame Chiang Kai-shek: China's Eternal First Lady*. New York: Atlantic Monthly Press, 2006.

Li, Wen. *Zongheng wushinian: Lu Hsiu-lien qianzhuan* (The first fifty years: a biography of Lu Hsiu-lien). With a Foreword by Lu Hsiu-lien. Taibei: Shibao, 1996.

Lim, Kok-ui. "Taiwan's Presidential Election." *Taiwan International Review* 2, no. 2 (March–April 1996): 5.

Lin, Yu-pao, and Ni Chia-chen. "Laoweihui kuoda xieban laogong tuor" (The Council of Labor Affairs expands the establishment of workers' childcare facilities). *Awakening*, 5 November 1995, 29.

Lin, Yu-sheng. *The Crisis of Chinese Consciousness: Radical Anti-Traditionalism in the May Fourth Era*. Madison: The University of Wisconsin Press, 1979.

Liu, Hsiu-fang. "Xinliangxing guanxi zuotan jilu" (Minutes of the panel discussion on the relationship between the genders). *Awakening*, 10 December 1986, 5–8.

Liu, Min-chu. *Shijie zhi nü: Lu Hsiu-lien* (Woman of the world: Lu Hsiu-lien). Translated from Korean to Chinese by Chin Hsuen-ch'en. Taipei: INK Publishing, 2006.

Lorde, Audre. "Cong chenmo dao yuyan xingdong" (The transformation of silence into language and action). Translated by K'ang Fen. *Awakening*, 1 February 1993, 10–11.

———. "Nianling, zhongzhu, jieji he xingbie: nüren chongxin dingyi chayi" (Age, race, class, and gender: women redefining difference). Translated by Li Wan-shu. *Awakening*, 1 February 1993, 6–8.

———. "Qingse zhi yong: zuowei yizhong liliang eryan" (Use of the erotic, the erotic as power). Translated by Wu Ching-yi. *Awakening*, 1 February 1993, 5–6.

———. "Qingyu de liyong: qingyu zuowei yizhong liliang eryan" (Use of the erotic, the erotic as power). Translated by Sun Ruei-suei, *Awakening*, 5 August 1995, 24–28.

———. "Shengqi zhi yong" (The use of anger). Translated by Chou Ch'ien-yi, *Awakening*, 1 February 1993, 11–12.

Lu, Hsin-yi. "Imagining 'New Women,' Imagining Modernity: Gender Rhetoric in Colonial Taiwan." In *Women in the New Taiwan*, ed. Catherine Farris, Anru Lee, and Murray Rubinstein, 76–100. Armonk, N.Y.: M. E. Sharpe, 2004.

Lu, Hsiu-lien. *Bangta zhengqu yangguang* (Helping him/her to compete for the sunlight). Taibei: Tuohuangzhe chubanshe, 1976.

——. "Fuyun sanshinian, nüren kuashiji (Thirty years of women's movement, women stride over the century)," delivered at Taipei, Taiwan (7 March 2001). Special Column of Published Speeches, The Office of the President of the Republic of China, Taipei, Taiwan.

——. *Liangxing wenti nüxingguan* (Looking at gender problems from women's perspective). Taibei: Qianwei chubanshe, 1990.

——. *Shuyishu tuohuang de jiaobu* (Counting the pioneering footsteps). Taibei: Tuohuangzhe chubanshe, 1976.

——. *Taiwan da weilai* (Taiwan's great future). Taibei: Zhibenjia wenhua shiyei youxian gongsi, 2004.

——. *Taiwan de guoqu yu weilai* (Taiwan's past and future). Taibei: Tuohuangzhe chubanshe, 1979.

——. *Taiwan liangxinhua: Lu fuzongtong de diyinian* (Taiwan's words of conscience: Vice President Lu's first year in office). Taibei: Tianxia yuanjian, 2001.

——. "Tan fatong" (On the discussion of the justice system). *Formosa: The Magazine of Taiwan's Democratic Movement,* 16 August 1979, 20–21.

——. "Xiang lishi wutai angran maijin" (We proudly forge ahead in history). *Awakening,* 10 January 1988, 6.

——. *Xinnüxing hequhecong* (What are the choices of new feminists). Taibei: Tuohuangzhe chubanshe, 1977.

——. *Xinnüxing zhuyi* (New feminism). 3d ed. Taibei: Dunli, 1986.

——. *Xunzhao linyisan chuang* (Searching for another window). 7th ed. Taibei: Shupinshumu chubanshe, 1978.

Lu, Hsiu-lien, Li Chin-mei, and Ts'ui Mei-lan. "Yi jianjie tisheng banfa qudai funü baozhang ming'e" (Replacing protective quota for women with incremental affirmative action). *Awakening,* 1 April 1992, 6–9.

Lu, Hsiu-lien Annette. "Women's Liberation: The Taiwanese Experience." In *The Other Taiwan,* ed. Murray A. Rubinstein, 289–304. Armonk, N.Y.: M. E. Sharpe, 1994.

Lu, Hwei-syin. "Transcribing Feminism: Taiwanese Women's Experiences." In *Women in the New Taiwan,* ed. Catherine Farris, Anru Lee, and Murray Rubinstein, 223–43. Armonk, N.Y.: M. E. Sharpe, 2004.

Lu, Meiyi. "The Awakening of Chinese Women in the Women's Movement in the Early Twentieth Century." In *Holding Up Half the Sky: Chinese Women Past, Present, and Future,* ed. Tao Jie, Zheng Bijun, and Shirley L. Mow, forward by Gail Hershatter, 55–70. New York: The Feminist Press at the City University of New York, 2004.

Mann, Susan. *Precious Records: Women in China's Long Eighteenth Century.* Stanford, Calif.: Stanford University Press, 1997.

——. "What Can Feminist Theory Do for the Study of Chinese History? A Brief Review of Scholarship in the United States." In *Women in the New Taiwan,* ed. Catherine Farris, Anru Lee, and Murray Rubinstein, 3–13. Armonk, N.Y.: M. E. Sharpe, 2004.

——. "Women, Families, and Gender Relations." In *The Cambridge History of China,* Vol. 9, Part 1: *The Ch'ing Empire to 1800,* ed. Willard J. Peterson, 428–72. Cambridge: Cambridge University Press, 2002.

——. "Women in East Asia: China, Japan, and Korea." In *Women's History in Global Perspective,* Vol. 2, ed. Bonnie G. Smith, 47–100. Urbana and Chicago: University of Illinois Press, 2005.

Mann, Susan, and Yu-Yin Cheng, eds. *Under Confucian Eyes: Writings on Gender in Chinese History.* Berkeley: University of California Press, 2001.

McCaghy, Charles H., and Charles Hou. "Taiwan." In *Prostitution: an International Handbook on Trends, Problems, and Policies,* ed. Nanette J. Davis, 284–87. Westport, Conn.: Greenwood Press, 1993.

Mead, Margaret. *Sex and Temperament in Three Primitive Societies.* New York: William Morrow, 1935.

Meilidao zazhishe. "Dangwai zhenglun: minzhu wansui" (Political discussion of the Democratic Opposition: long live democracy). *Formosa: The Magazine of Taiwan's Democratic Movement* 1, no. 1 (August 1979): 4–9.

Miller, Jean Baker. *Toward a New Psychology of Women.* Boston: Beacon Press, 1976.

"Minfa qinshupian xiufa yundong dashiji" (The record of major events in the movement to amend the section pertaining to family relationships in the civil code). *Awakening,* 5 April, 1995, 12.

Minjian tuanti minfa qinshupian xiuzheng weiyuanhui. "Xiuzheng minqin shupian wanren dalianshu" (Mobilizing ten thousand co-signers for the draft amendment to the civil code's section on family laws). *Awakening,* 1 March 1994, 29.

"Minzhongdang kai linshi zhongyang changwu weiyuanhui" (The standing committee of the [Taiwan] Populist Party held a provisional meeting). *Taiwan minbao* no. 181 (6 November 1927): 4.

Mo, Yan-chih. "Women's Groups Celebrate Passage of Harassment Act." *Taipei Times,* 15 January 2005, 3.

"Moni xuanju wanjie le, qingting minxuan yiyuan de zhengjian" (The mock election is now over, please listen to the legislator-elect's political views). *Taiwan xinminbao* no. 348 (24 January 1931): 8.

"New Law Will Boost Gender Equality at Work." *Min Sheng Daily* (Taipei), 5 June 2001.

Ngo, Tak-wing. "Civil Society and Political Liberalization in Taiwan." *Bulletin of Concerned Asian Scholars* 25, no. 1 (January–March 1993): 3–15.

"Nongmin zuhe dajia zhibu dahui juxing funübu fahuishi" (The Dajia chapter of Farmers' Union held a meeting for the creation of women's department). *Taiwan minbao* no. 199 (11 March 1928): 5.

Nüpengyou shuangyuekan bianji (Editor of bimonthly, *Girlfriends*). "Xishou zhi qian, fenli, youqi biyao" (Before we cooperate, there is a need to separate). *Awakening,* 5 October 1995, 16–18.

"Nüren lianxian, qingyu tuohuang yundong xuanyan" (The declaration of the movement to unite women and pioneer eroticism). *Awakening,* 5 July 1995, 20.

"Nütongzhi fuyun come out? Zuotan" (Panel discussion on whether lesbianism in the women's movement should come out). *Awakening,* 5 November 1995, 1.

Nüxingxue xuehui. *Taiwan funü chujing baipishu: 1995 nian* (The white paper on Taiwanese women's situation in 1995). Compiled and edited by Liu Shu-hsiu. Taibei: Shibao chuban, 1995.

"Nüzi jiaoyu zhi biyao" (The necessity of women's education). *Tai Oan Chheng Lian* no. 2 (15 August 1920): 19.

"Nüzi shengji wenti" (Problems of women's livelihood). *Taiwan minbao* no.129 (31 October 1926): 3–4.

Offen, Karen. "Defining Feminism: A Comparative Historical Approach." *Signs: Journal of Women in Culture and Society* 14, no. 1 (Autumn 1988): 119–57.

Office of the President, The Republic of China. *Milestones: The Honorable Lu Hsiu-lien.* Taipei, 2000.

Ono, Kazuko. *Chinese Women in a Century of Revolution.* Edited by Joshua A. Fogel. Stanford, Calif.: Stanford University Press, 1989.

P'an, Tse-hsiang. "Taiwan funü wenti" (The woman question in Taiwan). *Taiwan minbao* no. 221 (12 August 1928): 8.

P'eng Wan-ju. *P'eng Wan-ju jinian quanji: Wan-ju huojingu (Shang)* (The complete works of P'eng Wan-ju), Edited by Su Ch'ien-ling. Vol. 1. Taibei: Nüshu wenhua shiyei youxian gongsi, 1997.

Po, Ch'ing-jung. "Tekanci" (A word on the special edition). *Awakening,* 10 March 1983, 4–5.

Radicalesbians. "Nüren rentong nüren" (Woman-identified woman). Translated by Chang Chun-mei. *Awakening,* 5 July 1995, 2–4.

Ramusack, Barbara N., and Sharon Sievers. *Women in Asia: Restoring Women to History.* Bloomington: Indiana University Press, 1999.

Raphals, Lisa. *Sharing the Light: Representations of Women and Virtue in Early China.* Albany: State University of New York, 1998.

Reed, Barbara. "Women and Chinese Religion in Contemporary Taiwan." In *Today's Woman in World Religions,* ed. Arvind Sharma, 225–44. Albany: State University of New York Press, 1994.

Reed, Barbara, and Gary Marvin Davison. *Culture and Customs of Taiwan.* Westport, Conn.: Greenwood Press, 1998.

"Remembering P'eng Wan-ju: a Fighter for Women's Rights." *Taiwan International Review* no. 6 (November–December 1996): 12.

Report on Women's Rights in Taiwan. Taipei: Foundation of Women's Rights Promotion and Development, 2003.

"Riben funü canzheng wenti" (The problems of Japanese women's political participation). *Taiwan minbao* no. 207 (6 May 1928): 2.

"Riben ge wuchan zhengdang de zhenrong" (The various proletarian political parties in Japan). *Taiwan minbao* no. 199 (11 March 1928): 8; no. 200 (18 March 1928): 8; and no. 201 (25 March 1928): 8.

Rich, Adrienne. "Compulsory Heterosexuality and Lesbian Existence." *Signs: Journal of Women in Culture and Society* 5, no. 4 (Summer 1980): 631–60.

Rigger, Shelley. "Electoral Strategies and Political Institutions in the Republic of China on Taiwan." *Harvard Studies on Taiwan,* Vol. 1 (1995): 3–27.

———. *From Opposition to Power: Taiwan's Democratic Progressive Party.* Boulder: Lynne Rienner, 2001.

———. "Nationalism versus Citizenship in the Republic of China on Taiwan." In *Changing Meanings of Citizenship in Modern China,* ed. Merle Goldman and Elizabeth J. Perry, 353–72. Cambridge, Mass.: Harvard University Press, 2002.

———. *Politics in Taiwan.* London: Routledge, 1999.

———. "Social Science and National Identity: A Critique." *Pacific Affairs,* 74:4 (Winter 1999–2000): 537–52.

————. *Taiwan's Rising Rationalism: Generations, Politics, and "Taiwanese Nationalism."* Policy Studies, No. 26. Washington, D. C.: East-West Center Washington, 2006.

Roy, Denny. *Taiwan: A Political History.* Ithaca, N.Y.: Cornell University Press, 2002.

Rubinstein, Murray A. "Lu Hsiu-lien and the Origins of Taiwanese Feminism, 1944–1977." In *Women in the New Taiwan,* ed. Catherine Farris, Anru Lee, and Murray Rubinstein, 244–77. Armonk, N.Y.: M. E. Sharpe, 2004.

Rubinstein, Murray A., ed. *Taiwan: A New History.* Armonk, N.Y.: M. E. Sharpe, 1999.

Rupp, Leila J. and Verta Taylor. *Survival in the Doldrums.* New York: Oxford University Press, 1987.

Sang, Tze-lan Deborah. *The Emerging Lesbian: Female Same-Sex Desire in Modern China.* Chicago: The University of Chicago Press, 2002.

Sato, Barbara. *The New Japanese Woman: Modernity, Media, and Women in Interwar Japan.* Durham, N.C.: Duke University Press, 2003.

Schneir, Miriam. *Feminism: The Essential Historical Writings.* New York: Random House, 1972.

Schwarcz, Vera. *The Chinese Enlightenment: Intellectuals and the Legacy of the May Fourth Movement of 1919.* Berkeley: University of California Press, 1986.

"Sheizai bangzhu xingsaorao" (Who is collaborating with sexual harassment). *Awakening,* 5 December 1995, 23–29.

"Shelun: Furen jiefang de dangmian wenti" (Editorial: the impending problems of women's liberation). *Taiwan minbao* no. 76 (25 October 1925): 1.

Shen, Hsiu-hua. *Chamuoren de 228* (Women's February 28th). Taibei: Yushanshe, 1997.

Shen, Tzong-Ruey. "Modes of State Control of Labor Unions: an Analysis of the Taiwan Experience From the 1950s to the 1990s." In *Postwar Taiwan in Historical Perspective,* ed. Chun-chieh Huang and Feng-fu Tsao. Bethesda: University Press of Maryland, 1998.

"Sheshuo: pinjin feizhi wenti" (Editorial: problems of eliminating the bride price). *Taiwan minbao* no. 256 (14 April 1929): 2.

Shih, Chih-yu. "Jiangfuren yu Zhongguo de guojia xingzhi: Houzhimin fuquan wenhua de jiangou" (Madame Chiang and Chinese national character: post-colonial patriarchal cultural construction). *Research on Women in Modern Chinese History* no. 4 (August 1996): 167–200.

Shih, Shu-ch'ing, ed. *Cong nüren dao ren* (From being women to becoming human beings). Taibei: Tuohuangzhe chubanshe, 1975.

Shuai Jen. "Dui tade ganjue zhenhao" (Our feelings toward her are truly good). *Awakening,* 1 March 1991, 12–14.

Shuzi gaosu ni (Let the numbers tell you). Taibei: Caituan faren funü quanyi cujin fazhan jijinhui, 2004.

"Shuzi shang de ruxue nan" (The difficulties of school admissions based on numbers). *Taiwan minbao* no. 257 (21 April 1929): 2.

Sievers, Sharon L. *Flowers in Salt: The Beginnings of Feminist Consciousness in Modern Japan.* Stanford, Calif.: Stanford University Press, 1983.

Simon, Scott. *Sweet and Sour: Life Worlds of Taipei Women Entrepreneurs.* Lanham, Md.: Rowman and Littlefield, 2003.

Smith, Bonnie G., ed. *Global Feminisms Since 1945.* New York: Routledge, 2000.

Sommer, Matthew H. *Sex, Law, and Society in Late Imperial China*. Stanford, Calif.: Stanford University Press, 2000.

Stevens, Sarah E. "Figuring Modernity: The New Woman and the Modern Girl in Republican China." *NWSA Journal* 15, no. 3 (2003): 82–103.

Su, Yi-chen. "Xinshidai de funü he lianai jiehun" (Women of the new age and marriage based on love). *Tai Oan Chheng Lian* no. 1 (15 July 1921): 13–16.

Su, Yu-ling. *Liangxing pingdeng jiaoyu de bentu fazhan yu shijian* (The indigenous development and practice of gender equity education in Taiwan). Taipei: Fembooks, 2002.

Sui, Ping-chen. "Minfa qinshupian shiwen shida" (Ten questions and answers concerning the civil code's section on family relationships). *Awakening*, 1 March 1994, 25–28.

———. "Taiwan fuyun de luxian yu celue" (The direction and strategies of the Taiwanese women's movement). *Awakening*, 1 December 1991, 20–23.

Sun, Ruei-suei. "Congxin sikao qingyu!" (Rethinking the eros). *Awakening*, 5 August 1995, 29; and 5 September 1995,16–18.

———. Telephone interview with author, 14 July 2003, Wichita State University, Wichita, Kansas.

"Taibeishi funü xinzhi xiehui zhengshi chengli" (The Taipei Awakening Association is formally established). *Awakening*, 1 May 1994, 21–22.

"Taiwan de funü jiaoyu" (Women's education in Taiwan). *Taiwan minbao* no. 110 (20 June 1926): 3.

"Taiwan de funü yundong jinnian yao zhankai ma?" (Is the women's movement in Taiwan going to be launched this year?). *Taiwan minbao* no. 190 (8 January 1928): 2.

"Taiwan jiaoyu de jihui bujundeng" (The educational opportunities in Taiwan are not equitable). *Taiwan minbao* no. 265 (16 June 1929): 2.

Taiwan keimukyoku. *Taiwan shakai undoshi* (The history of Taiwan's social movements). Tokyo: Ryukei shosha, 1939.

"Taiwan minzhongdang chuxian" (Emergence of the Taiwan Populist Party). *Taiwan minbao* no. 166 (22 July 1927): 4–5.

"Taiwan shehui yundong tuanti diaocha (6)" (An investigative survey of the organizations in Taiwan's social movements [6]). *Taiwan minbao* no. 194 (5 February 1928): 8.

Taiwanshi yanjiu wenxian leimu bianji xiaozu. *Taiwanshi yanjiu wenxian leimu 2004 niandu* (Annual bibliography of studies of Taiwan's history, 2004). Taipei: Institute of Taiwan History, Academia Sinica, 2005.

Takenaka, Nobuko. *Shokuminchi Taiwan no Nihon josei seikatsushi: Meiji hen* (The history of Japanese women's lives in colonial Taiwan: the book on Meiji era). Vo1.1. Tokyo: Tahata shoten, 1995.

———. *Shokuminchi Taiwan no Nihon josei seikatsushi: Taisho hen* (The book on Taisho era). Vol. 2. Tokyo: Tahata shoten, 1996.

———. *Shokuminchi Taiwan no Nihon josei seikatsushi: Showa hen* (The book on Showa era).Vols. 3–4. Tokyo: Tahata shoten, 2001.

T'ang, Wen-hui. "Taiwan nügong chujing zhiduoshao: fuquan yu ziben tizhi shuangcong yapo xia de funü laogong" (How much do we know about women workers' situation: women's labor under the double oppression of patriarchy and capitalism). *Awakening*, 10 May 1988, 1–2.

———. "Zu gonghui zhishi nangong de quanli ma: funü laogong zai gonghui yundong zhong de xiankuang" (Is organizing labor unions the sole right of male workers: the current situation of women's labor in the labor movement). *Awakening,* 10 May 1988, 3–4.

Tang, Wen-hui Anna. "Explaining Social Policy in Taiwan Since 1949: State, Politics, and Gender." Ph.D. diss., Harvard University, 1997.

T'ao Hsin. "Yige nüren zhuzhi de chengzhang: huigu waijiaodu" (The growth of a women's organization: X-Centric in retrospect). *Awakening,* 1 March 1991, 9–12.

Tavares, Antonio C. "The Japanese Colonial State and the Dissolution of the Late Imperial Frontier Economy in Taiwan, 1886–1909." *Journal of Asian Studies* 64, no. 2 (May 2005): 361–86.

Teng, Emma. "An Island of Beautiful Women: The Discourse on Gender in Ch'ing Travel Accounts of Taiwan." In *Women in the New Taiwan,* ed. Catherine Farris, Anru Lee, and Murray Rubinstein, 41–58. Armonk, N.Y.: M. E. Sharpe, 2004.

Theiss, Janet M. *Disgraceful Matters: The Politics of Chastity in Eighteenth-Century China.* Berkeley: The University of California Press, 2004.

Thornton, Patricia M. *Disciplining the State: Virtue, Violence, and State-Making in Modern China.* Cambridge, Mass.: Harvard University Press, 2007.

Tien, Hung-mao. *The Great Transition: Political and Social Change in The Republic of China.* Stanford, Calif.: Hoover Institution Press at Stanford University, 1989.

Ts'ai, Hsiao-ch'ien. "Cong lianai dao jiehun" (From erotic love to marriage). *Taiwan minbao* no. 90 (31 January 1926): 15–16; no. 91 (7 February 1926): 13–14; and no. 92 (14 February 1926): 14–15.

Ts'ai, P'ei-huo et al. *Taiwan minzu yundong shi* (A history of the Taiwanese nationalist movement). Taibei: Zili wanbao congshu bianji weiyuanhui, 1971.

Ts'ai, Tun-yao. "Women Taiwan de funü jiefang wenti" (The problems of women's liberation in Taiwan). *Taiwan minbao* no. 219 (29 July 1928): 8.

Ts'ao, Ai-lan. "Taiwan fuyun xinshiyei: Toushi fuquan shehui he ziben zhuyi de hehuo guanxi" (New horizons of the Taiwanese women's movement: taking a close look at the partnership between the patriarchal society and capitalism). *Awakening,* 10 October 1988, 6–9.

———. *Xinshidai Taiwan funü guandian* (The perspectives of a new generation of Taiwanese Women). Taibei: Qianwei chubanshe, 1989.

Ts'ao, Yu-fang, ed. *Tamen weisheme chenmin?* (Why did they become famous?). Taibei: Tuohuangzhe chubanshe, 1976.

Tseng, Chao-nuan, ed. *Funü xinzhi 2005 niandu baogao* (The Awakening 2005 annual report). Taibei: Caituan faren funü xinzhi jijinhui, 2006.

Tseng, Chao-yuan. "Women zhexie bianyuan jiemei de taolun" (A discussion by we the sisters on the margin). *Awakening,* 1 February 1993, 12.

Tseng, Ch'i-hua. "Sheme shi nüxing zhuyi?" (What is feminism?). *Awakening,* 10 August 1986, 9–11.

Tsurumi, E. Patricia. *Japanese Colonial Education in Taiwan, 1895–1945.* Cambridge Mass.: Harvard University Press, 1977.

Tzu, Chuan. "Xiqu chengli de zhutiaojian zhi shangque—zhi Yeh Jung-chung shi de yifongxin" (A Discussion on the various prerequisites for being recognized as a play—a letter to Yeh Jung-chung). *Taiwan minbao* no. 278 (15 September 1929): 8

Uno, Kathleen S. "Women and Changes in the Household Division of Labor." In *Recreating Japanese Women, 1600–1945,* ed. Gail Lee Bernstein. Berkeley: University of California Press, 1991.

Vecchione, Judith. *Tug of War: The Story of Taiwan.* 90 min. WGBH Boston, 1998. Videocassette.

Wachman, Alan M. "Competing Identities in Taiwan." In *The Other Taiwan: 1945 to the Present,* ed. Murray A Rubinstein. Armonk, N.Y.: M. E. Sharpe, 1994.

———. "Taiwan: Parent, Province, or Blackballed State?" In *Taiwan in Perspective,* ed. Wei-chin Lee, 183–203. Leiden, The Netherlands: Brill, 2000.

"Waijiaodu huodongbiao" (The schedule of X-Centric). *Awakening,* 1 March 1991, 11.

Waley, Arthur. *Three Ways of Thought in Ancient China.* Stanford, Calif.: Stanford University Press, 1982.

Wang, Cheng-t'ung. "Fan nugong dayouxing" (The mass rally to oppose slave labor). *Taipei Awakening Association,* January/February 2006, 37–38.

Wang, Chun-lin. "2005 nian yazhou nüxing yimin/yigong NGO zuzhizhe guoji gongzuofang xingdong fasheng" (The activity and voice of NGO organizers' international workshop for Asian women immigrants and migrant workers in 2005). *Nüyan zongheng* no. 77 (January 2006): 1–19.

Wang, Min-ch'uan. "Duiyu feichang wenti de guanjian" (Opinions regarding the question of abolishing licensed prostitution). *Taiwan minbao* 3, no. 3 (21 January 1925): 4–6.

Wang, Shih-ch'ing. *"Taiwan yanjiu zhongwen shumu: shidi zhi bu* (Chinese bibliography for Taiwan studies: part one on history and geography). Taibei: Huanqiu shushe, 1976.

Wang, Tay-sheng. *Legal Reform in Taiwan under Japanese Colonial Rule, 1895–1945: The Reception of Western Law.* Seattle: University of Washington Press, 2000.

Wang, Tsai-wei. "Feminism and the Formation of Collective Identity within the Women's Movement in Contemporary Taiwan." Ph.D. diss., University of Pittsburgh, 1997.

Wolf, Margery. *Women and the Family in Rural Taiwan.* Stanford, Calif.: Stanford University Press, 1972.

Wollstonecraft, Mary. *A Vindication of the Rights of Woman.* New York: Penguin Books, 1992.

Women and Communism: Selections from the Writings of Marx, Engels, Lenin, and Stalin. Westport, Conn.: Greenwood Press, 1973.

"Women yao shuochu na bukeshuo de xingsaorao" (We speak out against the unspeakable sexual harassment). *Awakening,* 5 December 1995, 23.

Women zhijian (Between us). "Nütongxinglian yu nüxing zhuyi de guanxi" (The relationship between lesbianism and feminism). *Awakening,* 1 July 1990, 24–25.

"Workplace Gender Equality Law to Take Effect March 8." *United Daily News* (Taipei), 25 February 2002.

Wu, Suo-yun. "Nüzi xinhanxue yanjiuhui zhengqiu huiyuan shu" (A letter for recruiting members to launch the women's society for new Chinese studies). *Taiwan minbao* no. 5 (21 March 1924): 9–10.

Xinzhi gongzuoshi. "Chaijie hunyin shenhua: minfa yundong yu tongzhi yundong de duihua" (Dismantling the myth of marriage: a dialogue between the movement to amend family laws and the gay and lesbian movement). *Awakening,* 5 July 1995, 10–13.

"Xiuzheng minfa qinshupian, nüren chutoutian" (Women transcend the sky: amending the section of civil codes pertaining to family relationships). *Awakening*, 5 December 1994, 1–2.

Yang, Mei-hui, ed. *Funü wenti xinlun* (New theories on the woman question). Taibei: Lianjing chubanshe, 1979.

———. *Funü wenti xinlun* (New theories on the woman question). Vol. 2. Taibei: Chenzhong chubanshe, 1975.

———. *Funü wenti xinlun yucong* (A collection of translated works on the new theories pertaining to the woman question). Vol. 1. Taibei: Chenzhong chubanshe, 1973.

Yang, Ts'ui. *Riju shidai Taiwan funü jiefang yundong* (The Taiwanese women's liberation movement under Japanese colonial rule). Taibei: Shibao wenhua, 1993.

Yang, Wei-ming. "Lun hunyin" (A discussion on marriage). *Tai Oan Chheng Lian* no.2 (26 February 1921): 32–37.

Yeh, Ch'ih-ling. "Weisheme yao tan xiuzheng yousheng baojianfa?" (Why do we want to propose an amendment to the Eugenic Law for the Protection of Health?). *Awakening*, 1 December 1993, 5–6.

Yeh, Hsiu-wen. "Fansheng shouzha: xiangei xunzhao jiemei de nürenmen" (A letter of reflection dedicated to women in search of sisterhood). *Awakening*, 1 February 1993, 15–16.

Yeh, Sheng-hung. "Xinhuanjin zhufu lianmeng chufa le" (The Homemakers' Union for Environmental Protection is established). *Awakening*, 10 December 1986, 12–13.

Yu, Chien-ming. "Dang waishengren yudao Taiwan nüxing: Zhanhou Taiwan baokan zhong de nüxing lunshu, 1945–1949" (When Mainlanders met Taiwanese women: discourse on women in postwar Taiwanese newspapers and magazines, 1945–1949). *Jindaishi yanjiusuo jikan* no. 47 (March 2005).

———. "Taiwan diqu de fuyun" (Women's movements in the Taiwan area). In *Jindai Zhongguo funü yundongshi* (The history of women's movements in modern China), ed. Ch'en San-ching, 403–554. Taibei: Jindai Zhongguo chubanshe, 2004.

Yu, Chuan. "Jiu sixiang zhi diaozhong" (The knell of old-fashion thoughts). *Taiwan minbao* no. 102 (25 April 1926): 10.

Yu, Mei-nü. "Nannü gongzuo pingdengfa zhongshuoming" (The elucidation on the Equal Employment Bill for Men and Women). *Awakening*, 1 April 1989, 13–16.

———, Personal interview with author, 28 July 2006. Yu and Associates Law Office, Taipei, Taiwan.

Zheng, Wang. *Women in the Chinese Enlightenment: Oral and Textual Histories*. Berkeley: University of California Press, 1999.

Zhonghua funü fangong lianhehui. *Fulian sanshinian* (Thirty years of the Chinese Women's Anti-Aggression League). Taipei: The Chinese Women's Anti Aggression League, 1980.

"Zhuluo funü kenqinhui" (Zhuluo Women's Association). *Taiwan minbao* no. 126 (10 October 1926): 8.

"Zhuluo funü xiejinhui chuxian le" (The women's association for mutual assistance, collective action, and advancement has emerged). *Taiwan minbao* no. 118 (15 August 1926): 13.

Zouguo liangge shidai de Taiwan zhiyei funü: fangwen jilu (The Taiwanese career women who lived through two eras: records of interviews). Oral History Series No. 52. Taipei: Institute of Modern History, Academia Sinica, 1994.

Index

DORIS T. CHANG is an assistant professor in the Center for Women's Studies at Wichita State University. Her research interests include Chinese intellectual history, modern Japanese history, and women's history. She specializes in Taiwan studies.

The University of Illinois Press
is a founding member of the
Association of American University Presses.

Composed in 10.5/13 Adobe Minion Pro
at the University of Illinois Press
Manufactured by Sheridan Books, Inc.

University of Illinois Press
1325 South Oak Street
Champaign, IL 61820-6903
www.press.uillinois.edu